MORGAN AND DEESE'S CLASSIC
HANDBOOK FOR STUDENTS

HOW TO STUDY

AND OTHER SKILLS FOR SUCCESS IN COLLEGE

Fourth Edition revised by

James Deese
Ellin K. Deese

McGraw-Hill, Inc.

New York St. Louis San Francisco Auckland Bogotá
Caracas Lisbon London Madrid Mexico City
Milan Montreal New Delhi San Juan
Singapore Sydney Tokyo Toronto

JAMES DEESE is Hugh Scott Hamilton Professor Emeritus of Psychology at the University of Virginia.

ELLIN K. DEESE is former Assistant Dean in the College of Arts and Sciences and Associate Professor in the General Faculty and Lecturer in Religious Studies at the University of Virginia.

 This book is printed on recycled, acid-free paper containing a minimum of 50% recycled de-inked fiber.

2 3 4 5 6 7 8 9 10 11 12 13 14 15 16 17 18 19 20 MAL MAL 9 8 7 6 5 4 3

ISBN 0-07-016269-7

Sponsoring Editor: Jeanne Flagg
Production Supervisor: Paula Keller
Editing Supervisor: Patty Andrews
Book Designer: Meri Keithley
Cover Design: Jon Valk

Library of Congress Cataloging-in-Publication Data

Morgan, Clifford Thomas.
    How to study : and other skills for success in college / Morgan
and Deese's classic handbok for students.—4th ed. rev. / by
James Deese. Ellin K. Deese.
       p.   cm.
    Includes index.
    ISBN 0-07-016269-7
    1. Study. Method of. 2. College student orientation—United
States. I. Deese, James, 1921- . II. Deese, Ellin K.
III. Title.
LB2395.M595 1993
371.3'028'12—dc20   93-4010
                                                     CIP

CONTENTS

PREFACE

Knowing how to study efficiently doesn't come naturally. Even students who want to learn and who are eager to do well in college don't always know what to do. They may not know how much to study or how to use their time wisely. Many students don't know how to read a textbook, particularly the kinds of textbooks encountered in college. They don't know how to absorb and remember information from lectures. Indeed, they may not be prepared for the lecture style of teaching at all.

Furthermore, many potentially good students are deficient in some basic skills; they may not be able to read well enough for college-level material. They may have only the vaguest notions about English grammar. And many students have trouble putting their ideas into words in such a way that other people can understand them. Too many students fear and avoid mathematics and science.

Still others have sufficient preparation and are good at studying but don't know some particular things essential for success in college. They may not know, for example, how to use all of the resources of the college library. Or, in a very different vein, they may not know how to keep their personal problems from interfering with their academic work.

This book is intended for all of these students. It is for students still in high school intending to go on to college, for students entering college, for older people returning to college, and even for students who haven't really thought about college yet.

But through the years, students and colleges change; a new edition of *How to Study* was due. To meet those changes, we have updated, expanded, and added various sections, drawing on advice from students and critics, too numerous to cite. Most of those who read the book and gave us their

v

impressions are from the University of Virginia. Several anonymous reviewers provided us with invaluable insights into the weak points of previous editions. We particularly thank Jeanne Flagg, sponsoring editor in the College Division of McGraw-Hill, for her editorial guidance and helpful suggestions.

James Deese
Ellin K. Deese

TO THE STUDENT

Why should you read this book? Well, for one reason it might tell you something you don't already know. Even more important, it may tell you something you may be aware of but haven't thought about much. It may remind you of those things you do well and those things you don't do so well. This book is meant to be about both of these.

To put it simply, this book is about and for you as a college student or soon-to-be college student. The trouble with books for students is that there are a lot of you, and you are all different. Keep that in mind as you read or skim through this book. Look for those things for which you can say: "Yeah, that's my problem all right." At the same time, don't assume because you *think* you don't have a problem in using the library, organizing your time, or getting a good balance between your social life and the demands of schoolwork that there isn't anything that can help you here. A very good student—Phi Beta Kappa material—read an earlier edition of this book, and she said: "You know, I really learned something." We pressed her to tell us what, and she did in detail. We strongly suspect that her outstanding success as a student (and student leader, we might add) came from her ability to extract what was important and useful in everything she did. Use that as a cue, not only in reading this book but in dealing with everything that comes your way.

Now, don't overdo it; sometimes it's better just to sit back and enjoy. However, when you pick up a book titled *How to Study* you can be sure that it has information you can put to good use. There are bound to be things we have missed—things that relate to your particular circumstances. But we've included all sorts of suggestions for going after such things. Use this book to set yourself on the right track, or to help yourself out of a hole, if you think you're in one.

Good luck in your college experience.

1
GETTING OFF TO A GOOD START

WHY GO TO COLLEGE?

Going to college is one of the good things of American life. For many people, it is the first time they are really challenged by ideas; it is the time they look back on as the most exciting, significant, and enjoyable in their lives.

Perhaps because going to college is so much a part of the American dream, many high school graduates go for no particular reason. Some go because their parents expect it, others because it is what their friends are doing. Then, there is the belief that a college degree will automatically ensure a good job and high pay.

Some students drift through four years of college, attending classes or skipping them as the case may be, reading only what can't be avoided, looking for "gut" courses, and never being touched or changed in any important way. For a few of these people, college provides no satisfaction, yet because of parental or peer pressure, they stay on.

To put it bluntly, unless you are willing to make your college years count, you might be better off doing something else. Not everyone should attend college, nor should everyone who does attend begin right after high school. Many college students profit greatly from taking a year or so off. A year out in the world helps some people to sort out their priorities and goals.

EVALUATING YOUR PRIORITIES

Think about your own situation. You may be in high school trying to decide whether to go to college or not. Or perhaps you have been working for a while and think you might want to enter college or return to get your degree. Or you may already be in college and, for one reason or an-

1

other, wondering if you should stick it out just to get that degree.

A college degree is a kind of union card. You've got to have one to be accepted in many professions. But not in all. There are good high-paying occupations that don't require a college degree. What is more, people often develop an interest in ideas, books, and intellectual pursuits after they have been out of school for a while. One famous chemist dropped out of high school when he was sixteen and didn't return to his education until his mid-twenties. Recent statistics tell us that the median age of college students has been climbing into the high twenties.

Sad to say, high school is not the kind of place which, as a matter of course, fosters intellectual interest. Take Bill. He finished high school with satisfactory grades and very high SAT scores. He would have been a good prospect for any selective college. But he knew at that point he was not interested in learning from books. He liked working with his hands, and he liked being out of doors. His father was a well-known doctor, so you can imagine what pressure Bill was under to go to college. But he weathered the pressure, and he got himself a construction job. There he discovered that he had a real talent for carpentry. He began doing free-lance cabinetry work and he was great at it. After five years he found himself developing an interest in science. The kinds of books that bored him in high school now fascinated him. He bought books on physics, the weather, and chemistry. By the time he applied to college at age twenty-three, his goals were clear. He spent four happy and productive years as an undergraduate, supporting himself from loans, from his family, and from the jobs he could pick up. He graduated with honors, and he ended up doing top-notch work in the medical school where his father had gone. For Bill and for the world-famous chemist, taking a break from academic education was a good thing to do.

One of the things Bill did during his last year of high school was to think a lot about what he was interested in. Many students need to do that but in addition, they need to take stock of their abilities and interests. College requires abilities that are sometimes not touched in high school. It's a real shock to discover that high school math and col-lege math are as different as a country road and a freeway.

Rating Your Abilities

A lot of studies tell us that students often overrate themselves on traits and abilities that make for success in college. One of the most important things you can do is make an honest appraisal of your strengths and weaknesses. You will find a table on page 3, which you can use to rate your traits and abilities. Check where you honestly think you stand on the things listed. Discuss your ratings with people who really know you well—your friends, counselors, and teachers—and try to decide where you have overestimated and under-estimated yourself.

What You Can Learn from Your Test Scores

Standardized tests can be a real trap for some students, but they can help you. If you can learn what your test scores are, use them to evaluate yourself. Take into account the people who take a particular test, because they establish the norms. Suppose you scored in the ninetieth percentile on a test given to high school seniors. That means that you scored better than ninety percent of the students who took the test. Remember, however, that not all high school seniors go to college. For those students who do, you might have scored at only the fiftieth percentile. Because some colleges are more selective than others, you might find that the same score puts you at the thirtieth percentile of your fellow students. The meaning of a score is usually relative to the group of which you are a part. But don't let standardized tests tell you what to do. In recent years we have learned that stand-ardized tests can be influenced by coaching. We have more to say about this later.

Usually, your college's counseling services or your high school counselors can help you evaluate your test scores. Nearly every college has a coun-seling center for interviewing, testing, and coun-seling students about their academic and personal problems. Trained counselors know not only how to give and interpret tests but also how to put together a total picture of your academic and personal qualifications. Tests are not infallible, and they need to be interpreted. Some of that you can do on your own (after all, you are the person who took the test), but counselors can help.

Self-Rating of Traits and Abilities

In the spaces below, check where you honestly think you stand on the traits and abilities listed. After you have done that, discuss your ratings with some other people who know you really well—students, friends, parents, counselors—and who might show you where you have overestimated or underestimated yourself.

In my school, I think I am in the—

Upper Fifth	Middle Three-Fifths	Lower Fifth	
		x	in speed of reading textbooks
	x		in ability to understand textbooks
	x		in ability to take notes
y			in general preparation for college
x			in amount of time I study
x			in not wasting time
x			In work habits
	x		in vocabulary (words I know and use)
	x		in grammar and punctuation
		x	in spelling
x			in mathematical skills

How Motivated Are You?

One of the things we have learned over the years is this: The biggest difference between those who barely get by in college and those who get top grades is motivation. We're not sure this book will help you all that much with the problem of motivation itself, but it should help you sort out the reasons you are not enthusiastic enough about your studies to do well.

Are You Prepared for the Competition?

Some high schools are good at preparing their students for the level of academic work at college and some are not. Yet whatever the quality of your high school and however great your achievements, you may not be prepared for the competition you'll find. This is what every college admissions officer knows—some students who have been tops in high school are going to have trouble in college, and some students who were real goof-offs in high school can make the grade. But to make the grade takes work. College professors have different expectations than high school teachers. While they can be friendly and helpful, they are often not, as one student put it, "student-friendly." They expect that you are going to do a lot on your own. There will be more about this later in the chapter.

Examining Alternatives

Going to college or staying in college once you are there are not your only alternatives. You can enter the job market right after high school. If you are good at something and like doing it you can go into vocational training. Postponing college for a definite—or indefinite—time is a real alternative. Even jobs that are temporary and not particularly interesting can help you develop personal maturity. With some work experience behind you, you will appreciate college even more. If you are in college and feel that you are only marking time, see your dean or advisor about taking a leave of absence. Most colleges are pretty flexible about leaves of absence.

You or your parents may be upset about any departure from the traditional sequence of high school, college, and then perhaps graduate or professional school. A lot of people think of this as preparation for life and that we should get through it as quickly as possible. But we don't just prepare for life, we live it. We live it from the moment we are born to the day we die. The trick is to live it well—responsibly, productively, happily, meaningfully. We are all different. People don't develop at the same rate. Some experiences are wasted for some of us at one stage, but they can be important at another. If college is right for you now, fine. If not, postpone or interrupt your education, or find out what you can do to make it better. In the next few pages we will tell you about some of the things that might help it be better for you.

WHAT TO EXPECT

There are more than 2600 colleges and universities in the United States, and no two are exactly alike. Some are mainly for local students, others for people across the country or even the world. Some have fewer than 1000 students, and there are some with nearly 50,000. Some are private, some public; some have a strong religious orientation, and some, both public and private, make a point of being secular. Some have a four-year undergraduate program, some a two-year program, and some have affiliated graduate and professional schools. Some are hard to get into, while others will take any high school graduate.

If you are still facing a choice of a college, or if you want to transfer, you might consult one of the books that describes all American colleges. You can find these books in any bookstore, or in the library, and they are brought up to date every year. College counselors in high schools use them, and you and your parents can too. They will tell you about costs, programs, size, and even whether the school will offer the kind of social life you want. Whatever your decision is or has been, you should remember that no institution is perfect. Problems you may have had in high school aren't going to disappear just because you are in college.

LIVING ARRANGEMENTS

Living at Home

Most students go to a local college, and even though some of these colleges have dormitories, many students live at home or in neighboring apartments. This kind of arrangement has its advantages. It's cheaper. If you are home you are in a comfortable and familiar setting. It means you will get the kind of home cooking you are used to instead of what—even at its best—is institutional food.

However, if you commute, you need to go out of your way to get involved in the life of the college. That requires a certain amount of initiative. In all colleges, whether commuter or residential, students don't seek one another out nearly enough. They tend to form "safe" groups early on, gravitating to tables in the school cafeteria where they feel they will be immediately accepted. Yet one of the things college should do is help you break away from these kinds of patterns. But it will take some effort on your part. Just don't wait for somebody to seek you out.

If you live at home, you have to try for the same kind of independence you would have if you lived away. Home rules that would have been right when you were in high school don't apply. If your parents are reluctant to negotiate the matter, speed the process along by showing that you have the responsibility that goes with maturity. If, however, there is too much friction at home or too little room, think about sharing an apartment with some friends.

Living in a Dormitory

If you live away from home, the odds are that you will spend at least your freshman year in a dormitory. For some of you, dormitory life will be the greatest thing ever. A few of you will hate it. Not all dormitories are alike, however. Some consist of suites of four or five rooms with a common living room, while others are made up of individual rooms, usually shared by two students, opening on a corridor. Some are apartments for four to six persons, often in a high-rise building. But most of you will have to share; you will have roommates or a roommate. Students who have their own room at home and are used to privacy often find it difficult to live with roommates. Colleges often try to match people with similar interests and values, but they don't always succeed. Look upon getting along with your roommate or roommates as one of the things with which the collegiate experience provides you. Learn to give and take.

Many roommates, even when randomly matched, become close friends, and most get along well enough to survive the year. But sometimes they hate one another. If you are stuck with a roommate you can't stand, try to solve the problem. The first step is to try to work things out between yourselves. Often your roommate doesn't know what it is that bothers you. Sometimes just bringing grievances out in the open in as pleasant and unemotional way as possible improves the situation. If the problem persists, a resident staff member, typically an upperclassman or graduate student, may be able to help. If things are really bad, you may have to try to change.

Dormitory living offers tempting distractions. Nearly always there is something interesting going on. It is easy to put off studying in favor of a card game, a yak session, or even just watching *Jeopardy*. If you can resist these kinds of temptations when you have work to do, you've beat your major enemy in your pursuit of a successful college career.

Most places now give you a choice between coeducational and single-sex dormitories. Typically, the relationships between men and women in coeducational dormitories is that of being good friends. Pairing off is the exception rather than the rule, and dating is usually with persons living elsewhere.

Most schools have rules against alcohol and drugs in the dormitories. These rules are often ignored. Although this book isn't meant to deal with problems of alcohol and drug abuse, we have to say something about them, because they are often critical causes of poor study habits. It's your decision as to whether you are going to drink or use drugs, but you should be aware that the line between use and abuse is often hard to find. Students who regularly drink a lot or spend a lot of time stoned *always* end up in academic trouble.

That you should know. Don't be tempted to do something that doesn't fit in with your personal values. Life styles differ, and sooner or later at any institution you will find people you can be comfortable with.

Dormitory living or living in shared apartments gives you a chance to get to know different kinds of people. Take advantage of that. Students sometimes make their closest friends during their freshman year.

ORIENTATION AND ADVISING

Every place has some sort of orientation program for entering students, whether freshmen or transfers. Don't skip any part of this program if you can help it, even if the speakers are boring and repetitive. You might miss out on some crucial information (about drop dates, for example), but even more important you'd be passing up a chance to meet a broad range of your classmates. Everyone is floundering, and it is easy to strike up conversations with other students, if only to exchange gripes.

You're going to be given a lot of miscellaneous printed and mimeographed material. Read it and save it, because later in the year you'll have questions that didn't occur to you at first, and the handouts are your first line of information. If you have questions that the handouts don't answer, go to official sources—resident staff, faculty advisors, deans—rather than rely on guesses from the student grapevine.

Usually you are given a tour of the campus during orientation. Get to know the layout and the surrounding student community. You'll feel at home sooner when you know something about the place. Check out the library. You will—or should be—spending a lot of time there. The sooner you know how it works the more efficient you will be. Also check out the student union, if there is one. On most campuses this is the center of student activities. Wander through the classroom buildings. This is a good time to find out how long it will take you to bike or walk from your dormitory. On big campuses getting from one class to another sometimes takes more time than you are allowed.

Your student newspaper probably puts out an orientation issue. It will have a lot of useful information. We don't need to tell you to read the student paper regularly—most students do. But we urge you to check out those features that make it special—listings of concerts, films, plays, etc. Usually during orientation there will be a lot of things going on—parties, meetings, etc. Go to as many as you can. It will help you get over homesickness and, again, introduce you to a lot of people.

Placement tests in such subjects as mathematics, foreign languages, and English are usually given during the orientation period. Find out what tests you are required to take and which ones might be advantageous to take even if not required. Placement policies vary from school to school, but many colleges will give credit in addition to advanced placement if you score high enough. If you're still in high school and have taken some advanced placement courses, be sure to take the CEEB Advanced Placement Tests. If you do, you may find yourself exempt from some college requirements and ahead on credits.

LEARNING TO COPE

Academic Demands

High school is not college. You have probably heard that a thousand times. Even so, listen. If you went to a high school that falls in the statistically average range, a lot of your fellow students probably weren't headed for college. You could easily shine. And if you went to a below average high school, you could almost count on being in the upper half or even near the top of your class. In either case, you're likely to be in for a bad surprise. In most colleges, particularly four-year colleges, you are going to find yourself in the fast lane. Most college students were in the upper half of their high school class, and if they were lucky enough to go to a really good school, they've got a real advantage. A lot of your fellow college students are going to be people who were also student leaders—class officers, student body presidents, newspaper editors—in short, doers and achievers, some of them from the most prestigious high schools in the country.

What is even more important, college professors are not likely to gear the work to the average student. A well-known professor used to say (he's now retired) that if more than two students understood what he was talking about he wasn't doing his job. Professors like to aim their courses at the superior students, and they expect everyone to meet higher standards. The kind of work that got you A's and B's in high school could easily get you C's, D's, and even F's in college.

Because a lot of students aren't prepared for the tougher job of studying in college, they do badly in their first semester. They get discouraged, and they want to drop out. That's why we think this book is especially useful to students entering college. We hope that it will help you head off trouble. Remember that many students who drop out are just as able and motivated as those who finish.

Aside from the competition and the higher standards of work, there's another big difference between high school and college. Even if you went to a high school that demanded a lot of work, it was pretty well laid out for you. A lot of it was covered in class, and homework could sometimes be completely done in study hall. Long-range projects, such as term papers, are fewer and less demanding in high school. You were mainly graded on what you did in class and in daily homework.

This is reversed in college. You spend relatively few hours in class, and except for lab, discussion sections, and seminars, you are hardly graded at all for what you do in class. Instead of an hour or two of homework for five classes, you have two or three hours of work for every hour in class. If you carry the standard course load of fifteen semester hours, you can easily expect to spend about thirty hours a week in study and preparation. There are no supervised study halls in which you have little choice but work. Instead you will have all of your nonclassroom time to use profitably or to waste, as you choose.

Most professors won't require you to do your work on a daily basis. Sometimes you will be given a syllabus outlining an entire semester's work. Nobody checks to see if you are keeping up with the reading or working on your term papers. You might have an occasional quiz or midterm, but sometimes there will be only one exam, the final. Given that, it is all too easy to let all the reading slide until the night before the final. This approach yields, at the best, a C.

In college you are treated as an adult. Most of the selective colleges boast of this. You are on your own, not only academically but in how you behave. College abounds in distractions that invite procrastination. In later chapters we'll deal with the problem of structuring your time so that you can get the most out of studying. But for now, let us remind you that with your new freedom goes a lot of responsibility.

Social Pressures

We all like to be liked, and everyone needs friends. Making and keeping new friends will be one of the best things about your college years. But if you run into problems with your social life, your academic work will suffer.

Take Suzy, for example. A bright, hard-working student in the small-town high school she attended, she was liked and respected by her high school classmates. Although she was not the most popular girl in her class, she had a few close friends both from school and from her church youth group. She looked forward to attending the state university. When she got to the university she was placed on a dormitory hall whose residents all came from urban areas. They were sophisticated. All of them drank, two of them were experimenting with drugs, and most of them talked freely about their sexual experiences. Suzy had not faced this sort of thing before. She felt awkward and uncomfortable. Her roommate, with no intention of being unkind, dubbed her the "country mouse," and one of the other girls changed this to the "church mouse." She couldn't feel close to anyone, and she became more and more the outsider. As she withdrew from social contacts, the other girls became increasingly hostile. Lacking the social skills and the confidence to seek friends elsewhere, Suzy spent most of her time alone. Although she studied diligently, it became harder and harder for her to concentrate. Most of the time she was depressed and anxious. She began to wonder if she were out of step with the rest of the world. By late October she was thoroughly miserable. After a long, tearful weekend at home, she withdrew from the university.

The saddest part of the story is that Suzy made no attempt to solve her personal problems. She might well have weathered the semester if she had sought the help of her resident advisor, her dean, or someone at the counseling center. The only thing she knew how to do was to control her

environment by withdrawing to the safe, circumscribed life she knew.

There are all sorts of social pressures in college, most of them very different from the kinds of pressures you encountered in high school. You will be thrown in with people with different ideas, values, backgrounds, and ways of living. These will challenge things you have always taken for granted. So your first year in college can be painful and threatening. Even if you go to a community college, you are going to find a far more diverse social environment than you experienced in high school. A lot of the students will be older and perhaps hard for you to relate to. At the same time, remember, those students in their thirties are going to be equally challenged and threatened by students fresh out of high school. Perhaps some of your views should be challenged, and those that you stick to can't really be your own until you have examined them for yourself. The wider horizon of social life in college can help you do that. Be prepared for some uncomfortable moments. You may be the only person of your race or from your part of the country in your dormitory. If so, expect some of your fellow residents to be thoughtless. They may not mean to do so, but they can well offend you. Take it in stride.

There are ways of dealing with social problems in college without giving up or without continuing to be miserable. If you have trouble coping with social pressures, seek out the help of one of the support services at your institution.

Parental Pressure

Pressure sometimes comes from parents. Most parents mean well, but some of them really don't know how to help with the problems their sons and daughters have in adjusting to college. A few of them seem to go out of their way to add to their children's difficulties.

Parents don't know what kinds of problems you face because they are not you. They don't know about the competition, both social and academic, that you face, and they may not be aware of the standards, both social and academic, to which you are held. If you are at an academically competitive college, the easy A's and B's that you were used to in high school may not appear. Your parents are bound to be disappointed if your college grades fall way below those you got in high school. They may bug you about trying harder. At worst they may threaten to take you out of college, or cut off your funds. Consider that tuition, to say nothing of room and board, may be a real financial strain for your parents.

Sometimes parents regard their children as extensions of themselves and think it only right and natural that they control what their sons and daughters do. In their involvement and identification, they forget that we are all different and that each person must develop in his or her own way. They forget that you are now a young adult and that you must be responsible for yourself. Inevitably, students are going to do things that their parents regard as unacceptable. Even though what you do is perfectly consistent with your own values, you may come up against anger and resentment. If you are in conflict with your parents, you can help make things better by looking at the matter from their point of view. You don't need to sacrifice your own values or your right to live according to your own standards, but it will help if you can understand how they feel. If you are considerate about small but important things such as writing home and telephoning, and if you can demonstrate your adult status by doing your work and handling your finances, you may not eliminate conflict but you will keep it to a minimum.

Another big source of conflict between parents and students is the matter of what courses they take and what their majors are. Some parents are convinced that only certain subjects are worth studying and others are a waste of time. The engineer who can't understand why his son is taking courses in art and music, the artist who is horrified by his daughter's enthusiasm for economics and accounting, the physician who insists that his son follow a premedical curriculum, the lawyer who is upset because her daughter has no professional aspirations, the mother who is shocked because her daughter wants to be an electrical engineer are all cases in point. Parents who have never been to college themselves have, perhaps, the most difficult job of understanding what it is you want to study and to do. But remember one thing: Students who merely accept the courses that their parents map out for them are usually headed for trouble. They are living out someone else's aspirations, not their own. Sometimes students get entirely through college on someone else's plans.

Such people may discover when they are thirty-five or forty that they really don't like what they are doing. A few of the more courageous ones will go back to school to correct the mistakes they made earlier.

College is a time for exploring alternatives, for examining life, for moving gradually and smoothly from parental direction to autonomous commitment. At times it is hard for both students and parents. We hope that some parents will read this book and will get the message we are trying to send. Resolving conflicts requires cooperation.

Financial Pressures

You may have had some experience in managing money before you get to college, but, somehow, it is different when you are on your own. You may be careless in budgeting your money, and discover for the first time that no one is around to dole out cash when you run out. You'll save yourself a lot of headaches if you learn how to manage your money effectively. College is expensive, and if your parents are supporting you in whole or in part, you will do them a big favor by not being careless with money.

Students who go away to college usually open a checking account in the town where their college is located. A common arrangement is for a parent to deposit a certain amount of money in the student's checking account on a regular basis, usually once a month.

If you've never learned how to balance a checkbook, get someone to show you how. Keeping accurate records is important. It can save you the embarrassment and considerable cost of a bounced check. Get into the habit of withdrawing enough cash on a regular basis to meet ordinary expenses. Most banks charge from ten to twenty cents per check, and if you write a check for every little two-dollar purchase, you are wasting a lot of money.

Expenses at the beginning of the college year are likely to be heavy because you will be buying books and supplies. After a few months, however, you will have a good idea about how much it costs you to live. If you don't get enough money from home, look for a part-time job. These are often surprisingly easy to find in a college community. You may have heard—and it's true—that college students who pay part of their own way are more motivated than those who don't. But then again, a part-time job forces a student to budget time more carefully. Management of time is the most important aspect of effective studying.

Many students receive financial aid from their colleges. A typical pattern is to have some funds in direct scholarship, some as a loan, and some in a work-study job. Every institution has a financial aid officer to whom a student can turn if it is necessary to have his or her aid package changed. In addition, many institutions have an emergency loan fund to help students out of temporary difficulties.

Meet your financial obligations promptly. In our credit-oriented society, a good credit rating is a strong asset and a bad one a burden. Competition among banks makes it easy for college students to get credit cards. Don't abuse the privilege. The penalties are more than the monetary assessments. Don't let your college bills go delinquent. If you are behind in paying your college bills or library and parking fines, you may be barred from the classroom. In any event, your college won't grant you a degree or send out a transcript until you have paid all of your bills.

Being Involved

You probably know a good bit about college life by now. If you spend fifteen hours a week in the classroom, thirty or so hours in study and review, and fifty-six hours a week sleeping, you are not far from being the typical student. You still have more than sixty hours a week left for other activities. Even if you have a job that takes up twenty hours a week, you still have some time. You can use that extra time to learn a lot of things that are not part of the formal curriculum, particularly how to work with and relate to other people.

But don't overdo it; take it easy. Don't get involved in too many extracurricular activities, particularly during the first few weeks. There is a lot of waste motion in getting started in college, and it may be harder than you think to settle into a routine that makes time for study. You will need some time to assess just how hard college work will be for you. Take most of the first semester getting used to the academic schedule. Don't try to throw yourself into every activity that looks interesting or profitable.

Somewhere in your schedule, allow time for regular exercise. At the minimum, medical experts tell us, it should be the equivalent of a half-hour a day of walking. Jogging is the "in thing;" some evidence suggests that in addition to its physical benefits, it is a good antidote for depression. If you play a varsity sport, don't expect to do much else. Even nonrevenue sports, such as tennis and baseball, take up a lot of time. If you do play one of the varsity sports, you will have to be careful to budget time for studying. Some big institutions run study sections and tutoring services for varsity athletes. Make sure you take advantage of this or whatever other services your college offers to help you meet the time demands of playing on a varsity team.

Clubs and Organizations. Every campus is crowded with clubs and organizations. There is something for every taste. If drama isn't your thing, how about working on the campus radio station? Some schools even have a TV studio. There is always a student newspaper. There may be a debating society, a chess club, a folk dancing club, and even a mountain climbing club on some big campuses. Investigate those things that interest you. Find out what the people are like who are in organizations you might want to join.

There are a lot of reasons for choosing an organization to join. The most important one is to do something you like doing. Another is to give you experience at something you might want to do later in life or something related to your choice of a profession. If you are headed for medical school, you may join the drama club for fun and the premedical society because it sponsors activities which will help you meet your professional goals. And, of course, organizations provide opportunities for leadership and for learning how to work comfortably with other people.

A note of caution: Like varsity athletics, extracurricular activities place heavy demands on time. Putting out a newspaper is not a small job. You could find yourself giving so much time to your nonacademic activities that your grade point average will suffer. If you find yourself pressured by some extracurricular activity, drop out. No matter what the activity is, it isn't worth the risk of academic probation.

Student Government. Student government is a lot more important in college than in high school. On some campuses, students literally run everything but the academic curriculum. Student government may even have the sole responsibility for discipline. If you have a political streak or if you would like to have a say in how things are run, this is something to get into.

You will want to start at the local level. Go to your dorm council meetings or their equivalent (there are even such organizations for commuting students) and speak up. If you are active, there is a good chance that you will be elected to some position sooner or later. That can give you an opportunity to test your skills at management and leadership. Again, remember not to spend too much time at it. Some people who are heavily into student government get swamped by it and neglect everything else.

Sororities and Fraternities. Sororities and fraternities, to be found at most four-year colleges, offer a way of life that is very attractive to many students. They provide friendships and social activities with people who share your tastes. On some campuses they are very important and on others they are minor. At some schools, the majority of students belong; at others, only 10 to 15 percent. Whether they are for you or not depends upon your needs and interests. Don't automatically assume that you should join one or, for that matter, that you should avoid them at all costs. For some people they are the most enjoyable part of their college years. For others they are confining and narrow. Don't be pressured one way or another, either for the so-called social fraternities and sororities, or for the service fraternities and sororities. If you participate in rush, the chances are that you will end up in an organization that suits you or not in one at all. If the latter happens, it is probably for the best. It means that the chances are you would not have been happy in any of the sororities or fraternities on your campus. If you end up in *any* organization that you don't like or that conflicts with your values and beliefs, drop out. If you do drop out, the chances are that you will find congenial friends elsewhere.

Do be involved in some aspect of college life. It will add immeasurably to the quality of your college experience. You will find that you are a part of a living community and not merely an anonymous body in the classroom. And, of course, you know that you will get from an activity what you put into it. If you give some of your time and energy to your college community you will get something back in return.

Now that we've covered some of the things that help you get off to a good start in college, we're ready to get down to the main topic of this book: how to organize and use your time for effective study.

2 THE ART OF STUDYING

You may not be interested in some of your courses, or you may be interested but can't bring yourself to do the homework. People who are interested or who don't study as much as they should usually feel guilty. But that doesn't help. In fact it usually makes matters worse by adding anxiety and depression to the problem. Most people who advise students and who know what their problems are believe that lack of motivation is responsible for more failures than inadequate background or lack of ability. Not being motivated is about the worst academic problem a college student can face.

Before we tell you about some of the specific techniques of efficient study, we need to say something about the problem of motivation and what you can do about it. We can't make you want to learn, but we can say some things that might help you want to learn. First of all, you need to be clear about your reasons for going to college. On page 12 you will find a list of statements about motivation for college. By ranking these yourself, you can determine what things are important to you and what goals and values you have that may make for success in college. There are no right, wrong, or magical answers, but if you are honest you can see yourself more clearly than if you don't think about such things. Such a self-examination could lead you to change some of your goals or make you more aware of what you need to do in order to meet your goals.

IMPROVING MOTIVATION

Why is it hard to study? For one thing, there is the difference between high school and college. In high school someone is usually breathing down

Motivation for College

The following questions are designed to help you think about your motivation and to give you some insight into it. Read completely through each group of items; then rank them in importance by using 1 for the phrase that applies best to you, 2 for the phrase that applies next best, and so on.

I. I came (or will go) to college because—

_____ I know what I want to be, and college preparation is necessary for it.

_____ my folks wanted me to, even though I didn't.

_____ I thought it would be a lot of fun.

_____ I wanted to gain a better knowledge and understanding of the world I live in.

_____ many of my friends did, and I wanted to be with them.

_____ I wanted to get away from home.

_____ I am particularly interested in athletics and student activities.

_____ a college degree seems indispensable in this day and age.

_____ I like to study and am particularly interested in certain subjects.

II. I want to make grades that are good enough to—

_____ let me stay in college.

_____ meet degree requirements.

_____ let me participate in extracurricular activities.

_____ put me on the honor list and give me special recognition.

_____ make an outstanding record in college.

III. My motivation for making grades is to—

_____ prove to myself that I am learning something.

_____ secure a good job recommendation.

_____ please my family.

_____ do better than my competitors.

_____ live up to my reputation of being a good student.

_____ be respected by my teachers.

IV. I sometimes don't study when I should because—

_____ I worry about my personal problems.

_____ I simply can't get interested in certain subjects.

_____ I am too involved in extracurricular activities.

_____ I am bothered by illness and poor health.

_____ I get distracted by things going on around me.

_____ I tend to keep putting off my work.

_____ I am easily tempted to do more interesting things.

your neck every day to get you to do your work, and hardly any internal push is required just to get by. In college external pressure scarcely exists. You are on your own. For most students there are no study halls; homework is not assigned on a daily basis, and sometimes a single assignment may be given for the entire semester.

Another reason it's hard to study has to do with the absence of short-term goals. Most students who go to college express some kind of career interest. They want to be doctors, lawyers, engineers, business executives, teachers, and so on. But these aims are often pretty vague, and it is hard to see how day-to-day schoolwork relates to them. Then aims shift, and when they do, students are often left at sea. Few students are absolutely sure of what they want to do in life, and fewer know exactly what they must do in college to prepare themselves for their chosen careers. Not being sure makes students uncomfortable and anxious, but it doesn't provide any real motivation for studying.

There is nothing wrong with not knowing what you want to do, even after you've been in college for a while. One of the things college can do for you is to give you enough experience to help you find your career goals. But occupational choice is often difficult, particularly for students in a liberal arts program. In the absence of such a choice, many students can't work up much enthusiasm for studying. Or worse, they feel positively paralyzed without some clear goal in mind, even if they like their courses.

We can't do much in this kind of book to help you make your career decisions. This is something most people work out for themselves. Many campuses have career counseling services. If you are concerned about your career goals, you should take advantage of any such service available. Career counseling can help you find out what your interests and talents really are, and they can provide you with information about the kinds of careers that attract people like you.

But if you don't feel any clear-cut call to a particular occupation, don't let it worry you. One thing you can be sure of: If you haven't made a career choice by the time you are twenty-one or twenty-two you are not going to turn into a pumpkin. If you're in a liberal arts curriculum, remember that the subjects you study will have little or no direct relation to what you will end up doing. A liberal arts curriculum is not designed to train for some specific occupation. Rather its purpose is to make you into an educated, thoughtful person, and to give you skills in critical reading, writing, and thinking. What you study is useful and important in its own right, and you owe it to yourself to make the most of it.

The Importance of Grades

Grades are not the measure of a person nor are they even the sole measure of academic accomplishment. They are only one rather imperfect reflection of how much you have learned in your various courses. People can learn a great deal and acquire a good education without making high grades, and some students who make straight A's may concentrate so much on getting them that they really miss their education. But grades are one of the concrete and particular things society uses to judge what you are likely to accomplish in the future. They work, however imperfectly.

If you want to go on to graduate or professional school, grades are even more important than you think. The competition among applicants for law school, medical school, veterinary school, graduate business school, and most programs in graduate arts and sciences is formidable. Your college grades will probably be the most important factor in determining whether you are admitted or not (though letters of recommendation sometimes count even more—we'll say more about this later). Experienced admissions officers know that grades predict success in advanced work better than do test scores. Of course, a few people with the right connections or with a great record of achievement in extracurricular affairs will be admitted despite mediocre grades. But that happens less often than you think. The best graduate and professional schools have two to ten times as many applicants as they have spaces. They can afford to take only the best. In many fields, no one with less than a B average is even considered, and some schools seldom admit anyone with less than an A– average. So, if you plan to go on to advanced studies, you can't afford to dismiss grades as unimportant, even if you have reservations about them, as many of us do.

Satisfaction in Study

Learning, even studying, doesn't have to be a chore. It can be a real source of satisfaction. In the last chapter we pointed out that if you get no intrinsic pleasure from learning, perhaps you shouldn't be in college, at least for now. Part of the trick in liking to study is in knowing what to learn and how to learn it. If you can pick up a book, read it with reasonable speed, and know how to select the main points and remember them, you're the kind of person who probably does get satisfaction from learning. You're lucky. You will be the richer person for it. Besides acquiring some new information or being challenged to examine some new ideas, you'll have the kind of feeling of pride that a craftsperson has in work well done. Once you have done a good job at studying, you will be in a better position to do it again. The more you read and learn, the easier it is to read and learn. Instead of being a dull, frustrating chore, studying will be something satisfying in itself. If you develop a high level of skill in studying, we can almost guarantee that you will come to enjoy studying more and that you won't dread it. If despite your best efforts studying is still a dull task, it may be that you have a problem in reading, writing, or doing ordinary arithmetic. If so, do something about it. Your college almost certainly has some program for helping students for whom the ordinary procedures in studying are a monumental chore.

Good study habits will let you get more done in less time. The time you save can be used for the things you like to do best. If you earn part of your expenses, you'll have more time for work. We can tell you with complete confidence that if you learn to study in the way this book tells you to, you will have more time to do the things you like to do—even if it is only more studying. A good deal of evidence accumulated over the last fifty or so years indicates that—for whatever reason—students who have been taught how-to-study methods make better grades with less time spent in studying than do the same kind of students who have not been so instructed.

Of course, it is not *how much* you study but *how well*. Students who study all the time—those who study thirty-five hours a week or more—on the whole make poorer grades than those who study a shorter amount of time. This isn't because those who study long hours lack academic ability. Many bright and quick students study day and night without getting the grades they ought to. As it is with many other things we do, it's the quality rather than the quantity that counts.

DEVELOPING PERSONAL EFFICIENCY

Sara is chronically behind in her work. It is not that she doesn't try. Every evening after supper she goes to her room and picks up a book. Most of the time, however, something happens to interrupt her. The telephone rings, or someone has an urgent personal problem that he or she wants to talk about, or she can't find the book she needs. By the time she gets down to work, she's too sleepy to concentrate.

Scott, a premed, is so worried about his performance in chemistry that he spends four and five hours at a time studying it and neglects his other subjects. He doesn't think about them until exam time, when he realizes how far behind he is. Jack is so anxious about falling behind that he jumps from one subject to another and never stays with one long enough to master the material.

Sara, Scott, and Jack share the same problem. They have not learned how to organize their time

for effective study. Even if you're a student who studies long and hard, the chances are that you're wasting time. In fact, as we implied above, if you study many more hours than other people with the same kind of schedule, you're probably wasting a good deal of time. This problem can be corrected, but only you can do it. The remedies we suggest have to be, like a diet, faithfully carried out.

The Value of a Schedule

The most important thing you can do by way of organizing your life for studying is to make a schedule. A schedule makes time by cutting out waste motion. It keeps you from worrying about what you are supposed to do next. Most things in life are organized for you. If you have a job, you are supposed to turn up at a particular time, and your meal times are pretty much set. But in studying, you have to organize your own time.

And then there are minor benefits from organizing your study time. Assigning time where time is due keeps you from neglecting one thing for another. It helps you to study subjects at the best time for those subjects rather than at the wrong time. By having a schedule you can avoid the hit-or-miss approach that causes some students to tackle the hardest or dullest subject when they are least able to concentrate.

A Sample Schedule

We can't make a schedule for you. You have to make your own so that it fits your class hours, activities, and part-time work. But we can give you some tips on how to make one. Start with the example on page 15. There you will find a schedule for a student carrying a fairly heavy load. She is taking economics, psychology, German, organic chemistry, and English. She is also in ROTC and she holds a part-time job ten hours a week.

We have blocked out her schedule into one-hour periods because many of the gaps in a student's class schedule are only an hour long. These spare hours add up, and you should use them. Research on effective work shows that most people do best by working intensively for a reasonable period of time and then resting or switching to another task. There is an optimal cycle of work and rest for every job and for every individual. For the kind of work that studying requires and for the typical student, a period of forty to fifty minutes

Sample Schedule

Time \ Day	Monday	Tuesday	Wednesday	Thursday	Friday	Saturday	Sunday
7:00		DRESS	AND	EAT			↑
8:00	ECON.	Study	ECON.	Study	Study		
8:30	LECT.	Engl.	LECT.	Engl.	German		
9:00	Study	ENGL.	Study	ENGL.	ECON.		
9:30	German	CLASS	German	CLASS	DISC.		
10:00	GERMAN	↓	GERMAN	↓	GERMAN		
10:30	CLASS	PSYCH.	CLASS	PSYCH.	CLASS		
11:00	Study	LECT.	Study	LECT.	Study		
11:30	Econ.	↓	Econ.	↓	Psych.		
12:00			LUNCH				
12:30							
1:00	CHEM.	CHEM.	CHEM.	ROTC	CHEM.		
1:30	LECT.	LAB.	LECT.		LECT.		
2:00	Study		Study		Study		
2.30	Chem.		Chem.	↓	Chem.	Eight hours of	
3:00	Job		Job	Job	Job	study distributed	
3:30						as needed. among	
4:00						five subjects	
4:30		↓		↓	↓		
5:00	↓	Recre-		Recre-	Study		
5:30		ation	↓	ation	German		
6:00			DINNER				
6:30							
7:00	Study	Study	Study	Study	Recre-		
7:30	Engl.	Psych.	Engl.	Chem.	ation		
8:00	Study	Study	Library	Study	Recre-		
8:30	Psych.	Econ.	(Papers)	Chem.	ation		
9:00	Study	Study	or	Study	or		
9:30	Chem.	German	(reports)	Econ.	Library		
10:00			RECREATION				
10:30							
11:00			SLEEP				↓

of work followed by ten minutes or so of rest or change is just about right. We'll have more to say about this later, but, all things considered, an hour that is well used is pretty close to the best unit of time for most college study.

Notice that the hours in the sample schedule are blocked off for specific subjects. Assigning specific subjects will save you the time you might spend trying to decide what to study next, and it will help you put together the right books and materials.

The sample schedule is tough. This student is serious—she wants to do well. You may not want to settle for so rigorous a routine, but make your schedule as close to your own ideal as you can. Remember, however, you're supposed to stick to your schedule. Don't make it so ideal that you won't follow it. A schedule that you don't follow can be less than useless because it deludes you into thinking that you are doing something that you really aren't.

Put your schedule in a place where you are apt to look at it: in your notebook, over your desk, or even in your mirror or on your "must do" bulletin board.

Studying for Lecture Courses

One of the best things you can do for yourself in a lecture course is to schedule a review of your notes as soon after class as possible. First of all, you need to make sure that you really understand your notes. It's easy to think that you have assimilated the lecturer's main points just because you followed them when you were in class. Second, you need to be sure that there are no mistakes (errors can be fatal in something like organic chemistry).

Unless the lecture is unusually well organized and you are a top-notch note taker, you should revise or even rewrite your notes, eliminating trivial points and expanding those that are important or rewording those that are difficult. If you let too much time pass before you do a revision of your notes, you'll find it to be a hopeless task. Nothing can be worse than looking at your notes and saying to yourself: "Why did I write that down?"

If you have a study period for a particular subject just before the class, use it to read the assignment that goes with the lecture. Reading about a topic before you hear about it is effective because what the lecturer is saying will fall into

place. Even if you don't understand what you read too well, just being familiar with the vocabulary will help you. This is particularly important in the sciences. But, we must admit, some lecturers don't follow the organization of the reading assignments. If that is the case, there are a few things you can do. You can try to integrate your notes with your text or readings. And you can look for reading material that does parallel the lecture after you have heard it. Don't hesitate to ask the instructor for help in finding such material. Getting things from two sources—lectures and reading—really helps.

Studying for Recitation Courses

In most of your basic language courses, and in some math courses, you have to recite, in one form or another. Try to prepare for this as close to *before* the class as possible. Even an hour probably won't do for your major preparation, but if you even have fifteen minutes, use them to go over what you might say or write on the blackboard.

The really major problem with most recitation courses is almost never mentioned. It is that languages and mathematics, more than almost any other subjects, tend to be cumulative. If you miss the Jackson administration in American History you have missed a crucial episode, but the chances are you can still follow the events that led up to the Civil War. But in language and math courses if you miss something early on, you will find yourself totally baffled by what is going on later. Poor preparation snowballs in such courses. And it gets worse. If you don't know what's going on, you feel like an idiot asking questions. So as assignments pile up you fall farther and farther behind. The moral is: Keep up. But if you don't, seek help from your instructor or your adviser.

Making a Schedule

As we've said before, how you make your schedule is your own business, and a highly individual business it is. What you do depends upon your work habits, your abilities, and the courses you are taking. The old rule says that you should spend two hours in studying for every hour in class. Maybe yes, maybe no. But *know what it takes to make it.* One thing you may not know is how much time—realistically—it takes you to accomplish what you need to do. Are you a slow reader? Can you work out problem sets, but only by taking frequent breaks to relieve the tension? These are the kinds of things you need to think about to set time limits on your studying. Everybody—factory and office workers included—does a worse job working very long hours than working for reasonable periods. If you start out by trying to do too much, you will get discouraged and perhaps give up altogether. If we have any realistic advice to give you about a study schedule it is to be moderate and sensible. Know your limitations (more about this later) and your assets.

In the back of this book you will find several pages for a "Provisional Working Schedule." You can use these, or you may even find bigger (and hence better) work sheets in your college bookstores or in the binders you buy to keep lecture notes and other things.

As soon as you know when your classes meet, put these in your working schedule. *Don't do this at preregistration.* To put it bluntly, preregistration is a mess. Do it when you know exactly what classes you will be going to. Next, fill in the other regular activities you know about (job, ROTC, etc.). Now estimate how much time you'll need to do the work in each of your subjects. Later you can adjust the study time to suit the way things are really shaping up. If you're a quick study in languages, you can shave time for French in order to make room for math or organic chemistry. On the other hand, if languages are an uphill struggle, allow extra time for them.

You may want to compare your provisional schedule with the sample schedule on page 15. The student who made this schedule has allotted thirty hours a week to study, twenty-two hours of which are scheduled for particular subjects during the week and eight of which are to be used as needed. In addition, she has reserved one evening a week for working in the library or in the computer lab on papers, reports, and so forth. She has kept another evening on reserve for emergencies. Remember, this student has a heavy load, and she must be an efficient user of her time. Should you be also?

Of the five courses she's taking, organic chemistry will take the most time. It has a laboratory, and that requires lab reports. It's the killer course for premeds, so the competition is tough, and even a passing grade is hard to get. With good sense, she has assigned six of her scheduled hours to organic, and she expects to spend some extra time on it during the weekend. Three of her scheduled hours come right after the weekly lectures. A fourth she has put on Monday evening to prepare for the laboratory on Tuesday. The last two she's assigned to Thursday night in order to have a larger stretch to write up lab reports.

German is the most difficult of the remaining subjects. While she is moderately good at languages, her instructor has a reputation for being tough. In any language course there is a lot of memorizing and translating. So, she has allowed five scheduled hours for German. She has managed to put three hours just before the class so she can be prepared for recitation.

In planning her three other subjects, she's anticipated little trouble with economics. The course she is taking is in money and banking, something in which she has an interest. The course description includes the development of the banking system, and she has a good background in the Federal Reserve System from a history course. Moreover, the scuttlebutt on campus is that the professor teaching the course is an excellent lecturer who places the greater emphasis upon lecture material. She has scheduled four hours a week for economics, two of them after the lecture and one on Thursday evening before the meeting of the discussion section on Friday.

She also doesn't expect much trouble from her English lit course. She is a fast reader, and she has read some of the assigned readings before. Rereading these with an eye to putting them in the context created by the instructor will be fun. She needs, at this stage, only to keep up with the readings in order to be prepared for class. But she knows that she will have to find some extra time in the second half of the semester when she will have to produce a major term paper.

This leaves psychology. It is a large lecture course with a lot of different kinds of students. The course, she thinks, will be interesting, and probably easy. The course syllabus tells her that the main thing is to study the text; the lectures will mainly explain and illustrate it. But the textbook is a big one, and so she has assigned three hours a week to psychology and reserved a couple of hours on the weekend in case she needs more time.

This schedule was her first guess as to the

amount of time she would need to study. She knows that she might have underestimated the amount of work she will have to do. If so, she can fall back on Friday evening.

If you total up her assigned times you will find that she will be in class or lab about twenty hours a week, studying from thirty to thirty-five hours a week, and working ten hours a week. No doubt about it, this is a heavy schedule, but this student is ambitious and disciplined, and she thinks, probably correctly, that she can hold to it. Then there is more time left over than you might think. She can quit studying at ten. That gives her an hour or so, depending upon how much sleep she needs, for going to the local hangout, watching TV (she's a news freak), or taking part in a rap session. She has scheduled leisurely hours for meals. She has time for exercise, and most of the weekend is free. For at least part of the semester, she will be able to take off one or two evenings a week (Wednesday and Friday) in addition to Saturday. What she hasn't done is scheduled time for student activities—meetings, dorm council, and so forth. She may have to make time for these kinds of things later on. Though her schedule is a rigorous one—it calls for more studying than most students do—it is still leisurely compared with the schedule of a doctor, lawyer, business executive, working mother, or someone who moonlights on a second job.

Blocking Out Your Study Time

In summary, here are our suggestions for blocking out your study time:

1. Assign less time to easier subjects, even those you like, and more for those that are hard for you.

2. Spread out study time. People learn more and remember better when studying is spread out over several sessions rather than being crammed into one session.

3. As a general rule, schedule a study review session, particularly of class notes, as close as possible after the class. This way you can correct and add to your notes while the information is still fresh in your head. But if your class is mainly recitation, as in a beginning foreign language, you should schedule a review period just *before* the class.

4. Before final exam time, set up a special schedule. Also work into your schedule a time plan for researching and writing a term paper.

Revising a Schedule

Your first schedule for the semester should not be the last. You may have been unrealistic about your total study time—either underestimating or overestimating. If so, revise. Use the schedule as a guide, particularly if you don't do as well as you think you should. After you have settled down to some regular routine, you can revise your schedule to better suit your demands. Demands vary, and you will want to trade around study times now and then. The whole purpose of a schedule is to get you into regular habits of work. If you establish good work habits you won't need to rely on your schedule as much, and you can use it only as a convenient reminder.

What if you're a total goof-off? We've known students who were stoned most of the time, or spent most of the day in bed in their rooms. You are not likely to be that extreme, but if you think you have a serious problem in keeping to any sort of schedule, seek some help. The chances are it isn't just that you're lazy or overwhelmed by a new life, or all the socializing you've suddenly discovered. Rather it is probably something that you don't recognize yourself. Take advantage of the services provided by your dean, by counseling services, or by any other person or agency that you think you might be comfortable with. Putting off looking for help just makes the problem worse.

Using Time Effectively

Many students start out with a schedule but then abandon it because they can't seem to make it work. Take Pete, for example. His schedule called for him to read for English literature from seven until ten o'clock. With the best of intentions, he would sit down at his desk promptly at seven. On an all too typical day, he began to read, but when he reached for his pen to make notes, it wasn't where he thought he'd left it. It wasn't in his jacket pocket, either, and he didn't find another in his desk drawer. He went across the hall to borrow one from a friend, but he got taken in by a hot discussion of the prospects of the Washington Redskins, and he forgot that he was supposed to be studying English. When he finally got around to leaving, somebody said something about a great TV show at eight o'clock. Pete managed to persuade himself that he could study English during the commercials. But then there was daydreaming about the next weekend. Should he try to go home to borrow one of the family cars? Ten o'clock and time to go out for a beer, and still no work done.

Dribbling away time is the single biggest block to effective study. If this is a major problem for you, you need to seek help. There are several possibilities. One is an assigned study session. Many institutions have them. They are common in varsity athletic programs, but usually everyone is welcome and in many places they have become standard. Even campus ministries sometimes sponsor them. Another is to seek some guidance. You may not be aware of the origin of your problem, and having somebody to talk to who has had experience with a lot of similar cases may be just what you need.

Here are some practical measures you can take to help you use your study time more effectively.

Establish Definite Study Periods. When you establish a study period, make up your mind that during that time you'll *do nothing else but study*. Start by making your study periods short, interspersed by definite periods of rest or relaxation. Planning for three hours at one crack and then doing nothing is worse than useless; it makes you feel guilty and hopeless. Settle for one hour at a time. If you really have a problem concentrating, cut that down. Twenty minutes spent actually studying is better than an hour procrastinating. With a modest goal, you'll be more likely to do what you set out to do, and you will have the feeling that you have really done something. If you opt for a twenty-minute study time, take a ten-minute break and then go back for another twenty minutes. If you can't concentrate for even such short periods of time, you're in trouble and need help. Something to consider is that you may not really be ready for college yet. Dropping out for a year or two is better than massing a lot of rotten grades.

Once you've gotten used to an easy schedule, gradually change it. The satisfaction that comes from working well when you work will help you reach for longer times. Even students who are very

proficient at studying, however, should take periodic breaks in order to sustain concentration.

Find a Good Place to Study. Some people can study in the middle of the year's biggest party, but most of us need a good place to do our work. The best place is to sit at a table or desk, not on a bed. If you read or study in a prone position, you're much more likely to daydream or doze off to sleep. Sitting up straight provides the degree of muscle tone necessary to keep you alert.

If you're easily distracted, keep your table or desk clear of everything not connected with study. That means no pictures, trophies, radios. For the same reason, a table or desk that faces the wall or is away from people is a good idea.

Good lighting that covers the entire working area is important. Avoid strong shadows on your work. If it's hard to see part of your work, you'll tire more easily and give up more quickly. Strong light that is comfortable, pleasant, and evenly distributed will make your task easier. If you are working with a computer, you don't want a glare on the screen. Glare is particularly a serious problem if you are working with a backlit screen, as is the case with lap-tops.

When you sit down to study, make sure that everything you need is at hand. Textbooks, notebooks, pens, pencils, computer discs, erasers, and a good dictionary are all included. Having to hunt for something not only wastes time but invites distraction. Remember, Pete's wasted evening started with a missing pen.

Any place that provides the best combination of the conditions we have described is a good place to work. Your own room, if other people can't distract you, is a good place. Even if you have a roommate, your room can be a good place, provided your roommate is willing to respect your privacy.

Of course, other people in your dormitory, fraternity, sorority, or apartment are on different schedules and are probably no more disciplined than you are. They interrupt you; they carry on interesting conversations within earshot; they listen to the radio or the stereo. In the war against time dribbled away, our worst enemies can be our friends, family, and roommates.

So there will be times when you'll want to find a place to work where other people can't bother you. A good place is the library. Find as isolated a spot as you can in the library. Face away from the entrance. Libraries are usually pretty good about enforcing rules against talking and other kinds of distractions. There are no TVs, no pictures of boyfriends or girlfriends to look at. The atmosphere discourages daydreaming. Nobody should be surprised to learn that students who regularly study in the library make, on the average, better grades than those who do not.

A lot of students say that they don't like to study in the library (or learning center as a lot of them are now called). That may be because a lot of students aren't really motivated to study. If you are worried that you may miss out on something interesting in the dormitory or sorority house, you may feel itchy in the library. The important thing is to find some place where you can concentrate on studying. Experiment if you have a problem here.

In some large institutions or places in which facilities are tight, the library may be too crowded. But in most places you can find a location that is free of distractions. Unused classrooms make good places to study. Then, some people who have learned to use their time well can study effectively in most unusual places—on park benches, on buses, trains, and airplanes. Neither of us works on airplanes; therefore we marvel at those people who can sit there with their lap-tops or note pads and work away. But if you are still learning the art of mental concentration, pick the library or some other place designed for and restricted to studying.

Many dormitories and fraternity and sorority houses, as well as such places as student unions and campus ministry houses, have special study rooms which are quiet and mainly free from distractions. These make good substitutes for the library.

Improving Your Ability to Concentrate

No matter how well you organize your time or how good your place to study is, you will have to use your mind effectively in order to accomplish something. There are a lot of things that make it easier to concentrate. Physical fitness is one of them. Eat regular meals and get enough sleep. Don't try to live it up and study at the same time. Drinking and some drugs, marijuana and cocaine included, give you the feeling that you are really doing a great job

at what you are doing, but nothing could be more mistaken.

Of all of the enemies of concentration probably the most common is a lack of regular sleeping hours. If you are away from home it is very tempting to stay up until the morning hours, even if it is only to watch late movies, and then sleep until eleven o'clock. Try to keep your sleeping hours on a reasonable schedule and get what is for you the right amount of sleep.

Keeping fit means both exercise and recreation. If you like tennis or squash, set aside regular times to play. If you're not all that wild about sports, then jogging, tossing a frisbee around, or even regular walking can give you the kind of exercise you need.

Sleepiness is the curse of the college student. Of course you are going to be sleepy if you don't have regular hours of sleep during the night. But some students are sleepy in class anyway, and some fall asleep while they are trying to study. Study is a quiet activity, and sometimes it is boring. Don't yield to the temptation to put off studying until you are fresh, because doing so will only get you off your schedule. The best way to fight sleepiness is to take five-minute breaks during which you rest or even nap (if you do so, make sure you have some way of waking yourself up). Most people snap back quickly after a short rest. Move around for a minute. Pace the floor. Read out loud. Activity gets the adrenalin up. Another way of fighting sleepiness is to identify those times when you are likely to feel sleepy—for most people that is after meals—and schedule for those times the things you find easiest to concentrate on.

Different from but related to sleepiness is the feeling of being tired. After a period of reading or study you may feel mentally fatigued. Mental fatigue is not the kind of fatigue you feel after doing heavy physical work. For college students it is often the result of boredom and diminished motivation for study. Take it into account in making or revising your schedule. Study for shorter periods of time those subjects that tend to make you tired or fatigued. Schedule the longer stretches of studying for those subjects that absorb your attention.

The whole point is to maintain your schedule of study. Anything that keeps you alert is what you need. You may need to use a little ingenuity to discover what works for you.

How Good a Student Are You?

Read carefully each of the following questions, and answer it honestly by writing a "yes" or "no" in the margin to the left of the question. When you are finished, see the directions for scoring at the end of the test.

1. Can you think of anything that prevents you from doing your best work?
2. Do you usually study every day in the same place?
3. Do you usually know in the morning just how you are going to spend your day?
4. Does your desk have anything on it that might distract you from your work?
5. When studying, do you frequently skip the graphs or tables in your textbook?
6. Do you frequently make simple charts or diagrams to represent points in your reading?
7. When you find a word in your reading that you do not know, do you usually look it up in the dictionary?
8. Do you usually skim over a chapter before reading it in detail?
9. Do you usually glance through a chapter, looking at the paragraph headings, before reading it in detail?
10. Do you usually read the summary at the end of a chapter before reading the chapter?
11. Do you keep your notes for one subject all together?
12. Do you usually take your notes in lecture in outline form?
13. Do you usually take your notes on reading in outline form?
14. Do you usually try to summarize your readings in a sentence or a short paragraph?
15. After you have read a chapter and taken notes on it, do you usually write a summary of the chapter as a whole?
16. Do you sit up studying late the night before an examination?
17. In preparing for an examination, do you try to memorize the text?
18. When you memorize something, do you usually do it all at one time?
19. Do you at times try to analyze your work to see just where you may be weak?
20. Do you often write an answer to a question and then realize that it seems to be the answer to some other question on the examination?
21. Do you consciously try to use facts you learn in one course to help you in your work on some other course?
22. Do you usually take notes in class just as rapidly as you can write?

Some years ago Luella Cole Pressey gave questions like these to fifty good students and fifty poor ones at Ohio State University. Good students more often than poor ones answered them as follows: (1) no, (2) yes, (3) yes, (4) no, (5) no, (6) yes, (7) yes, (8) yes, (9) yes, (10) yes, (11) yes, (12) yes, (13) yes, (14) yes, (15) yes, (16) no, (17) no, (18) no, (19) yes, (20) no, (21) yes, (22) no.

STRENGTHENING BASIC SKILLS

How do your basic skills measure up? Are they up to the kind of studying you have to do? Some years ago, Luella Cole Pressey gave some questions like those listed above to fifty good students and fifty marginal students at Ohio State University. These questions appear to differentiate between good students and poor ones. Answer the questions yourself and compare the pattern of your answers with those given by good students.

Identifying Your Weaknesses

If you have answered the questions honestly, you will be able to pick out those aspects of your study skills that need improvement. But the list is almost endless.

Reading, for example, is something most students take for granted. A lot of problems with reading you can identify yourself. Have you thought about how fast you read? Nearly everyone can read faster than he or she does even without special speed-reading training. Do you adjust your reading speed to what you read? One of us tends to read everything fast, and in order to slow down, he resorts to reading aloud. How much of what you read do you remember? Most students don't remember more than half of what they read right after they have read it. Can you decide what is worth trying to remember? Can you interpret charts and tables? The captions for them? What do you do when you first start to read an assignment? What do you do when you finish reading an assignment? How many times do you read an assignment? Do you read a textbook in chemistry or political science in the same way you read a novel?

How well do you grasp the meaning of what you have read? Some students can read and correctly interpret whole sentences in an assignment, but they somehow can't put the sentences together. The passage makes no sense to them.

Do you take notes? Not all students do. What kind of notes do you take? Are they adequate? Do you sometimes have the feeling that the instructor springs things on you in exams that were not in the lectures or in the reading assignments?

Some college students do not know the precise meaning of important words, words that instructors assume all students know. How good is your vocabulary? Do you pay attention to new words you encounter? Do you look at the dictionary regularly? Do you know the difference between the general and the technical use of words you en-

counter? Can you identify technical words? Are you sure about the meaning of common prefixes and suffixes?

A lot of students are paralyzed by simple arithmetic or elementary algebra. Are you able to deal with fractions, to carry out the ordinary operations of addition, subtraction, multiplication, and division accurately and rapidly? Sure, you may say, I just use my hand-held calculator. You may find situations in which that option is not open to you. Can you translate a word problem into the necessary arithmetic? Do you know how to deal with exponents? With fractional exponents? Can you read graphs? Can you move a term from one side of an equation to another?

Correcting Your Weaknesses

Even the best students can't answer all these questions in the right way. When they do think that they know the answers, they are often wrong. But it is still a good idea to evaluate yourself by thinking about questions like these. In the chapters that follow we will give you some specific suggestions for getting the most from the classroom experience, improving your reading skills, studying textbooks more efficiently, taking examinations, writing papers, and studying foreign languages, mathematics, and the sciences. These suggestions, if you put them to use, will pay off in more efficient study, better grades, and greater satisfaction from your college experience.

3 THE CLASSROOM EXPERIENCE

By now you know that college is very different from high school. The demands are tougher, and you have to work on your own. The relative importance of class and homework is reversed. In high school, you probably spent twenty-five to thirty hours a week in class and no more than a third of that doing outside reading and other assignments. In college you can expect to spend fifteen to eighteen hours in class and lab and approximately twice that preparing outside of class. That is one of the reasons we emphasize the skills you will need outside of the classroom. But learning in both high school and college starts in the classroom, so that is where we begin.

HOW TO GET THE MOST OUT OF LECTURE COURSES

College classes vary in size more than do high school classes, and size often determines what the course is like. Some small colleges and a few private universities that have a relatively large faculty-to-student ratio may be able to maintain most classes at no more than thirty and keep a few below ten. But most schools let the nature of the subject set class size. Freshman English, math, and foreign language courses are taught in small sections because such courses require recitation and discussion. On the other hand, a lot of courses in your first year will be so large that no discussion is possible. These courses are planned as a series of lectures. The teacher, who might well be an internationally known expert in the field, will do nearly all the talking. It doesn't matter, therefore, how many students are in the class, for the lecturer can just as easily talk to three hundred as to a hundred students. Even relatively small institutions have some such large classes.

Attending Discussion Sections

Often the one-way flow of large lecture courses is offset by small discussion sections. These meet once a week in small groups. The purpose of these sections is to allow students to ask questions and to put the lectures and readings into their own words. Because such teaching is time-consuming it is usually done by graduate students or by junior members of the faculty, some of whom may be relatively inexperienced at teaching. Moreover, little new is likely to be introduced in such sections. The result is that students who are not particularly interested in the subject have little incentive to attend. To provide such incentive, section leaders may give frequent quizzes.

Nevertheless, students are tempted to cut discussion sections, especially if the instructor appears to be inept. Before you do this, make sure that attendance is not required in your particular course. Your absence can be easily noticed, and you may find yourself with a lower grade as a result. If quizzes are given, it is your responsibility to find out when they are scheduled and what material they will cover. Then, even when sections are not particularly well taught, it is possible to get a lot out of them if you take the trouble to do so.

Our advice to all students is to attend classes, even discussion sections, regularly. Even if the lecturer goes over the same ground as the textbook, it will probably be worth your while to attend. Students who frequently cut classes usually end up having academic trouble. After you have had some experience in college and know your own strengths and limitations, you may be in a better position to make sensible decisions about cutting classes.

Understanding How the Course Is Organized

Large courses are usually well planned. The instructor doesn't just assign a textbook, start lecturing, and periodically announce a quiz or exam. Most instructors pass out an outline or syllabus at the beginning of the semester. That will include a schedule of the lectures, the reading assignments, and examination schedules. Students who are used to having assignments given every week or every day sometimes don't grasp the importance of the syllabus, and they may lose it or ignore it. Hang on to your course syllabus and consult it regularly. That will save you a lot of grief. Think ahead and make sure everything is clear for the exam dates. If you have a real problem making a particular exam, consult your instructor or the teaching assistant as soon as possible. Most instructors will allow you an alternative date if you have a good reason for requesting one.

If you happen to be sick at the time of an examination, it is your responsibility to notify the instructor or teaching assistant and request a make-up exam. Instructors differ in their policy on make-ups, but most don't like them and some even assign handicaps or penalties to students who need them. So unless it is absolutely necessary, don't miss exams.

Some instructors will tell students how exams will be weighted. For instance, half of the exam may be based upon lectures and half upon readings. Other instructors won't tell you, and they may even be annoyed if you ask. The best rule is to be prepared for any eventuality.

A lot of examinations in big lecture courses are objective. These are examinations, as you surely know, in which you write little or nothing, but rather choose among alternative answers, mark statements as being true or false, match words and phrases, or fill in the blanks. The instructor will usually tell you early in the course what kinds of exams you will have. This is very important information, for the nature of the exam will determine how you study, as we shall point out later.

Another thing you will want to know about a course is how the lectures are related to the assigned readings. This is sometimes difficult to tell, but the syllabus should help. Look through the textbook and compare the topics with those listed as lecture topics. Some instructors will not cover anything in the readings, while others follow the readings closely. Knowing ahead of time how the readings are related to the lectures will be a big help.

Improving Listening Skills

Listening to lectures in a large class can be boring. Being one of three hundred people often makes you feel like you are part of a faceless herd that is being talked down to by some remote, impersonal figure. Because there is nothing to do but listen, some people slump in their seats, take no notes, daydream, or, worse, drift off to sleep. This last is the hardest thing to fight, but you can do it if you adopt the right attitude.

To be a good listener, you have to do something active about it. If you sit up straight, tell yourself that you are going to concentrate, and take notes, you will lessen your chances of falling asleep. Even if the lecture is a bore, keep your mind on what the lecturer is saying, not on his or her mannerisms or voice, the pictures on the wall, or the view from the window. You can learn something from the worst lecturer. Taking good notes and keeping your mind on what is being said will pay you back at exam time. A lot of students have the feeling of not even recognizing what some of the exam questions are about, but if you don't go to sleep or daydream, you won't suffer from that handicap.

Taking Good Lecture Notes

Being a good listener and taking good notes go hand in hand. Some students can get by without taking notes, but they are a small minority, and you may not be one of them. A lot of students don't know how to take notes the right way, even though they had some practice in high school. Some students scribble away frantically because they don't know how to pick out what is important. Others write down an isolated word or phrase that doesn't jog their memory later on. Taking good notes from lectures is an art that develops through practice. It means that you must have an alert mind in class and that you spend some extra time after class in editing and rewriting notes. Time spent developing note-taking skills is time well spent.

Surveying, Questioning, Listening. A successful politician from the backwoods once explained how he gave speeches: "I tell 'em what I'm gonna tell 'em, then I tell 'em, and then I tell 'em what I told 'em." Good speeches, chapters, articles, whatever, give you some idea ahead of time what is to come. When you read something, you can survey by skimming the headings and reading the summaries, but when it comes to lectures, you can't survey unless the lecturer does it for you. One of the best teachers we ever knew came into his lecture hall and put an outline of what he

was going to say on the board. But don't count on that.

Try to pick up clues from what the lecturer says at the outset. When she or he says, "We're going to talk about the economic collapse of Germany after the Thirty Years' War," write that down. This gives you something to hang on it, no matter how far the lecturer wanders from the topic.

Questioning is one of the things you should do. Use the few moments before class to think of questions that might arise about the topic of the day. If you can't think of any, ask yourself "What do I already know about this topic?" If you do something like that, you will be in the right frame of mind to take part in what is going on, even if that only means listening in an intelligent mode. Keep asking questions of yourself during the lecture, even if it is only "What is he talking about?" That will help you be an active participant in what is going on, even though you are one of three hundred faceless students in an amphitheater. Keep mentally active. That is the primary rule. Even a dull lecture can become interesting if you keep working at understanding what is being said. If we have one message above all others in this book, it is that effective learning demands active participation.

Getting the Organization. If you are going to understand what you hear, you have to organize it in some way. Lecturers have little tricks to tell you about what is in their minds. Tone of voice is one. Another is such throwaway phrases as "And now let us turn to. . . ." These tell you when something new is about to be mentioned. You know then to start a new heading in your lecture notes. Some lecturers talk so fast or are so deficient in telling you what their organization is that all you can do is to write down everything that seems to be important. If that is the case, you have to organize your notes after class.

To help you provide that organization, here are some of the clues instructors give you to tell you what is important: (1) Statements such as "The main point is . . ." or "Remember this . . ." tell you directly. (2) Anything that the instructor says repeatedly is probably important. (3) Probably even more important is something that the instructor says in three different ways. (4) A change in pace may serve as a clue; when a lecturer slows down and says something very deliberately, it is important.

Lecturers each have their own style. They all have different ways of telling you what is important. Get to know the style of your lecturers. Compare your reactions to those of others. Other students may pick up things you miss.

Identify the major points the lecturer makes. Listening carefully will tell you that the lecturer organizes what she or he has to say into the equivalent of paragraphs and sections. Your job is to extract the essential information from those paragraphs. When you rewrite or edit or comment on your notes, do so in your own words. That way you will make sure that you understand what you've taken down. Watch for technical definitions or other kinds of statements that are meant to be recorded word for word.

If you have trouble organizing your notes, remember that any notes at all are better than none. If the subject is new to you, or the instructor gives you so much information that you are overwhelmed, just try to get as much down as you can and to understand it. Sometimes it can only be organized when you put it together with what you pick up in your reading assignments.

How much in the way of notes you take down will depend upon you, the course, and the instructor. Practice note taking. It is a skill that doesn't come automatically. But whatever you do, don't give up on note taking altogether. Only a tiny minority of students can get by without notes. The chances are you are not one of them.

Reviewing and Revising

No matter how good they are, your lecture notes compared to your textbook will be incomplete, imperfect, and not too well organized. Revision helps. It also provides you with a chance to review and recite what you have learned. Review and recitation are the only tools you have to fight forgetting.

Your first review should be right after the lecture or as close to that as you can manage. That way you can fill in information you may not have gotten down while it is still fresh in your mind. The worst thing you can do is to let your notes go to the point at which you cannot even decipher them before you get around to trying to review them.

Don't rewrite notes mindlessly. Having them neatly copied may make them easier to read in the future, but copying will be an empty exercise if you don't engage your mind while you do it. This is probably a good place to comment on canned notes. At some large institutions you can buy published notes. These are okay as an auxiliary aid to studying, but don't let them substitute for your own notes, or worse, substitute for not going to class. The are going to be, at best, a semester out of date, and they may even be for the wrong instructor. And no matter how "good" they are, they aren't notes you took yourself with all the thought and associations that went into taking them.

Keeping Lecture Notes

How should you keep your classroom notes? If you use a large, looseleaf notebook, you should have dividers for each subject you are taking. You may prefer having a separate spiral notebook for each course. The only trouble with that is that you may take the wrong notebook to class. Nothing is more inconvenient for study than a hodgepodge notebook in which several courses are jumbled together.

While some good students make do with almost any arrangement, the best size for most people is letter size—eight and one-half by eleven inches. A notebook of this size allows plenty of room for marginal comments and spare copying. It cuts down on the amount of page turning you must do.

For lectures, date your notes; for textbook notes, indicate the chapters or pages. Do so for every page, so that you can tell at a glance where you are in reviewing your notes. If for some reason you are caught without a notebook or with the wrong notebook, transcribe your notes at the first possible chance.

The Five R's of Note Taking

Professor Walter Pauk of the Study Center at Cornell University once described five essential aspects of note taking, which he referred to as the five R's. They are important enough to mention here:

1. Recording. Get down all the main ideas and facts.

2. Reducing. To reduce is to summarize. Pick out the key terms and concepts. You can make from your notes what some students call "cram

Illustration of Reduced Notes

Original notes	Reduced notes

History 121   February 2, 1992

The Normans (cont'd)
I. Gov't of Henry II 1154–1189
  A. Chancery
    1. Documents became uniform.
    2. All executive orders dependent on written orders from king—per breve regis.
  B. Exchequer
    1. Administrative agents of the king: Sheriff, Viscount.
    2. Revenues were collected at Easter and Michaelmas.
      a. At Easter, Sheriff would pay one-half and be given a notched-stick talley as a receipt for what he had paid. He kept one-half, the exchequer the other.
      b. Revenues computed on principle of abacus.
    3. Every item of income was recorded year by year on pipe rolls (rolled skins of parchment). These are extant from second year of Henry II's reign.
  C. Judicial
    1 Tried to develop a system of courts and judges that would not require his personal intervention.
    2. Itinerant judges on circuit.
      a. Extended over all England.
      b. Broke down local privileges.
      c. Led to Common Law.
    3. Early court was an assembly of the king's barons; after Henry II the court became a body of professional judges.
II. Breakup of Anglo-Norman Empire . . .

The Normans (cont'd)
Gov't of Henry II 1154–1189
1. Organization
  A. Chancery
  B. Exchequer
  C. Judicial
II. Administrative reform
  A. Uniform documents
  B. Per breve regis for executive orders
  C. Sheriff, Viscount as administrative agents
  D. Revenues collected at Easter and Michaelmas
  E. Pipe rolls record yearly income
  F. System of courts
    1. Extended all over England
    2. Broke down local privileges
    3. Body of professional judges
    4. Led to Common Law

sheets." These are lists, usually in outline form, that give you the bare bones of a course. You can use them as cues for reciting the details of what you have learned. On each page of notes you take, allow room to write down such cues. An example of some notes and their reduction is illustrated above.

3. Reciting. The advice above gives you an important principle. Recite to yourself. Don't assume you know something just because you've read and understood it. You have to tell someone else—your instructor—about what you have learned. So recite. In your own words.

4. Reflecting. Ideas from your courses are meant to be thought about. Even though you know that, you may not practice it. It's easy to fall into just giving back the information you have learned. Don't do that. Then too, if you reflect about what you are learning, you won't be surprised when ideas turn up on examinations in an unexpected form.

5. Reviewing. The most important part of the art of studying is knowing when, how, and what to review. But however you do it, reviewing is essential. Even the accomplished performer—the pianist or the actor—knows that a review, no matter how well he or she may know the material, is essential to a professional performance.

By Way of Caution

Good students sometimes find eccentric ways of studying. If you are such a student, you can ignore nearly everything we've said. You can take notes on the backs of old envelopes if you want. If you are really good at studying you can get by with just about anything. But before you try, you had better be sure you are a virtuoso student. Even if you are, there are two pieces of advice you can't ignore. The first is to be active. Don't just listen passively. Argue with your instructor mentally. Be as aggressive as you can without actually challenging the lecturer out loud. That is one of the easiest ways of making sure you are active. The second but even more important piece of advice is to review. Few of us are gifted with the kind of memory that allows us to reproduce something new and difficult after only one exposure.

HOW TO GET THE MOST OUT OF RECITATION COURSES

Most recitation courses require little in the way of note taking. The main thing is to be actively involved. That means knowing the assignment, and it may also mean being prepared to contribute ideas of your own as well as being attentive to the ideas of your classmates.

Contributing to Discussion

Discussion classes are only as good as their contributors make them. Don't sit back and expect to be entertained. Not only will you not be doing your bit, but your instructor will probably notice. You may tell yourself: "But I can never think of anything to say." If that's the case, ask questions. It's hard to ask a dumb question. Don't be afraid to ask for information. That's what you're there for—to learn. When the instructor asks questions of the class, volunteer, even though you are not sure of the answer. Volunteering for questions is a good, active form of studying. Even if you are wrong, the instructor will sense that you are interested in what is going on and put you on the right track.

Exchanging Ideas with Classmates

Sometimes small recitation and discussion sections degenerate into discussions between the instructor and one or two students. A good discussion section is run like a seminar in which all students are expected to participate. What is more, the students are expected to talk to one another, not just to the instructor. If you are lucky enough to be in a discussion section in which the students really do talk to one another, you will have experienced one of the best and most satisfying forms of education. In a really good discussion, the instructor needs to intervene only to get people back on the track or to supply some missing information. But such a good discussion depends primarily on you, not on the instructor.

HOW TO GET THE MOST OUT OF INDEPENDENT STUDY

Almost every college or university offers opportunities for independent study. Usually, such courses are taken for a variable amount of credit depending upon an agreement between the student and the faculty member. These sometimes function as do the tutorials in British universities, but often in the sciences they involve the student's taking part in a research project sponsored by the faculty member. Whether you do original research, write an essay, or merely report to the faculty member on what you have read, independent study can be one of the best experiences of your college life. But as the phrase "independent study" tells you, it requires some discipline.

Planning Your Work

If you are working on an independent project it is tempting to put it off while you get your assigned chores out of the way. Don't fall into this trap. If you do, you will end up with an unfinished project and an incomplete for the course, or what is worse, a hastily done project and a poor grade. Students and faculty alike know that grades for independent projects are inflated, and getting a C in independent study is like getting an F in a class. You will also have made a poor impression on the instructor, from whom you may have to ask for a letter of recommendation.

So if you are on independent study, get started immediately. Decide what you need to do and build time into your schedule so that you can do some work each week. If you work in the library, set aside the necessary library hours each week. If you are working in a lab, make sure that you arrange for regular hours. If your project requires that you do interviews or make observations in the field, schedule these so that you have all of your data in time to prepare a final report.

As with any other course, make provisions to

keep your notes or whatever else you need in an organized way. Nothing makes a worse impression on a professor than to have some student who is working on a research project come into her or his office with a handful of odds and ends of paper with penciled notes and data scrawled every which way on them.

Conferences with Your Faculty Advisor

Make sure you meet regularly, at least once a week, with your faculty advisor. Don't depend on him or her to make the schedule. You do it. Faculty members have heavy demands on their time, and they are apt to forget about you or be hard to track down unless you have a regularly scheduled time to meet. Sometimes in independent study you will be part of a research team, and you will meet regularly with a group. But if you are on your own, make sure you have a regular time for conferring with your advisor. When a faculty member agrees to sponsor you in independent study, he or she has an implied commitment to spend time with you, no matter how busy he or she is.

Preparing Your Paper or Final Report

The worst mistake students make in preparing a paper or final report is not to allow enough time. If it is a typical term paper, follow the procedures described in Chapter 7. If it isn't a typical paper, make sure you have in mind the form the final report will take when you begin to gather the material. Any independent project you have worked on for an entire semester is worth the effort of a presentation that will do it justice. Don't let a hasty or sloppy presentation disguise all of the work you have done.

Sometimes when you prepare a final report in one of the sciences, the instructor will want you to follow the typical form of a scientific paper. If so, learn what that is and gear your work to fit that format.

Some Tips about Independent Study

Independent study can be one of the highlights of your college education, but don't overdo it. A student who spent half his or her junior and senior years doing independent study may be looked upon with suspicion by law school admission officers, graduate schools, and potential employers. That's mainly because of the grade inflation that goes along with independent study. If you have done a great deal of independent study, be sure that you have copies of whatever you've produced. You may want to submit these with your graduate application or give them to a prospective employer. But if you have put in a lot of time on independent study with little to show for it, those who look at your record will entertain the suspicion that you were really looking for easy A's or a way to boost your grade point average without doing too much work.

If you do a really good job on an independent project in, say, your sophomore or junior year, keep in touch with your advisor. He or she will know you well and be able to write a good letter of recommendation for you.

A FINAL WORD

This chapter is one of the shortest in the book. And for a good reason. We've already told you that in your college years you will spend about twice as much time in study outside of class as you will in class. In high school you were mainly taught in class. In college, you teach yourself. It's not that going to class is not important—for most students it is an absolute must—but it has a different flavor in college. The chances are your high school teacher monitored your work carefully. That was part of his or her job. In most colleges, the role of the teacher is different. Your professor knows more than you do, and it is her or his job to tell you what she or he knows, or lead you to discover it yourself, or better yet, show you how to discover knowledge completely on your own. Learning is vastly easier if you go to class. If you take advantage of your new freedom to cut class, to sleep, or generally to goof off, you're in trouble. Once again, we remind you that if you find going to class such an awful chore that you can't get out of bed in the morning, you ought to think about whether or not you are ready for college. You can come back if you drop out, but it is much harder if you rack up a semester of F's.

4 THE ART OF READING

But thanks to my friends for their care in my breeding,
Who taught me betimes to love working and reading.

Isaac Watts (1674–1748)

Isaac Watts is a bit stuffy for modern tastes (he also wrote "For Satan finds some mischief still for idle hands to do" and "How doth the little busy bee improve each shining hour"). But he has a point. You are lucky if you have learned to read well and you like reading. Usually, these things go together. What is certain is that if you are a poor reader you will regard reading with all the enthusiasm you have for carrying out the garbage. In college you must do more reading than you have ever done before, and if you don't read well, you need to work at improving your skills in reading. Even if you are a good reader, the chances are that you can be even better at it. When you are better at it, you will like it more. This chapter is meant to help you improve your reading skills. Some parts of the chapter may help you decide whether you need special help in reading.

Here are some questions that are meant to help you decide if you are deficient in any of the most basic aspects of reading. Answer them carefully and honestly. If you can't answer a particular question, keep the question in mind, and when you are next reading something—this book will do as well as anything—try to determine whether you have one or more bad habits in reading. Any question to which you answer "yes" marks a fault.

1. Do you move your lips or vocalize when you read? Silent reading isn't as old as you think. Until nearly modern times readers read aloud (even in the library!). But that was when books were few and much of learning was oral. Reading aloud is too inefficient for the modern world. When you move your lips, you are going through exactly the movements made in reading aloud. There are times, particularly if you are a fast reader, that you will have to slow down in order to understand something difficult. Then moving your lips or reading aloud may help. But most of the time it is terribly inefficient.

We could go on to say that moving lips is a bad habit that you ought to break. It is a bad habit all right, but it is a symptom rather than a cause of poor reading. Simply holding your lips still will not improve your reading, but if you learn to read better and faster, lip movements will disappear.

2. *Do you read words one by one?* Good readers know that some words are more important than others, and they do not give equal emphasis to each word. Reading words one by one is, like moving lips, a symptom rather than a cause of poor reading. People who read word by word have a hard time putting together the words to make sense out of them. They can understand each word as it comes, but they have no idea what the words are saying when they are put together in phrases and sentences. A lot of people who read this way are likely to write poorly and have a limited understanding of English grammar. If you think you read this way, you probably need some help from one of the study, learning, or reading skills centers in your institution.

3. *Do you often find words you do not understand or are unfamiliar to you in our assigned readings?* If so, you need to work on your vocabulary. This is probably the easiest of reading problems to correct. We will discuss some techniques for helping you to do this later in this chapter.

4. *Do you backtrack and find it necessary to reread what you have just read?* This is usually a symptom of inattention. Sometimes, though, it happens because you have not learned the technique of putting ideas together as you read so that they make sense to you.

5. *Do you read everything at the same rate and in the same way?* Francis Bacon told us that "Some books are to be tasted, others to be swallowed, and some few to be chewed and digested." Some things need only be skimmed. Other things such as good stories can be read as rapidly as possible by a mixture of reading and skimming. Still others must be read very carefully; you must go through each sentence as if every word were a mine ready to be exploded. If you don't adjust your rate to the nature and difficulty of what you are reading, you are not a good reader. More about this in the next section, Reading for a Purpose.

6. *Do you often complain that you don't understand what you read?* Some things you won't understand. All of us at some time or other are going to have difficulty understanding what we read simply because we are ignorant of the technical details of the subject. If you don't know what a spreadsheet is you can read an article on programming spreadsheets fifty times to no useful end.

You should be able to understand *most* of the textbooks assigned to you. If you don't, there are several solutions. The obvious one is that you need some tutoring in the subject matter. But then, you might just be a poor reader, something that you can correct by improving your basic language skills.

There are other faults, but these are the main diagnostic ones. If your reading is characterized by any of these things, you have room for improvement. And as we said earlier, everyone can improve his or her reading skills in some respect. There are a few people whose difficulties with reading are so fundamental and deep-seated that their problems must be described by a special word, "dyslexia." If you think you are dyslexic, you really need special help, but for most of you, just attending to a few details will improve your reading skills.

READING FOR A PURPOSE

Many students when they sit down to study just read. They don't think about the special purpose for which they are reading. The result is that they read everything—the comic pages, literature, history, chemistry, political science—in the same way. But there are almost as many different ways to read as there are things to read. How you read should depend upon your purpose at the moment. That is mainly what the next few pages are about.

Skimming

One aim in reading is to find out what something is about. You may want to know what kinds of things are in a particular book, or you may want to know if something you are interested in is mentioned, or if what the book discusses is something you already know. The way to find out is to skim.

There are several ways to skim. One is to look for signposts. In most textbooks and technical books that is easy, because the headings do most of the work for you. You can leaf through a book chapter just looking at the headings and subheadings. Another way to skim, particularly in books that don't have headings, is to look at the first sentence in each paragraph. Chances are, the first sentence contains the main idea in the paragraph. On the same principle, you may want to read the opening paragraph of each chapter or section. A third way to skim is to run your eyes over the page looking for key words. This is useful even in books that have indexes.

Skimming is a first step in studying. Because it is so important we shall have more to say about it later in this chapter and in other chapters.

Getting the Main Idea

Sometimes we read just to get the main idea. Busy professional people do that, and it is a good thing to learn how to do. A lot of the time the whole purpose in reading is just to get the main idea and then use *your own* background of knowledge to pick up the details. Reading for the main idea is what you do in the first stage of study, as part of your survey; it is the last thing you do when you review.

How do you find the main idea? This depends upon what level you are looking at. There are main ideas for entire chapters, sections, subsections, and paragraphs. Paragraphs are the smallest unit, and we'll start with them.

The usual definition of a paragraph, as a matter of fact, is that it is a section of prose that contains a single topic. Ideally, everything in the paragraph centers around that single topic (that this doesn't always happen, you will understand, is because even the best writers are not always alert). Incidentally, one of the ways you can help organize your own writing is to look for both main ideas and sloppy writing in what you read. We'll have more to say about that in Chapter 7. Suffice it to say right now, learning to identify the main or topical idea in reading will help you with your own writing.

In a lot of courses in expository writing you are told to begin a paragraph with a topical sentence, then explain it, illustrate it, support it with additional information, and finally wind up with a summary statement or a transition to the next paragraph. That is good advice. However, it is not always practical or desirable to have the first sentence contain the topical information. Sometimes a transition sentence comes first. Such a sentence shows the connection between one paragraph and the next, and it depends on a lot of things whether it should be the last sentence in one paragraph or the first sentence in another.

Sometimes authors can't give you their main idea first because you wouldn't know what they were writing about. A good way for authors to tell you something new—for example, to set forth a principle—is to illustrate it by an example or an analogy. This is a common practice in textbooks. It helps remind the reader of something she or he already knows. Keep in mind, it is the principle itself, not the illustration or analogy, that is the main idea.

Because locating the main idea is not always easy, we have provided an example on page 33. This is from a textbook on economics. There are some things we ought to say about this example.

First of all, in looking for the main idea, don't always look for whole sentences. Sentences often have more than one idea in them. The main idea is likely to be the principal clause or phrase in a sentence. You can usually boil that clause or phrase down to a few words.

To see what we mean, pick up one of your textbooks and find some sentences with main ideas. Try throwing away the modifiers. Keep only the simple subject and the essential words in the predicate (if you don't know what modifiers, simple subjects, and predicates are you are in trouble; you need some help in English grammar). The chances are you will have the main idea.

Sometimes, however, modifiers or qualifiers are important to the main idea of a topical sentence. For example, if you throw away the adjective in the sentence "Even tame lions bite," you will miss the point of the sentence. On the other hand, if you read, "The person who reads rapidly, scanning each line in the fewest number of glances and not stopping to daydream, is typically the person who learns a great deal in a

Analyzing Paragraphs

Here are two paragraphs from C. R. McConnell and S. L. Brue, Economics: Principles, Problems, and Policies, 11th ed., McGraw-Hill, New York, 1990, p. 452. In the first of these paragraphs, we have analyzed the words and phrases to illustrate how to analyze paragraphs. The second paragraph is for your own practice. Underline the important words and phrases and then write your diagnosis of them in the margin.

Main Idea →

Explanation by Example →

Economists put forth the idea that specific consumer wants can be fulfilled with succeeding units of a commodity in the <u>law of diminishing marginal utility</u>. Let us dissect this law to see exactly what it means. A product has utility if it has the power to satisfy a want. <u>Utility is want-satisfying power.</u> Two characteristics of this concept must be emphasized: First, "<u>utility</u>" and "<u>usefulness</u>" are <u>by no means synonymous</u>. Paintings by Picasso may be useless in the functional sense of the term yet be of tremendous utility to art connoisseurs. Second, and implied in the first point, <u>utility</u> is a <u>subjective</u> notion. <u>The utility of a specific product will vary widely from person to person.</u> A bottle of muscatel wine may yield substantial utility to the Skid Row alcoholic, but zero or negative utility to the local temperance union president. . . .

→ *Important Detail*

→ *Important Detail*

→ *Explanation by Example*

By marginal utility we simply mean the extra utility, or satisfaction, which a consumer gets from one additional unit of a specific product. In any relatively short time wherein the consumer's tastes can be assumed not to change, the marginal utility derived from successive units of a given product will decline. Why? Because a consumer will eventually become saturated, or "filled up," with that particular product. The fact that marginal utility will decline as the consumer acquires additional units of a specific product is known as the law of diminishing marginal utility.

short period of time," you can eliminate most of the words, translate them, and come up with "The fast reader is usually the fast learner" as the main idea.

You can also find paragraphs in which the main idea is not expressed at all. That doesn't happen very often in textbooks, but it does in literature, and particularly in fiction. A writer may spend a paragraph describing a house. The purpose, however, is not to tell you about the house, but by describing it to tell you about the people who live there. From the description you may know, for example, that they are old, fussy, and aloof. You need to be alert to these kinds of things in reading imaginative literature.

Incidentally, almost nothing you read is complete in itself. Most writers don't tell you everything essential about the subject. A writer who did so would bore you beyond endurance. He or she takes it for granted that you know certain things already—that you have had certain experiences—and that you can draw the necessary implications

from what you read. If you don't understand something you read it may be because you don't already know something needed to make sense out of the material or because you did not draw the correct implications from what was said.

Practice finding the main ideas of paragraphs. If you do, you may become so skillful that you won't have to think about it. Not only will you have mastered one of the most important aspects of efficient reading, but you probably will have improved your own ability to write.

What about main ideas for sections, chapters? If you master finding the main ideas of paragraphs, that will become natural. In one of the greatest textbooks ever written, William James's *Principles of Psychology*, a chapter of more than twenty pages is titled simply "Habit." That tells you what the chapter is about, but it does not tell you the main ideas in the chapter. To get them you have to extract the essential information from the paragraphs. So to find main ideas, concentrate on paragraphs.

Extracting Important Details

Because you can't always spot *important details* in what you read, don't think that the instructor maliciously looks for unimportant or trivial details for examination questions. More often than not, this is just a rationalization for poor reading. Getting the main idea and remembering important details usually go hand in hand. If you have really grasped the main idea, you can use it as a kind of tree on which you can hang the details. For example, if your history textbook tells you that "the Congress of Vienna was a triumph of reaction" you will be able to remember all sorts of important details—the restoration of the balance of power, the elimination of republican governments everywhere, and the attempt to reestablish old values and systems.

What is an important detail? It is often nothing more than an illustration of a general principle. This happens regularly in science texts. For example, a biology textbook may tell you that sparrows in urban centers in England in the nineteenth century were darker and grayer than sparrows in the country. The text may go on to tell you that this is an example of protective coloration and that it illustrates natural selection in operation. City birds lived in an environment of sooty, coal-dust-stained stone rather than in the woods. The ones not seen by predators (alley cats, for example) survived to breed. The result was that urban sparrows became darker than their rural relatives. The important idea is that protective coloration results from natural selection. The sparrows just provide an example. If you are really on to the problem, you can probably come up with some possible examples of your own.

What is important is a matter of judgment, and people don't always agree in their judgments. But most of the time, particularly in textbooks, which are organized to present information in an orderly way, it is easy to pick out the main idea and *important* details. If you get in the habit of reading in such a way as to identify them without thinking about it, you will be a superior student.

Reading for Pleasure

The more you read because you like to read the better reader you will become. Some people read little beyond *TV Guide*, the sports section, and supermarket tabloids. We don't mean to knock interest in any of these, but one of the things a college education should do for you is to expand the list of things you like to read. Also be aware that you can read for pleasure in all the ways you read in order to learn. Some things you will want to read very slowly, even out loud or saying the words to yourself as you read. Other things you will want to skim. Some things you won't want to remember after you have finished reading; others you will. Some things you will want to read just for the way in which they are written, others because they tell you something you want to know. Our point is that, if you learn to like to read all kinds of things, your college education will have more than paid for itself.

Evaluating What You Read

Another purpose that will guide your reading from time to time is *evaluation*. We hope that you will read controversial things, new stories, and other things that can't always be taken at face value. We even hope that you will read things that offend your beliefs and values. The important thing is to evaluate—to determine why you agree or disagree with what you read. Even textbooks are sometimes not going to square with your beliefs and preconceptions. When you disagree with something, use it as an opportunity to examine your own beliefs and determine whether you want to keep them. Sometimes you will say a resounding "yes," and at other times you will want to change what you think in certain ways.

If you take an evaluative stance when you read, it will keep you alert and you will absorb knowledge more selectively. You will become more skillful at dissecting arguments. We warn you, though, you won't be satisfied with accepting everything you read at face value.

Expanding What You Read

One of the really important purposes in reading is to expand or amplify what you read so that you can apply it to things perhaps not even imagined by the author. Sometimes you can apply what you read to your own problems. When you read this book, for example, certain things will apply to the way you do things and others won't. Are you alert enough to expand upon things that apply and in so doing make this book more relevant to your own problems? Once again, this is part of the process of making reading an active and not a passive process.

USING YOUR EYES

It may help you to improve your reading if you know something about what goes on when you read. You use your eyes, of course, when you read, but you use them in a special and in some respects a rather strange way. In this section we're going to tell you how your eyes work in reading and how knowing that may help you improve your reading. You need to know, however, that your eyes are only tools. It is your purpose, your attentiveness, your knowledge, and your attitude that really determine what you get out of reading. When these are improved, proper use of the eyes almost always follows automatically.

Eye Movements

When your eyes move across a line of print, they move in a series of quick movements broken by very brief pauses. The movements are called "saccades." They are so fast that you are not aware of them. Your brain manages to blank out whatever signals come from your eyes during these saccadic movements. You are only aware of what you see during the pauses.

You aren't even really aware of the pauses, so it is easy to believe that your eyes move smoothly across the page. But if you watch another person read you can clearly see the quick, jerky movements. Get somebody, such as your roommate, to sit next to you and read. You can then train a hand mirror on his or her eyes and so can see them as they move.

What you probably can't do, because they are so quick, is to count the movements. The pauses, which are called "fixations," last only one-quarter to one-fifth of a second. The number of pauses per line varies, of course, with the length of the line of print, the nature of the material being read, and your own skill at reading. Good readers fix, on the average, once every three words of print. The typical college reader, however, is going to average about one and one-half words per fixation. Surprisingly, there is very little difference in the speed of the saccade between good and poor readers. About ninety percent of the total reading time is spent in fixations anyway, so the speed of the saccadic movements makes little difference.

The most important difference between good and poor readers is in something else—*regressive movements*. All of us move our eyes backwards from time to time in reading. Poor readers do it more often than good readers, but there is a further difference: Good readers know *where* to regress to. They go back to the beginnings of phrases and sentences, and they can pick out important and difficult passages to reread (because that is what regressive movements amount to). Poor readers just move their eyes back because they don't understand what they have just read.

Another difference between skilled and unskilled readers is in the return movement. Return movements occur when you move your eyes from one line of print to the next. Good readers make a single, clean movement from the end of one line of print to the beginning of the next. Poor readers overshoot or undershoot, so they have to make corrections to find the beginning of the line.

Improving Eye Movements

Eye movements in reading are automatic. That means that there isn't much you can do directly and consciously to improve them. In fact, knowing about them may make you a little uncomfortable and self-conscious about reading for a while. While some reading clinics have devices that may be of some help in correcting poor eye movement, recent emphasis is on improving eye movements indirectly by improving the *mental* habits in reading. If you improve the way in which you approach reading, your eye movements will almost automatically become more efficient. One of the things that will help, however, is to keep a record of your reading speed. We'll say more about that later.

There is an upper limit to reading speed. You can't push your fixation time down to much less than one-fifth of a second. You can't increase the speed of your saccadic movements, and even the best readers, unless they are skimming, must make a fixation, on the average, about once every three words. Thus, even if you make no regressive movements and if your return movements are absolutely on target, you can't read faster than 900 words a minute. No matter what anyone tells you, reading faster than that is skimming. Some things, of course, can be skimmed, and it is useful to know how to skim well. But remember, any claim that someone can read faster than 900 words a minute is based on skimming, not reading.

Most people have a lot of room for improvement in reading speed. A typical student reads easy textbook material at a rate of between 200 and 300 words a minute. That rate can be pushed quite a bit higher, and as it increases, your eye movements will improve.

HOW TO IMPROVE YOUR READING

There are a few things nearly everyone can do to improve reading. Some of these will come naturally as you learn better habits of study, for often poor reading is the result of wandering attention, or an inability to organize what you are reading into coherent knowledge. But there are some specific steps—aside from general improvement in study skills—that will improve your reading.

Building a Vocabulary

If you're going to make sense out of what you read, you're going to have to enlarge your vocabulary as the material you read becomes more difficult. In college you are going to learn about a lot of things that are new to you. It stands to reason that you will acquire many new words. Many of these will be technical terms, peculiar to a discipline. If you take economics, you will learn about "demand curves" and "marginal utility." In psychology you will encounter "libido" and "ganglion." In philosophy you will be lost unless you grasp the meaning of "epistemology," "positivism," and "natural law." Furthermore, philosophers will use words you already know, such as "materialism" and "idealism," in very different and specialized ways. Technical terms aside, you will be asked to read books that contain words like "heuristic," "peroration," and "reticular." Knowing the vocabulary is often more than half the battle in the effort to understand.

One of the most obvious marks of a good student is command of a strong vocabulary. Good students not only recognize and correctly define more words than do poor students, but they also discriminate more carefully among the multiple meanings of words. They don't often have to go back and say, "Huh, what was that?" To read efficiently, and thus faster, you should be able to perceive the meaning of words at a glance. You shouldn't have to stop and think. Paradoxically, one of the ways to help build a good vocabulary is to stop and look the word up.

Paying Attention to New Words. Be on the lookout for new words. When you see a new word or encounter one that you have seen before but which you can't pin down, don't pass it by. Not only is that being lazy, it's a sure way to poor academic performance. The meaning of a whole sentence may hang on the new, unfamiliar word. And this is often the sentence with the main idea.

Using a Dictionary. The most important tool that a college student can have—even more important than a personal computer—is a good dictionary. Use it. Once you have spotted a new word, an old word in a new context, or a word you think you know but are not sure about, the first thing to do is to look it up in a dictionary. We repeat: *Your dictionary is the single most important study aid you own.* When you buy a dictionary, make sure you buy a good one. There are a lot of cheap dictionaries available in drug stores and supermarkets, but a cheap dictionary is like a cheap automobile tire. If that's all you can afford, okay, but as with tires you are better off sacrificing something else to get a good one—one that is well edited and not likely to fall apart.

If you don't already own one, get a dictionary intended for use at the college level. If you are lucky, your parents may have an unabridged dictionary at home, and you will find a lot of them in the library. But you need something that is portable. Some college dictionaries are available in paperback, but you are better off getting one in a sturdy binding, because it *should* get a lot of wear. One of us has a dictionary that he received as a birthday present many years ago. The binding has had to be repaired with masking tape, but its pages are still intact, and it sits right on the desk next to the word processor.

When you look up a word in the dictionary, find out the particular meaning for the context in which you found it. Many words have general meaning, but they also have particular meanings in particular subjects. A good dictionary will give you those, though it may be way down in the entry. So when you look something up, don't just settle for the first meaning that is listed, look through

What You Can Learn from a Dictionary

Here is a reproduction of the entry for "memory" in Webster's New Collegiate Dictionary. The entry tells you how to pronounce the word and how to spell the plural; it also tells you what part of speech the entry is (n = noun). It gives the etymology of the word (ME = Middle English; MF = Middle French; L = Latin). It then gives a series of definitions, and finally under synonyms (syn) it gives a number of words with similar meanings. A careful reading and study of this one entry can teach you about the correct use of a half-dozen words. (By permission. From Webster's New Collegiate Dictionary, copyright 1977 by G. & C. Merriam Company.)

mem·o·ry /ˈmem-(ə-)rē/ *n. pl.* -ries [ME *memorie,* fr. MF *memoire,* fr. L *memoria,* fr. *memor* mindful; akin to OE *mimorian* to remember, L *mora* delay, Gk *mermēra* care, Skt *smarati* he remembers] **1 a:** the power or process of reproducing or recalling what has been learned and retained esp. through associative mechanisms **b:** the store of things learned and retained from an organism's activity or experience as evidenced by modification of structure or behavior or by recall and recognition **2 a:** commemorative remembrance <erected a statue in ⁓ of the hero> **b:** the fact or condition of being remembered <days of recent ⁓> **3 a:** a particular act of recall or recollection **b:** an image or impression of one that is remembered <fond *memories* of her youth> **c:** the time within which past events can be or are remembered <within the ⁓ of living men> **4 a:** a device in which information esp. for a computer can be inserted and stored and from which it may be extracted when wanted **b:** capacity for storing information <a computer with 16K words of ⁓> **5:** a capacity for showing effects as the result of past treatment or for returning to a former condition—used esp. of a material (as metal or plastic)

the whole entry. An example of the kinds of things a dictionary entry can tell you about a word is shown above.

Every educated person should acquire the dictionary habit. Accomplished writers, who have a better command of English than most people, often have a half-dozen dictionaries for different purposes. They are forever looking up new words and even words they have used all of their lives, simply to sharpen their understanding of the language.

Vocabulary Cards and Other Aids. If you have a poor vocabulary, you will have to work extra hard to do something about it. One good old-fashioned way is to use vocabulary cards. Three-by-five index cards are best for this purpose. Carry some around with you, and when you come to a new word or a word about which you have some question, write it on the card. It would probably also be a good idea to write some hint about the context in which you found the word. Then when you have access to a dictionary, look up the word and write its definition on the other side of the card.

When you have accumulated a batch, take the cards out and look at the side with the new word. Rehearse the meaning of the word, then turn to the other side to see whether you are correct. Some people keep tabs on themselves by putting a dot on the corner of the card each time they miss the definition. The use of vocabulary cards is particularly helpful when you are in a course that makes heavy use of technical terms. Some people use the technique for general self-improvement. They set goals for how many new words they are to learn each week.

If you are a computer buff you might want to modify the technique for a computer, but that is probably a waste of time. First of all, the cards are really portable—more so than a lap-top. Second, with a computer you have to have a program to retrieve the information in a way in which you can use it for study. Speaking of computers, a lot of people have the idea that they can dispense with dictionaries because there are computer programs for checking spelling. True, we use dictionaries less to check on spelling than we used to, but spelling is not the major information you get from a dictionary. Computerized dictionaries are possible, but as of this writing, the old-fashioned book format is clearly the more useful.

Then too you can buy some canned programs—either for computers or for tape recorders—for building your vocabulary. These are useful, but they are not nearly as useful as cards you make yourself. First of all, they convert you to the passive observer or listener rather than the active participant. Second, you are the victim of what the authors of the program think you ought to learn, not what you yourself choose. Our guess is that the best use for these kinds of programs is in your car tape-deck, when you are forced to commute long distances or drive in heavy traffic.

General vs. Technical Terms. We've already referred to the distinction between general and technical words. Be sure to remember that distinction in building your vocabulary. For many technical words and technical uses of ordinary words, you may have to consult a specialized dictionary or a glossary. Many textbooks carry glossaries of technical terms. Use them. If you are going into a specialized field such as law or medicine, you may want to own a dictionary that is essentially a glossary for that field. These specialized dictionaries are expensive, but often worth it. They can be found in libraries—even strictly undergraduate libraries carry them. If you have any doubt as to whether or not you are using a technical term correctly, particularly in a term paper, consult the appropriate specialized dictionary.

We remind you once more: Technical terms are often more important than students realize. In some courses, more than half of the subject matter lies in knowing what the technical terms mean. List these terms separately, and study them. Make up your own glossaries.

Dissecting Words. You can improve your own vocabulary by learning how words are put together. English is a complicated language, with many roots. Some words are Germanic in origin, some Latin, some Greek (indirectly, for the most part, through Latin), and still others French (also basically Latin). Furthermore, we have borrowed words from many languages of the world. It happens that, in the kind of writing you have to read in college, there is a heavy Latin influence. These words are built from elements, many of which are used over and over in combination to produce new words. There are three kinds of elements: prefixes, suffixes, and roots. If you know the meaning of a particular prefix and root or a particular suffix and root, you can guess the meaning of an unfamiliar word.

The root is the main part of a word. The prefix and suffix are syllables added at the beginning and the end. In the word "premeditation," for example, "pre-" is the prefix, "meditate" is the root, and "-ion" is the suffix. The prefix "pre-" means before, and the suffix "-ion" tells you that the word is a noun. "Meditate" means to contemplate or think about. Thus a premeditation is an act that is contemplated or thought about beforehand. So if you read that someone was murdered with premeditation, you will know that the murderer thought about it beforehand.

In a separate table (page 39) we have listed some of the more common prefixes and suffixes. Guess at the meaning of these (we have provided a space for that), then check in a dictionary. If your guess is off the mark, rehearse the correct meaning.

We have also provided a short list of some common Latin roots and their meanings. Since most of you will not have taken Latin, it would be unfair to expect you to know the meaning of these, though you can probably make some informed guesses from the English words you do know that contain them. These Latin roots appear over and over again in a huge number of English words.

If you have a good dictionary, the chances are that it will give you something of the origin of the word in question. For example, one of the dictionaries college students commonly use tells us that "domestic" is an adjective and that it derives from the Latin word *"domesticus,"* a word itself based upon another Latin word, *"domus,"* meaning house. The word did not come directly from Latin into English, however. Instead, the dictionary tells us, it is directly derived from the French word *"domestique."* Indeed there are two major routes by which Latin words entered English. The older of these is through French. If you have studied English history, you know that the language of the ruling classes in England after the Norman con-

Common Prefixes, Suffixes, and Latin Roots

The prefixes and suffixes listed below occur often in English words. Any good dictionary will list and define almost all of them. You can help improve your vocabulary by looking up their meanings and writing them in the space provided. Also listed are a few of the many Latin roots upon which English words are based. The English meaning is given for each. Try writing beside each root as many English words derived from it as you can.

Prefixes	Meaning
ab-, abs- a-	away
ad-, a-, at-, ap-	about or around
be-	
bi-	together
co-, com-, con-	reversal
de-	
dis-	not or lack of
en-	not
in-, il-, im-, ir-	before
non-	
per-	back or backward
pre-	not
pro-	
re-	
sub-	
un-	

Suffixes	Meaning
-able, -ible, -ble	able to be
-al	action
-ance	
-ent	established, estsad
-est	action or process
-ful	
-ing	inhabitant
-ion	
-ity	prctive or ingage in
-ive	action or result/ng stk
-ize	
-less	
-ment	
-ous	

Some Common Latin Roots	English Equivalent	English Words Containing Them
capio	take, seize	
duco	lead	
facio	do, make	
fero	bear, carry	
mitto	send	
muto	change, alter	
probo	test	pro boscis
recipio	take back	introspection
specto	look at	
tendo	stretch	
terreo	frighten	terr

quest in 1066 was French. When the nobility began speaking Anglo-Saxon, they incorporated many French words into what became modern English. The later route by which Latin words entered English was a direct one. That was partly because in the Middle Ages, books and other documents began to be written in English rather than in Latin or were translated from Latin to English. Either way, many of the Latin words remained or were pressed into service.

Some Greek words have found their way into English, mostly by way of Latin. While Greek-based words are encountered much less frequently than words of pure Latin origin, some of them are very important. *"Logos,"* which in Greek had a broad spectrum of meanings including word, speech, symbol, thought, and knowledge, is the basis for the English word "logic" and for the suffix "-ology" (as in psychology, sociology, etc.), as well as the root of words such as "prologue." Greek roots can be found in a number of specialized words coined by scientists, but not nearly as frequently as Latin roots. If you find the derivation of words to be interesting, you might want to look at an historical or etymological dictionary. At least one of them (Skeat, *A Concise Etymological Dictionary of the English Language*) is available in paperback.

Learning to Read Faster

We've already pointed out that there is an upper limit to how fast anyone can *read*. Most of us, however, seldom even come close to that upper limit, so there is room for improvement. Also, sometimes we read when all we need do is skim. Those of you who have taken one of the so-called speed-reading courses may know that you can skim a whole page in a few seconds. However, you can also skim in a more detailed way, so that you pick up almost as much information as you would in reading. In fact, good readers usually mix skimming and reading, and all good readers, when reading, adjust their rate to the difficulty or unfamiliarity of the material.

Practice at Reading. "I get plenty of practice at reading," you might say. "I read several hundred pages a week." True enough, you do get a lot of practice, if you are a college student. But practice doesn't necessarily lead to improvement. Many years ago, a famous educational psychologist, Edward L. Thorndike, demonstrated a fundamental truth: You can't improve your performance the next time unless you know what you did the last time. Thorndike asked blindfolded people to draw a line exactly three inches long. People could go on drawing hundreds of lines without coming close to making their lines exactly three inches long. But if they were told after each attempt how long the line was that they had just drawn, they could draw a line almost exactly three inches in length after only a few tries. Obvious, you say. Perhaps, but we often ignore that principle in practice. People do try to improve their reading speed without knowing how fast they are reading. The first step toward improving your reading speed is to keep a record of how fast you read.

Devote a special period each day to training yourself in fast reading. It can be at any time, as long as you can count on it and don't let other activities interfere. Figure on spending a half-hour—certainly no less than ten or fifteen minutes—at your practice in fast reading.

Choose something that you like to read and that is not too difficult: a novel, a book of short stories, a magazine such as *Time* or *Newsweek*. However, try to choose something that will not distract you with pictures and that does not ask you to look at tables and graphs or read formulas. Whatever you choose, keep the same kind of material for the duration of the first phase of your self-training course. If you choose something like *Time* which has multiple columns and an irregular format, keep on reading that kind of material. If you choose a book with only a single column per page, keep on reading other books like it.

Get a watch or clock that has a second hand and note the time to the second when you start reading. Read as fast as you can while getting the meaning of what you have read. When you have finished reading three or four pages, note the time. Subtract the first time from the second and divide by the number of words you have read. You don't need to count all the words. Count the words in ten or so lines, and multiply by the number of lines you have read.

You will find a chart on page 41 in which you can record your results. List on the chart the source and the page numbers that you have read, the number of words, the times, and your rate. You will also find it useful to make a graph of the

Chart for Increasing Reading Speed

Use this chart to keep track of your progress in your daily practice in reading faster. For instructions see text (to find reading rate, multiply the number of pages by the number of words per page and then divide by time).

Magazine or book	Pages	Time	Rate

results. Put on the horizontal axis of the graph the practice session—first, second, third, etc.—and on the vertical axis the words per minute. Make a mark on the graph for the reading rate at each practice session. That way you will not only be able to tell if you are improving or not but whether you are improving at an increasing rate. Make sure that you do not sacrifice comprehension. You will need to check from time to time to see how much you remember of what you read. You can do this informally just by trying to rehearse the material you have read.

If you are typical, you should reach a *near* maximum rate of reading after a couple of weeks of daily practice sessions. You ought to be able to tell from your chart or graph whether you are leveling off in your increase in reading speed. This will *not* be the best you can do, but it is a good start. Then it is time to begin practicing material that is more difficult, such as the textbooks you use. You will need to work on material in which there are unfamiliar words and in which the sentences are long and complicated. If you are doing things the right way, you should be reading more slowly during the first few sessions with the difficult material.

At the same time you should be conscious of reading your regular assignments more rapidly and efficiently. Reading efficiently means gearing reading speed to the difficulty of the material. Also, you will need to practice moving back and forth between reading and skimming.

One psychologist who spent a lifetime studying how people learn complex skills gathered evidence to show that we never stop improving. He studied workers who had been operating the same machine for more than twenty years. Even after all that practice they still got better year by year, though naturally the improvement was small. The chances are that you can improve your reading skills all of your life. The biggest improvements are going to come early, however, and just a few weeks of practice will be a big help, particularly if you are not a good reader to begin with.

If, when you start out to measure your reading speed, you find that you are a very slow reader— that is, you cannot read easy material at more than 150 words a minute—try to find some place for remedial work. Most institutions have such places, though they go by a variety of names. Consult your advisor, a teacher to whom you are close, or friends, until you find out where you can go to get help in reading. Or, if after a good bit of practice on your own, you find that you cannot read easy material faster than 250 words per minute, the chances are that you are doing something wrong. Again, look into some of the possibilities for getting special help.

Practice at Skimming. You will need practice at skimming too. Skimming is mainly a matter of knowing what you are doing.

There are two ways to skim. One is to look for key words and phrases. Often that may mean a search through headings. But sometimes it means more. While writing the material a few pages back one of us wanted to check a point about how Latin came into English. He took an appropriate book, looked up Latin in the index, and then skimmed through the indicated pages looking for entries such as "Latin," "Norman French," "growth of the vernacular," and similar words and phrases. In less than a minute he had skimmed through some ten pages and found what he wanted. Although it was in a book he had not previously read, he was familiar enough with the material to know what to look for. For this kind of skimming you must have some idea ahead of time of what you are looking for. It is the kind of thing you do when you review, or when you are looking for some specific statement which you may want to read in detail.

Another kind of skimming is the kind you do when you pick up something new. We've already commented on that, so we will only remind you of a few things. You just let your eye wander down the page, getting a feel for what the book or article is about, how it is written, and what kind of vocabulary you are going to need. It is a kind of scouting expedition that, among other things, can tell you how fast you are going to have to gear your reading rate.

More useful to most people is a mixture of reading and skimming that we might call "browsing." When you browse through a book, you let your eye run down the page, catching a word or phrase here or there. When you find something interesting or important, you read in detail. We ordinarily think of browsing as a kind of passive activity—the sort of thing we do when we are in the dentist's office—but it really isn't, because it requires you to be alert to the kinds of things you might be interested in.

Browsing is a good technique for looking over secondary reading—the kind of material your instructor may put on the reserve shelf in the library. Make it a practice early in the semester to browse through some or all of the books on reserve. You'll have an idea of what they are about and how difficult they are. When you find something that interests you later in the course, you will have a better idea of where to go. And, of course, if you have to write a term paper, browsing at the beginning of the semester may prevent that panic about what you are going to write about.

5 STUDYING FROM TEXTBOOKS

Let's assume that you have read the first four chapters of this book and have tried to carry out the advice in them. You have made a workable schedule, found a good place to study, and assured yourself that your reading skills are up to college level. You understand the plan of the course you are taking, have set up a notebook in the right way, and have begun to take notes.

You have a copy of the textbook for the course, and it is on your desk along with all the other materials you need, including a notebook and writing implements. You are now ready to read the assignment in the text. How do you make the best use of the time you've allotted for this study period?

FIVE STEPS TO EFFECTIVE STUDY

Every student has her or his own approach to studying textbooks. Two students, both outstanding, can go about studying the same material in very different ways. There are, nevertheless, some general principles for the effective study of textbooks. People who are good at studying use these rules in one way or another, even people who don't realize they are doing so, just as the man in Moliere's play was surprised to discover that he had been talking prose all his life. Where they will differ is mainly in their individual styles and the degree to which they emphasize different aspects of the principles of good studying.

What are these principles? One way of phrasing them originated with the late Francis P. Robinson of Ohio State University, who spend a long career guiding students in their study habits. Robinson put it in a formula: Survey Q 3R, or merely SQ3R. It is a good slogan and one that is easy to remember. It is a way of summarizing the

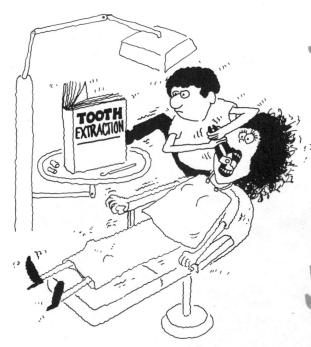

five specific steps in effective study. These steps are the following:

Survey.
Question.
Read.
Recite.
Review.

Robinson's plan has been widely adopted, and while there have been suggestions to change it in minor ways, it is still, after all these years, a very good approach to studying from textbooks. It is something that all students, good and poor, can do, and if they do, their study habits will improve.

Survey

The first of the five steps is survey. It tells you to get the best possible overview of what you are going to be reading before you study it in detail. Surveying does for you what reading a road map does before you take a trip on unfamiliar roads. You know what you are going to run into before you start.

Surveying a Textbook. Surveying a textbook goes in steps, from big ones to little ones. When you first pick up a book, look at the whole book. Start by reading the preface to get an idea of why the author wrote the book and what he or she says in it. By reading what the author has to say you can find out what kind of textbook it is and for whom it was written. It may even tell you what background you need for reading the text.

Next, look at the table of contents. Find out what's in the book. You will want to do this several times as you get into the course. The more you read in the book the more meaning the table of contents has.

Finally, leaf through the book. In a short period of time you can turn every page of a good-sized textbook, glancing at the headings, reading sentences here and there, and looking at the illustrations. The effort is worth it. You will have a feel for what is in the book, how difficult it is, and how it is organized. More textbooks (these days) have summaries. Skim these too.

Surveying a Chapter. When you settle down to read a chapter, look through it first. When most authors write textbooks, they go to some pains to organize what they have to say under the various headings. They do this mainly to help you know what to expect. In a lot of textbooks it is hard to find a page without one or more headings.

Yet many students ignore the headings and try to read textbooks as they would read novels. When they do that they ignore the most significant and useful clues to the content of the text. Use headings. As you actually read some section try to think why the author used the particular headings he or she did. This is part of the active, as opposed to passive, process of reading.

Pay attention to the *order of headings*. Most textbooks use two or three orders, or levels. This is really like an outline. This book, for example, has three: a main heading, two or more side headings under each main heading, and sometimes, headings indented into paragraphs. In many textbooks there may be even more complicated schemes, with different levels of headings distinguished by type size or style.

We have gone into some detail about headings because you use them at nearly every stage of the study process. You first use them in your initial survey. Then when you begin to read, you can use them to identify what is really important.

We also know that most students do not do enough surveying. They've acquired the habit of plunging right into the text without first making a map of what they are going to find.

Question

The Q in Survey Q 3R stands for "question," and it emphasizes the importance of asking questions while learning. Most things worth remembering are answers to some sort of questions. Moreover, people seem to remember better what they learn in answer to a question than things they have merely tried to memorize. This is probably because asking oneself questions is a more active process than merely trying to memorize.

Your Questions. If you make use of the question technique in reading this book, you should already have a number of them about this section. Why is asking questions so helpful? What kind of questions should I ask myself? Should I write them down? These are some of the things you might have asked by now. Some questions have already been answered for you, and if you keep the others in mind, you will find that most of them will also be answered. But if you are clever about asking questions, you may come across something we didn't think about. Those kinds of questions you have to answer yourself.

Our really major point is that you are the best source of questions, if for no other reason than that you are the one who knows what you are trying to learn, if for no other reason than that you know what you know already.

How do you go about asking the right sort of questions? The most direct way is to use the headings. A simple question is "What is _____?" This will happen most often when you are reading something technical and when the heading takes the form of a technical phrase. For example, in a textbook in astronomy you might find the phrase "retrograde motion." You ask, "What is retrograde motion?" If you can't get a clear definition from the section with that heading you need to consult either other parts of the same book (remember, most technical books have indexes) or another source.

Some people advocate writing down questions, but we don't. It is time-consuming. Eventually, the art of asking questions will become so habitual that you won't even be aware of forming them. Remember, the main purpose of asking questions as you read a textbook is to direct you to the main idea in a section and to help you assimilate that idea into what you already know.

An example of the types of questions that might occur to you about a portion of text is shown on page 47.

The Author's Questions. Although you are the best source of questions, the author of the book you are reading may provide you with some. Use them. They are often the most neglected parts of textbooks, particularly when they are stuck at the end of chapters.

Authors' questions have many uses. You can use them in your survey. You can use them while you read, and again when you have finished reading, as a way of testing yourself. If you test yourself before the instructor does, you will have a much easier time on examinations.

Stop for a second. When you started to read this section, did you pause to ask questions? What are the author's questions? Where are they? How do you use them?

Some textbooks, particularly in the social sciences and the natural sciences, are accompanied by workbooks. If the workbook to a text you are studying has questions or sample problems, use them to tell you what you don't know and to suggest questions to ask about the main text.

Read

The next step to effective study is reading. Any book, of course, is meant to be read. But reading is neither the first, last, nor even necessarily the most important part of studying a textbook. It provides the details. It fills out the framework you should already have if you have been surveying.

Reading Actively. A lot of things you can read passively. A good detective story or a column in the sports section of the newspaper are written mainly for your entertainment. You don't need to worry about remembering things about them because either you will (to tell your friends about) or you won't. It isn't that important. The kind of reading you will do in a literature course is likely to be a different matter. You must read in such a way that there is a kind of dialogue between you and the author.

Most textbooks need to be explored. You can't just walk through them. You have to be alert to them every step of the way. Questioning while you read is one way to avoid reading passively. You must keep asking yourself, "Am I following what I am reading? Can I remember what I have just read?" Stop every so often and try yourself out. If you do this, you will no longer voice the familiar complaint: "My head is just like a sieve; I forget what I read the minute I am through."

The Use of Questions

Here is an excerpt from a textbook (Janet L. Hopson and Norman K. Wessells, Essentials of Biology, *McGraw-Hill, New York, 1990, p. 28). The kind of questions you would want to ask about this excerpt are written in the margin.*

Why is water slow to change temperature?

What does this property provide for living creatures?

What is cohesion?

Tensile strength?

Adhesion?

Capillarity

Because of its high specific heat, water is slow to change temperature, and considerable amounts of heat must be added or removed to make the temperature change much. This property provides special insurance for living creatures, which often function best within a narrow temperature range. The seawater surrounding a kelp or a barnacle, as well as the water within the organisms, tends to heat or cool more slowly than the surrounding air or soil, and this provides a natural buffer against potentially damaging temperature fluctuations.

Water molecules also exhibit physical properties, such as strong cohesion, adhesion, tensile strength, and capillarity. **Cohesion** is the tendency of like molecules to cling to one another (such as water to water). **Adhesion** is the tendency of *unlike* molecules to cling together (such as water to the molecules of silicon dioxide on the walls of a drinking glass). **Tensile strength** is related to cohesion and is a measure of the resistance of molecules to being pulled apart. And **capillarity** is the tendency of molecules to move upward in a narrow space against the tug of gravity.

Here is another excerpt from the same source (p. 29). Try writing your own questions.

Let us see how these properties apply to some easily observed biological phenomena. You can observe the results of adhesion when you pour water into a flowerpot full of soil. The water sinks in and "wets" the soil, rather than remaining on top, because of water's inherent "stickiness," its tendency to adhere to the dissimilar molecules in the soil. Adhesion, cohesion, and capillarity also help explain why much of the water remains in the soil rather than running straight through. The molecules of water can resist the downward tug of gravity by first adhering to the surface of soil particles and then moving into tiny air spaces between them via capillarity. The water molecules enter the spaces and pull others along by means of cohesion, and thus remain in these tiny spaces rather than flowing out the bottom of the pot.

Reading important novels, plays, poetry, and stories requires more than passive reading, but the specific recommendations we give here do not by and large apply to them. They require a different set of skills. Toward the end of this chapter we'll have a few words to say about reading history and literature. What we have said thus far mainly applies to books that you read to get the information that is in them.

Reading for Important Details. Thus far we have said that when you read a textbook you read for the main ideas. But you also have to pick up the details—examples of a principle, historical anecdotes, things on which you can hang the main ideas.

Noting Important Terms. Authors have a way of telling you what is really important—they use italic or boldface type for key words and phrases. These are signs to stop and take heed.

If a technical term is italicized or set in bold type, repeat it to yourself and make sure that you know what it means. Also, though you may think it is a small point, make sure you know how to spell technical terms. Instructors sometimes get impatient with students who can't seem to learn how to spell important words.

Let's face it, authors do not always emphasize important words or phrases by italics or boldface, in which case you will have to look after that for yourself.

Looking at Graphs, Tables, and Illustrations. When you read, read everything. One of the worst things you can do is skip tables, graphs, and diagrams. Give them more than a casual glance. Authors put things in diagrams and graphs for a reason. Even a simple photograph or drawing can tell you what a whole section is about. It is true that some textbooks have pictures just because they are pretty, but even in a textbook in history, a picture of Henry IV in the snow outside of Canossa can help you remember about the conflict between the Holy Roman Emperors and the Pope. We'll have more to say on the topic of tables and graphs in Chapter 9.

Recite

Reciting is the oldest way of learning. Long before books were in common use, recitation was the heart of learning. In parts of the world where the tradition of using books is not firmly established, recitation is still the primary means of learning. Have you ever seen a documentary on TV about some school in a remote part of the world in which all of the children recite in unison? Such rote recitation is less valuable than the kind of recitation we are concerned with here because it favors memorization over understanding and questioning. Rote recitation does have its uses, however. Getting the multiplication tables into your head so that you can do fast calculations when you don't have your handy pocket calculator requires a lot of plain rote recitation. To a lesser extent rote recitation can also be applied to the study of foreign languages and similar things. But our main emphasis here is on reciting for comprehension and recall.

Reciting as a Means of Recall. Reciting is probably the best single way of keeping your reading active. As long as you merely read a textbook, you can, without challenge, comfort yourself with the belief that you understand and will remember what you have read. But if you recite to yourself as you read, you may make the unpleasant discovery that you don't really understand, that you can't really remember.

The only way to find out if you really understand and can remember what you have read is to recite to yourself just after you have read it. Recitation is an effective study method not only because it forces you to read actively but because it immediately reveals to you your own ignorance. If you recite, you can correct yourself on the spot. It is one way of providing your own programmed learning.

Reciting is recalling. Stop as often as you need to and try to recall what you have just read. At this point, for example, you might stop and ask yourself, "What have I learned in this chapter? What are the main headings and what do they stand for? What are the general principles and the details that support them?" Check your recall against the book.

The general rule is as follows: As you read, stop at intervals to recite the substance, in your own words, of each major section in a chapter. When you do your first reading of the material, the amount of time you spend in reciting will probably be less than that spent in actual reading. But when you review for an examination, most of your time should be spent reciting rather than reading.

Recitation both at the original reading and at the review is necessary. Older research on the value of recitation for remembering showed that the earlier you recite, the less you forget later on. The first recitation helps to keep the forgetting process from getting started. Because some forgetting is almost inevitable no matter what you do, you need that review just before the examination to correct for the fact that you will have forgotten some things, despite your earlier review.

More recent research tells us why early review is important. Remembering the kind of thing you find in a typical textbook is not merely remembering how to string words together, as you might do in trying to remember a poem in a language you don't know. When you read something you understand, you form a structure in your own way of thinking. Just reading is a lazy process; the structure you form from just reading may be so simple and bare of detail that it will never do for an examination. In one investigation in which college students were asked to write down what they had just read, some students read so superficially that all they could say was, "This passage was about how evolution makes different species of animals." All the details in the passage about the classification of animals, about the relationship between genetics and evolution, about natural selection, were ignored.

How Much Recitation? How much time should you spend in recitation? That depends on what you are studying. If it is something rich in detail and full of confusing relations or unrelated facts, you need to spend a lot of time reciting. That is because it is hard to form a rich structure for such material in your head. In some cases you may want to spend as much as ninety percent of your time in recitation. If, for example, you have to learn a number of rules, items, names, laws, or formulas, then recitation should be the principal mode of study.

If, on the other hand, the material is organized, or in the form of a story or historical narrative, less recitation is required. You may need only to pause here and there to make sure you know names and dates. It is hard to recommend a precise figure, but perhaps as little as twenty percent of your total study time would be spent in recitation. For courses such as economics, political science, and the like, fifty percent of the time is as good a figure as any. But remember, these are ball-park figures. How much time you actually spend in recitation will depend upon how active your normal reading is (if you read attentively all the time, you needn't spend so much time reciting), the particular course, and a lot of other circumstances.

This you can be sure of: The time spent in recitation pays off. One famous study showed that students who spent up to eighty percent of their time reciting did better than those who spent the same amount of time reading without reciting. Also, the time you spend reciting actually saves time. The amount you remember when you recite is so much greater that you don't need to spend nearly so much time in rereading and review.

When do you stop to recite? To wait until you have finished a chapter is too long. On the other hand, stopping to recite every paragraph—with some exceptions—is too much. It breaks up the material; you can't form sensible structures because you haven't got a complete scheme to do it with. Your best guides are the headings. Stop each time you get to a new heading and recite what you have read in the section you have just finished.

Besides giving you a chance to put things in your own words, recitation keeps you attentive. When you just read, it is easy to do so with only half a mind—to read the words without really taking them in. When you know you have to recite something, you can't daydream.

Recitation also helps you correct mistakes. It shows you where you have missed something or where you have misunderstood it. If you make notes of these mistakes when you recite, you'll know exactly what points you're going to have the most trouble with in a review.

Review

The fifth and final part of SQ3R is review. We don't need to make a big thing out of this because most students review anyway before examinations (assuming they have studied before exam time). We can, however, make suggestions about how to review and when it should be done.

Surveying the Material. Reread enough to make sure that you haven't omitted anything and to refresh your memory. Recite both before and after you read. The recitation before reading a section will tell you how carefully you need to read again. Reciting after your reading will tell you what you have learned. If you have taken notes on what you have read, use these to guide your reviews and as a prompt for the recitation before your review.

When to Review. If you have done a good job at surveying, questioning, reading, and reciting, you won't have trouble knowing what to do when you review and how often. Most students wait until just before an exam to do their reviewing. This is a good time for a review, but really careful students review before that time as well.

The first time to review is immediately after you have studied something. For example, after you have read a chapter, reciting between each of its sections, you should immediately go back and review it. This means trying to recite the important points of the whole chapter and rereading as necessary to check yourself. This first review may be fairly brief, but it is important. One study showed that an early review reduced forgetting by a factor of 10.

If you are really well organized, you will plan for one or two reviews between the first review and the final review before an examination. These intervening reviews are the ones most often skipped by students, but they make the final review easier.

The final review should consist of as much unprompted recitation as possible. Use the book to check the accuracy of your recitation, but try to recite without first reading. Go over all the material you think you will be responsible for. Plan your time so that you can review *all* of the material. You don't want to run out of time when you are halfway through. It goes without saying that trying to cram a review into the last few hours before an examination is not a winning strategy.

We've stressed studying for examination, but we have really been writing about studying for mastery. Mastering something doesn't mean that you will not "forget" it, though in a sense if you have really mastered something it is always with you. When faced with a problem in statistics years after you have studied the subject, you may feel that you remember nothing. But after a few minutes of working with the problem, the whole thing will come back. Things that you have mastered—that you have studied well—become part of you. They never leave you, and they allow you to understand and appreciate your world in a deeper and more knowing way.

UNDERLINING, HIGHLIGHTING, AND OUTLINING TEXTBOOKS

Most students underline or highlight textbooks or make notes. These are good ways to prepare for review. Note taking in particular, if done the right way, provides for recitation. Because these techniques are so important to studying from textbooks, we have a special section on them.

Underlining and Highlighting

A typical practice of poor students is to sit down with a book in front of them and read away in a listless manner. When they see something they think is important they underline or highlight it. They do this without surveying or asking questions. The result is a hit-or-miss selection of passages, something that reflects a chance judgment rather than any sense of the overall organization of the material. If you do this you are stuck with what you have done. You may think that you have underscored the important points, but you have probably not only missed some but have

selected others that are of minor importance. You can correct this somewhat by checking when you review to make sure you have hit the major points.

Incidentally, if you are buying a secondhand textbook, make sure you get one that has not been underlined or highlighted. Otherwise, buy a new one, because the handicap of seeing someone else's underlining is far too serious to be worth the amount of money you save by buying a used book.

Underlining and highlighting have their place. Some people find them useful and others do not. But if they are to be useful to you, they must be done wisely at the right time and according to a plan. The plan is this: First survey what you are going to read. Then ask yourself questions and try to answer those questions as you read. *In this first reading it is better not to underline or highlight.* You won't really know what is important until you have grasped the whole. As your questions are answered, or as you think that you spot main ideas and important details, make a checkmark in the margin. The next time you read, read for the main ideas, important details, and technical terms. It is these you will want to underline or highlight.

Even on the second, careful reading, don't underline or highlight the sentences as you read them. After you have read one or two paragraphs, go back and decide what it is you are going to mark. As a guide, use your checkmarks in the margin. If they don't designate the main points, you can ignore them.

Don't underline or highlight whole sentences. Many of the words in a sentence that contains an important idea are unimportant. Leave these out when you underline. (We know that it's easier just to move the magic marker across the page, but that's the point. Anything that's easy to do does not allow you to be an active student.) Underline only the words and phrases which are essential. If you do this, when you go back at reviewing time you can pick up only the important words; that will *force* you to reconstruct the rest. On page 51 you will find an example of good underlining. Look at this example carefully and try to figure out why we underlined the things we did.

If you follow these rules, you will not underline or highlight as much as most students do. On the average, a half-dozen or so words per paragraph will do the trick, though, of course, how much you

Underlining a Textbook

Here is an example of underlining to pick out the main points (from C. R. McConnell and S. L. Brue, Economics: Principles, Problems, and Policies, *11th ed., McGraw-Hill, New York, 1990, pp. 40–41).*

Extensive Use of Capital Goods

All modern economies—whether they approximate the capitalist, socialist, or communist ideology—are based upon an advanced technology and the extensive use of capital goods. Under pure capitalism it is competition, coupled with freedom of choice and the desire to further one's self-interest, which provides the means for achieving technological advance. The capitalistic framework is felt to be highly effective in harnessing incentives to develop new products and improved techniques of production. Why? Because the monetary rewards derived therefrom accrue directly to the innovator. Pure capitalism therefore presupposes the extensive use and relatively rapid development of complex capital goods: tools, machinery, large-scale factories, and facilities for storage, transportation, and marketing.

Why are the existence of an advanced technology and the extensive use of capital goods important? Because the most direct method of producing a product is usually the least efficient.[2] Even Robinson Crusoe avoided the inefficiencies of direct production in favor of "roundabout production." It would be ridiculous for a farmer—even a backyard farmer—to go at production with bare hands. Obviously, it pays huge dividends in terms of more efficient production and, therefore, a more abundant output, to fashion tools of production, that is, capital equipment, to aid in the productive process. There is a better way of getting water out of a well than to dive in after it!

But there is a catch involved. As we recall our discussion of the production possibilities curve and the basic nature of the economizing problem, it is evident that,

[2]Remember that consumer goods satisfy wants directly, while capital goods do so indirectly through the more efficient production of consumer goods.

with full employment and full production, resources must be diverted from the production of consumer goods in order to be used in the production of capital goods. We must currently tighten our belts as consumers in order to free resources for the production of capital goods which will increase productive efficiency and permit us to have a greater output of consumer goods at some future date.

Specialization

The extent to which society relies upon specialization is astounding. The vast majority of consumers produce virtually none of the goods and services they consume and, conversely, consume little or nothing of what they produce. The hammer-shop laborer who spends his lifetime stamping out parts for jet engines may never "consume" an airplane trip. The assembly-line worker who devotes eight hours a day to the installation of windows in Camaros may own a Honda. Few households seriously consider any extensive production of their own food, shelter, and clothing. Many farmers sell their milk to the local dairy and then buy margarine at the Podunk general store. Society learned long ago that self-sufficiency breeds inefficiency. The jack-of-all-trades may be a very colorful individual, but is certainly lacking in efficiency.

In what specific ways might human specialization—*the division of labor*—enhance productive efficiency? First, specialization permits individuals to take advantage of existing differences in their abilities and skills. If caveman A is strong, swift afoot, and accurate with a spear, and caveman B is weak and slow, but patient, this distribution of talents can be most efficiently utilized by making A a hunter and B a fisherman. Second, even if the abilities of A and B are identical, specialization may prove to be advantageous. Why? Because by . . . .

mark your textbook in this way depends upon the material you are studying.

Taking Reading Notes

Taking notes from your textbook is one way to be active in the learning process. If you write down in short form what the author says, you make it part of your own mental processes. You can't fool

yourself into believing that you have really been studying, when your mind has been elsewhere. The best way to take notes is in outline form.

Methods of Outlining

How do you go about outlining? First, use whatever clues the author gives you for her or his own outline. If there are headings, you can get the

Outlining from Books

Here is an outline of Chapter 4, "The Art of Reading." It illustrates how you might outline material found in a textbook.

I. Reading well and liking to read go together.
II. If you are deficient in reading you will:
  A. Move your lips or vocalize when you read.
  B. Read each word one by one.
  C. Find many unfamiliar words while reading.
  D. Backtrack and reread what you have just read.
  E. Read everything at the same rate and in the same way.
  F. Not understand what you have read.
III. Reading with a purpose.
  A. Skimming.
    1. Look for signposts.
      a. Look for headings.
      b. If there are no headings read the first sentences of paragraphs.
    2. Skimming is the first step in studying.
  B. Read to get the main idea.
    1. Finding the main idea.
      a. At different levels: chapters, sections, paragraphs.
      b. Paragraph contains a single topic.
        i. Topic sentence usually at beginning of paragraph.
        ii. But sometimes it occurs elsewhere in paragraph.
    2. Main idea not necessarily whole sentence.
      a. May be the principal clause of a sentence.
      b. May need to be boiled down in your own words.
      c. Often can throw away qualifiers.
    3. Sometimes main idea not expressed, only implied.
  C. Extracting important details.

    1. Details often examples—particularly in science.
    2. Often a matter of judgment.
    3. Make identifying them habitual—without thinking about it.
  D. Reading for pleasure.
    1. The more you read for pleasure, the better reader you will be.
    2. Read for pleasure in all the different ways you read to learn.
  E. Evaluate what you read—examine your own beliefs.
  F. Expand what you read to apply to situations not mentioned by author.
IV. Using your eyes.
  A. Eye movements.
    1. Saccades are quick movements broken by brief pauses.
    2. Pauses are fixations.
      a. Fixations last one-quarter to one-fifth of a second.
      b. Read during fixations.
    3. Very little difference between good and poor readers in speed of saccades.
    4. Good readers fix on the average only once every three words.
    5. Poor readers make more regressive saccades.
    6. Good readers make a single return movement at the end of a line; poor readers overshoot or undershoot.
  B. Improving eye movements.
    1. Eye movements in reading are automatic or reflexive.
      a. Can't improve them much consciously.
      b. Major emphasis now upon improving mental

---

skeleton of your outline from these. Don't just copy them, however. Most headings are not sentences; they are just a few key words. Sometimes converting them into full but terse sentences helps. (For example, using the heading for this section: Here are some Methods of Outlining." Or better yet: "Here are some ways of outlining.") Sometimes, in order to make a sentence out of the heading for a section, you will have to read the complete section.

Your outline should be orderly. There are two ways of doing that. One way is to indent one order of statement under another, so that the main statements are to the left and the subsidiary statements begin slightly to the right. The other way of structuring your outline is to use a consistent system of lettering and numbering the different orders. There are several ways of doing that, and if you have one already there is no need to change it. If you don't, try using Roman numerals (I, II, III, . . .) for the highest-order headings, capital letters (A, B, C, . . .) for the second order, Arabic numerals (1,

a. Can't improve them much consciously.

b. Major emphasis now upon improving mental habits of reading.

c. Keeping a record of reading speed helps to increase speed.

2. Upper limit to reading speed about 900 words a minute.

3. Most students read at a rate of 200 to 300 words a minute.

  a. That rate can be pushed quite a bit higher.

  b. As you do so, your eye movements will automatically improve.

V. How to improve your reading.

  A. Building a vocabulary.

  1. Lots of new words encountered in college.

  2. Vocabulary mark of a good student and good reader.

  3. Be on the lookout for new words.

  4. Use the dictionary often.

    a. A good dictionary is essential.

    b. In looking up a word, find out its meaning in the context in which you found it.

  5. Use vocabulary cards to improve a poor vocabulary.

  6. Distinguish between general and technical terms.

    a. May need glossary or special dictionary for technical terms.

    b. Sometimes half or more of the subject matter may be in knowing what technical terms mean.

  7. How to dissect words.

    a. Many words consist of roots, prefixes, and suffixes.

    b. Knowing the meaning of commonly used prefixes and suffixes may help you guess the meaning of new words correctly.

    c. Many English words built on Latin and Greek roots.

  B. Learning to read faster.

  1. Very few people read at their maximum rate.

  2. Reading faster requires practice.

    a. For practice to be effective, you must know whether you are improving or not.

    b. Therefore, you must keep a record of how fast you are reading.

      i. Devote a special period each day to practice at fast reading.

      ii. Use the same kind of material every day.

      iii. Use the same format.

      iv. Use material of moderate difficulty.

      v. Time yourself.

      vi. Count the words and calculate your reading rate.

      vii. Make a chart or graph of your reading rate.

      viii. Be sure you are not sacrificing comprehension for speed.

  3. If your reading is exceptionally slow or you don't improve, you will need help.

  4. Practice skimming.

    a. There are two kinds of skimming.

      i. Searching for key words.

      ii. Searching for key words and phrases on your initial survey.

    b. Use browsing for secondary or less-important reading.

2, 3, . . .) for the third order, and lowercase letters (a, b, c, . . .) for lowest order. More often than not, these two methods are combined, as in the sample outline on pages 52 and 53.

Content of Notes

Your notes should contain the main ideas and important details. Be sure to put enough into your notes so that you can understand them later. If, for example, you are outlining a section in a physics text on the idea of the "wave front," don't just write down "Huygens' Principle." Tell what Huygens' Principle is. You might write, "Huygens' Principle: Every point on a wave front is a point source for waves generated in the direction of the wave's propagation."

Write as legibly as you can. Even people who have a good hand get in such a hurry when they take notes that they can't read them later on. (If your writing is hard to read anyway, make a special effort to improve it when you take textbook notes. With practice, your writing should become clear enough for instructors to read it without difficulty. While almost no teacher wants to admit it, clear writing is probably worth some points on an examination.)

When Not to Outline

Making outline notes of textbook material helps you understand and remember what you read. There are some subjects, however, for which outline notes are not appropriate. You would not want to outline a foreign language text. Such texts consist of mixtures of grammatical rules, vocabulary, and sentences to be translated. In the physical sciences, your text is likely to be almost in outline form to begin with, and it is hardly worth your while to copy the outline. Instead, you would do better to emphasize silent recitation or written recitation as you read. When you read literature you do not read in order to understand particular facts or theories; you read in order to interpret. What you need to do instead of putting what you read into your own words is challenge yourself about what the author is trying to say. You need to think about why the author wrote the story or essay in the way he or she did. You should be alert to the imagery and ready to interpret any symbols you may come across. Some people like to make notes in the margins of the book; others keep a separate notebook for writing comments.

The first time you read through a story, don't make notes. On rereading you may want to take notes or make comments. A useful form for making such notes is to cast them in the form of questions. Why did the characters react in the way they did? In some high school texts and in a few college anthologies, you will find questions of this sort already included to help you understand what you are reading.

In reading stories and novels, be on the lookout for things which superficially are incidental but which really are central to the understanding of characters or to the mood which the author wishes to convey. Watch for allusions. Good writers often make allusions to classical mythology or to biblical texts. Do you understand these allusions? *Do you know where they came from?* If you have a demanding teacher you will be expected to know that.

Not all literature is in the form of fiction, drama, or narrative poetry. You will be expected

to read some essays, and you may be asked to read works like Darwin's *Origin of Species* or Marx's *Das Kapital* not just for the information they contain but because of the enormous influence they have had and because of the *way in which they were written*. Essays and such important works as those we have mentioned are not like textbooks. They are discursive. That means that the writers let their minds wander over a vast landscape instead of merely telling you something you don't know. So often these things need to be read in the way in which you would read stories. Ask yourself: "Why did the author say things in exactly that way? Is there anything in the work that reflects the author's personal life?" In brief, you need to read such works in their literary and historical contexts.

But—and this is a big but—you are expected to know what the literary works are about. It is a good idea to write summaries of them, summaries which incorporate something of your own views. That brings us to our next point.

Writing Summaries

Summaries are helpful for almost anything you read. They are useful for textbooks, particularly those that do not include chapter summaries themselves. For textbooks, however, don't try to write the summary until you have mastered the material. Summaries should be as brief as possible, but they should contain all the essential information.

If you write a summary of a story, be sure that it is more than just a bare recital of the narrative. Characterize the people in the story, and include your reactions to them. Try to capture the atmosphere of the story, the feeling it evokes in you. Comment on any irony, imagery, and symbolism that you may have come across.

Taking Notes for History Texts

History texts often have a unique organization, and it isn't just that things are arranged chronologically. Modern texts and history instructors tend to place less emphasis upon dates than used to be the fashion, but still you'd better be prepared to place the Treaty of Ghent or the founding of the Federal Reserve System in their right times. The easiest way to do this is to get the exact dates *right*.

Example of a Summary

Here is a summary of Chapter 4, "The Art of Reading." Compare the statements in this summary with the headings and main ideas in the chapter. Also, compare it with the outline on pages 52 and 53 to see how an outline and a summary differ.

In college you will have to do more reading than you have ever done, and you will need to work at doing better at it. When you read better, you will like it more. If you move your lips when you read, or read word by word, or find a lot of unfamiliar words, or backtrack, or read everything the same way, or fail to understand what you read, you are a poor reader and will need to improve.

There are different purposes in reading and different ways to read. Skimming is one way to read. In one kind of skimming you look for headings and subheadings. Another way to skim is to search for critical words. We also read to get the main idea. The main idea of a paragraph is the topical sentence, often found at the beginning of the paragraph. In looking for the main idea, don't look for whole sentences. Pick out the key words and phrases. Sometimes the author will not state the main idea but only imply it. This happens often in literary texts. Sometimes you will want to read to extract important details. Important ideas are often examples, particularly in scientific texts. Often you have to use your judgment to find important details. When you read for pleasure, you will want to suit your reading to your purpose, just as you do when you read to learn. Keep an active attitude toward reading, evaluate what you read.

When you read your eyes move in a series of quick movements broken by brief pauses. The movements are called "saccades," and the pauses "fixations." The pauses last about one-quarter to one-fifth of a second and they occupy about 90 percent of the total time in reading. There are also regressive movements. These occur more often in poor readers. Another difference between good and poor readers is in the return movement at the end of a line. Poor readers overshoot or undershoot.

The best way to improve your eye movements in reading is to improve your mental habits. You can't read faster than 900 words a minute, but since the typical student reads only 200 to 300 words a minute, there is a lot of room for improvement. To improve your reading you need to build your vocabulary. You will learn many new technical terms in college, and you must pay attention to these. Use your dictionary frequently. If you have serious trouble with vocabulary, use vocabulary cards. For technical terms you will need to consult glossaries and technical dictionaries. Learn to dissect words into prefixes, roots, and suffixes. Know the meaning of as many prefixes and suffixes as you can.

Practice timing yourself at reading. Do this every day with the same kind of material. Make a chart or graph of the results to see if you are actually improving. If your reading rate is very poor or if you don't improve, you will need to find special help. Practice skimming as well as reading.

The typical organization for a history text is to deal with some span of time that has some natural significance. The history of France (or the whole of Western Europe, for that matter) has a kind of continuity from 1815 and the Congress of Vienna to the revolutions of 1848 and, in France, the establishment of the Second Republic. So after you have surveyed and read your text, you might make notes by blocking off in your notebook a couple of pages devoted to the period from 1815 to 1848. Then you can indicate the significant events, ideas, and people in a sensible order. Since modern history courses stress social, intellectual, and technological history as well as the traditional political history, you might rule off your note pages into parallel columns with these things as headings. This way you can see, for example, how the development of railroads and industry paralleled changes in where people lived and the kinds of clothes they wore as well as the politics of the time.

While it is not strictly a matter of making notes, there is one feature of studying from history texts (and lecture notes) that is of particular importance. Make sure you know how to use maps. Look at the maps in your textbook very carefully, and make sketches of them if that is the way you can impress them upon your mind. On an examination, you may be given a blank map and told to indicate certain features on it. You could be given a blank map of, say, North America and asked to indicate the limits of the French and British settlements on the eve of the French and Indian War. Or you could be given a map of the Atlantic and asked to diagram the elements of the slave trade. Even if there are no maps on the exam, maps are a good way to hold information that you may be asked to produce. For example, it is much easier to remember that the provinces of Alsace and Lorraine were ceded by France to Germany after the War of 1870 if you know roughly where Alsace and Lorraine are. Otherwise you are forced to memorize a statement that has no real meaning for you.

Summarizing a Chapter

The time to recite what you have read in this chapter is now. If you haven't already made an outline, do it now. Then run back through the chapter to make sure you haven't missed something. Write a summary using your outline. We've provided a summary of Chapter 4 on page 55. It is somewhat long, but better to err on the side of being too long than on the side of leaving something out.

6 TAKING EXAMINA-TIONS

If you believe in miracles, then you may think that you can pass examinations without studying for them. For most of us, however, that's not possible. After all, the main purpose of examinations is to determine how effectively you have studied. If you have followed all the rules for effective study you should be ready for examinations, and you will have no need of miracles. In this chapter we offer a few additional ideas for taking examinations.

PREPARING FOR EXAMINATIONS

You all know the best rule: Be prepared. Be prepared for the *kind* of examination you are to take and for *all* the possible questions, not just for some of them. Master the subject thoroughly and organize it well. Be in good physical condition, rested, and in a confident frame of mind.

The Final Review

If you have kept up with your studying, preparing for an exam is mainly a matter of review. The final review should be an intensive one. You will go over your lecture notes and textbook notes, look at the main ideas, and review lists of technical terms, dates, etc.

A review is just that—a review. It should be an attempt to recall things you have learned earlier. If you're reading material for the first time just before an exam, you had better hope for a miracle. You are in deep trouble. If the exam is easy and the material not difficult, you might be able to scrape by. But then you should ace an easy exam; getting a respectable B won't do.

In some subjects, you may want to make a set of review notes. These can be of two kinds. They can be condensations of your detailed notes, or they can be compilations of all the things you found difficult, are apt to forget, or need to commit to memory.

Schedule of Reviews

Surprisingly, it is easy to overestimate the time you will need for a review. If you have kept up with your work, reviewing for an exam will not take a lot of time. Just allow enough time to cover *everything.* Keep your review periods short. When your attention begins to wander, do something else for a while. If you work too hard at reviewing a mass of material, you will have trouble organizing it.

Make a definite plan for review, just as you schedule your regular hours of study. For the week prior to finals, revise your regular study schedule to accommodate reviewing. You may need to cut down on some of your free time, but don't cut into it too deeply. You won't need to if you have been following a good study regime.

This brings up the subject of cramming. All of us at one time or another have boasted about some cram session. We've all heard stories about staying up all night and living on black coffee. Most students do more talking than cramming, but this kind of frantic, disorganized studying does occur, and it is inefficient and even harmful. Going without food, sleep, and rest is physically draining; if you have been doing that, it will take a superhuman effort of will to do your best at exam time. If you are really in poor shape, your judgment will be affected; you may not even know whether or not what you are doing in an exam is right or not. It doesn't take pep pills to disorient you. Students who have spent all night studying sometimes write gibberish under the impression that they are making sense. Even if you are not in that bad a shape, if you don't have your wits about you, you can't organize your answers or recall easily, and you are apt to lose your ability to discriminate the right from the wrong answers on an objective exam.

It goes without saying (but we'll say it anyway) that taking an exam after a night's session on alcohol or drugs is about the worst thing you can do. Students sometimes try to calm themselves down or get to sleep by taking alcohol or drugs. You may feel a little better when you finally get to sleep, but you will probably feel awful at exam time, and since you will have residual alcohol or whatever in your bloodstream, your mental efficiency will be impaired.

Organize your life so that you can live as normally as possible during exam time. Get your meals, sleep, and recreation. Keep up with all your subjects. You may not have much to offer in a bull session on cramming, but you will be way ahead in taking examinations.

How to Review

Emphasize recitation. Keep rereading to a minimum. Go after the job chapter by chapter, topic by topic. First try to recall the main ideas without referring to notes. Then check your recollections against your notes or the book. For each main heading in a chapter, do the same thing. First recall the main points, then check. If you can't remember something or can't understand or explain a point, go back to the book and reread the passage covering it. If you attempt to do more reading than this at once, you will lose sight of the important points.

It is easy to fall into the trap of trying to outguess the instructor. Don't try to guess what the instructor's favorite topics are. He or she knows that you will try to do that and will make an end run in making up exam topics. Yes, it may be useful to see past exams (many instructors keep them on file in the library), but don't rule out unpleasant surprises. Keep a balance in the material you study. That way you won't end up saying those famous sad words, "I studied the wrong things."

If you try to predict all that *could* be asked instead of concentrating on a few topics, you will be able to deal with anything that turns up. As you review, turn what you review into questions. How would you word a question about this topic? One way in which you can outguess the instructor is to take advantage of any hints, direct or indirect, about the *way* in which questions will be asked.

Types of Exams

Most exams are either objective or essay. Objective exams do not require you to write. All you do is decide whether certain statements are true or false, which of several statements is true, or how statements should be matched. Objective exams stress your ability to recognize the right answers when you see them, not your ability to recall or organize the information you have learned.

The essay examination, on the other hand, requires you to recall. You have to organize what you know in order to present it in a coherent way. In science and mathematics courses, you will be given problems to solve. Like essays, problems stress your ability to recall rather than recognize information. That is true even when they are presented in a multiple-choice or some objective format. If you aren't just going to guess at the most plausible answer, you must remember how to solve the problem and then work it out.

There are some exams that are in between traditional essay and objective exams. Completion questions, for example, require you to fill in a word or phrase. Or sometimes, the instructor will ask you to identify or describe something in a short sentence. These kinds of questions don't require you to organize a lot of information, but they do test for recall.

Because objective exams require only that you select (or guess at) the right answer, many students don't study as thoroughly for them as they do for essay exams. This could be a mistake. Most objective exams are graded on a curve. Thus all students have the same advantage or disadvantage. If you have only an average preparation, that is where you will end up—in the middle.

Many students also think that objective exams are picky. They emphasize trivial details. If you feel this way, consider the role of details in an essay. Well-chosen details serve to support and develop the points made. If you can enrich your answers to essay questions with details, the instructor or his or her reader is going to judge that you really know what you are talking about. In short, while getting the main ideas is the name of the essay game, don't neglect the details.

The really important difference between essay and objective exams lies in organization. Essay questions are harder because they require you to organize what you know. They don't require you to know *more* but they do require you to make what you know form a coherent pattern. If essay questions throw you, practice by making up your own questions and try writing up answers to them. You might even take your questions to the instructor or the teaching assistant to check out how well you are doing in this respect.

EXAMINATION ANXIETY

Examination anxiety is real. We've known students so upset that a couple of minutes into the exam they have to leave the room to go throw up. Some students break out into a rash. A few shake so badly that they can't write. What's the best way to avoid such reactions? The answer is simple: Be prepared. Of course, even the best prepared students are occasionally going to have rumbly guts at exam time, but the chances are they are going to be better off in this respect than their fellow students who are not as well prepared. A good way to approach exams with confidence is to assess your preparation. Exams that come early in a course let you do that. Use the first exam in a course to correct your preparation. Are you doing things the right way? Is this course going to require more study and review than you thought? If so, revise your schedule.

Besides being well prepared, there are a few other things you can do to reduce your anxiety. Some of them are little things such as getting to the exam well before it begins. Avoid being rushed; rushing only aggravates your nervousness. Spend the few minutes before an exam in small talk or reading the campus paper, or doing anything that will put you in a relaxed mood. A last-minute frantic review while waiting for the exam to be handed out will only increase your panic by telling you there are things you don't know. For the same reason, don't talk about the exam with other students; they may have studied things you overlooked. That also invites panic.

Don't let yourself get rattled in the course of the examination. If you feel that you can't remember your own name, you need to be better prepared than other students. Some people are impervious to the kinds of challenges an exam provides, while others go to pieces. If your tendency is to go to pieces, you've got to be thoroughly prepared. You will find that, as you gain confidence in your ability to cope with the stress of an exam, you will gradually lose the tendency to fall apart. Above all *don't use the excuse of test anxiety to take the blame that belongs to poor preparation.*

The last and most important thing you can do to bolster your confidence is to have a strategy for taking the exam. People who know what to do in emergencies don't panic. This holds for taking exams. You probably know what kind of exam to expect. There is a sensible way to go about taking each kind. Know what it is and be prepared to carry out your plan as soon as you get the signal to go ahead.

If, in spite of being well prepared and rested before an exam, you are still crippled by anxiety, you will need to do something about it. Many counseling services offer special sessions on how to reduce examination anxiety. And even if such a particular service is not offered at your institution, being counseled about your problems with examination may help. Panic before examinations even when you are well prepared is a symptom of an underlying problem. Doing something about it will help you not only with examinations but with other issues of personal adjustment as well.

TAKING OBJECTIVE EXAMINATIONS

Here are some of the things you should do when you are faced with an objective examination:

1. Survey. When you pick up an objective exam, flip through the pages to see how long it is and how many kinds of questions are on it. Note how many questions there are of each type—true-false, multiple-choice, matching—so that you can determine how to divide your time among them.

2. Read directions carefully. Make sure you know what you are supposed to do. Indicate your answers in exactly the way the directions tell you to. If you don't you may be in trouble.

3. Be sure you understand the scoring rules. If there is no penalty for guessing, you have nothing to lose by trying to answer every question. If, on the other hand, there is a definite penalty for guessing—taking off points for a wrong answer—follow a conservative strategy. How conservative your strategy should be depends on the penalty. If the instructor takes *two* points off for a wrong answer and gives only one point for a correct one, you will want to be very careful indeed. True-false tests are more likely to have such a severe correction for chance because you have a fifty-fifty chance of being right just by flipping a coin.

If, on a true-false test, the instructor arrives at a score by taking the number right and subtracting the number wrong, you should guess and try to answer every question because, on the average, your guesses will be right more often than wrong if you know *anything* about the material at all. But as we pointed out earlier, if the instructor corrects for this by taking the number right minus *two* times the number wrong, be very careful about your guesses. Guess only when you have a strong feeling that you might be right.

Whatever you do, read the instructor's directions. If the instructor says, "There is no penalty of guessing" or "Don't guess, because wrong answers will be penalized," adjust what you do accordingly. Don't hesitate to ask for clarification about penalties if it is not clear.

4. Answer easy questions first. If speed is a factor in objective tests, you will want to work as rapidly as is consistent with care. After you have surveyed the test and gotten the instructions straight, go right to work. Some questions will be easy and some will be hard. Some are so easy that you can answer them as soon as you have read the question. If you have to stop and think, put a checkmark in the margin and go on to the next question. Come back to those hard ones after you have done all the easy ones. Whatever you do, don't get bogged down on some particular question. Unless the test is unusual, every question of a given type will have equal weight, and you're just wasting good time fussing over a particular question. Know how much time you have left and how many tough questions remain to be answered so you can apportion your time sensibly.

This is particularly good advice for an objective test in which the questions are problems that must be worked. Work first those that you are sure you know how to work and then, if you have time, go back to those that take time to figure out.

5. Place the question in context. As you read the questions, remember their context. Ask yourself how this question ought to be answered in the light of your textbook or what has been said in class. Identify the source, if possible. Don't fall into the trap of answering a question with your own personal opinion or what has been said in some other course you are taking. Most answers are relevant to a given context. Don't handicap yourself by ignoring that context. Even if you think that the instructor or the textbook is wrong, it is still your job to show that you know what the correct answer is from the point of view of the course you are taking.

Some Tips on True-False Questions

True-false questions usually consist of some simple statements which relate two things. "Attitudes are learned." "Roses are red." "The stock market crashed in 1929." These could be examples. Such statements may be true some of the time and not true at other times, or true in some contexts and not in others. You can't be expected to answer anything as ambiguous as these examples, and instructors usually don't intend that you should. Instructors, if they are doing their job, are interested in knowing whether you know when and under what circumstances something is true or not. So statements in true-false exams are usually provided with qualifiers.

Analyze Qualifiers. Here are some important qualifiers you may run across:

> All, most, some, few, none, no.
> Always, usually, sometimes, rarely, never.
> Great, much, little, no, none.
> More, equal, less.
> Good, bad.

Pay attention to qualifiers. You can test qualifiers by substituting for the one in the question one of the others in the same series. If your substitution makes more sense than the original, the statement is probably false. If your substitution does not make a better statement, the question is likely true. For example, suppose the statement is "Some roses are red." The alternatives are "All roses are red," "Most roses are red," "Few roses are red," and "No roses are red." The two extreme statements are clearly not true. You may have some questions about "Most roses are red" and "Few roses are red." But even if one of these statements is true, "Some roses are red" would also have to be true. None of the substitutes makes a better statement than the original.

Don't labor over qualifiers, however. Take the time to test them only if you think you might be misled by the one in the question.

Pick Out Key Words. Even more important than analyzing the qualifiers is finding the key word or words. There is always a key word or a key phrase. It is the word or group of words upon which the truth or falsity of the statement depends.

Some students have picked up the idea that certain words automatically make a statement true or false. And, to be sure, it is difficult to construct true statements with such qualifiers as "no," "never," "always," or "every." But don't automatically mark statements containing these as false. In creating tests, instructors discard statements that can be answered correctly by taking a cue from extreme modifiers, and they do manage to construct some statements containing such modifiers that are, in fact, true. So judge each statement in the light of what you know. The exercise on page 62 will give you some practice in identifying key words and modifiers.

Finally, don't try to guess your way through a true-false test by trying to find a pattern to the sequence of answers. It's unlikely there is any.

Answering Multiple-Choice Questions

Multiple-choice questions are true-false questions arranged in groups. A lead phrase at the beginning of each question combines with three or more endings to make different statements. Sometimes the questions are made so that more than one answer can be right. For example: Roses most often grow (1) on bushes, (2) on trees, (3) in winter, (4) in summer. By checking the key words, "most often," we see that both "on bushes" and "in summer" are true. In such cases, the directions will probably tell you to mark all words or phrases that complete the statement as true. However, if only one alternative is correct, you should choose "on bushes" because roses also grow in early spring and late fall. Be sure to read the directions carefully so that you know whether you can mark two or more alternatives as being correct.

Most often, however, just one of the alternatives will be correct. Here, your job is to pick out the best alternative—that is, the one that is *most nearly true*. It is usually a relative matter, not one of absolute truth or falsity. For this reason, you will want to adopt a strategy of elimination. Take, for example, the following question: "The American philosopher most influential in the philosophy of education is (1) William James, (2) Bertrand Russell, (3) John Dewey, (4) Nathaniel Hawthorne." If you remember that Hawthorne was the author of *The Scarlet Letter*, you will know that he is not, technically speaking, a philosopher, and he can be easily eliminated. The other three are all

Exercise in Key Words

Here is a list of true-false questions that you might encounter early on in any introductory psychology course. It is designed to point to commonly held misconceptions. The answer to each of these true-false questions is "false." However, what you need to do is to pick out the key words that make them false. When you are finished, check your selections with the ones listed below.

Key Words

1. Geniuses are always neurotic.
2. You can accurately tell what someone is thinking from facial expression.
3. Cats can see in total darkness.
4. There is a clear distinction between normal people and emotionally disturbed people.
5. If people were always honest we would get along with one another better.
6. Your IQ is completely determined by heredity.
7. Psychology can never be objective.
8. Stuttering is usually the result of poor speech training.
9. If you practice enough, you can read anything at the rate of 1000 words a minute.
10. Darwin was the first person to advocate a theory of evolution.
11. With statistics you can prove anything.
12. Urban legends always have some basis in fact.
13. It has been proven that animals can sense a coming earthquake.
14. It is possible to classify everyone as either extroverted or introverted.
15. Slow learners remember better what they learn than fast learners.
16. You can size up a person very well in an interview.
17. All people are neurotic.
18. Studying mathematics will necessarily make you a better thinker.
19. A psychologist is someone trained to psychoanalyze people.
20. A first experience at intercourse can never make a girl pregnant.

The key words for each question are as follows: (1) always, (2) accurately, (3) total, (4) clear, (5) always, better, (6) completely, (7) never, (8) usually, (9) anything, (10) first person, (11) prove, anything, (12) always, (13) proven, (14) everyone, (15) better, (16) very well, (17) all, (18) necessarily, (19) psychoanalyze, (20) never.

philosophers, and unless you know something about philosophy and the philosophy of education, you will have a hard time reaching the most probable right answer. All three wrote about education. But the key words will help. They are "American," "philosophy of education," and "most." Bertrand Russell is British, and if you know that, you can eliminate him. Thus, you have to choose between William James and John Dewey. Both wrote on education, so the key word in choosing between them is "most." John Dewey is undoubtedly the choice the instructor had in mind, for he was and still is the towering influence on American education.

Once you have made your decision, mark the answer and go on to the next question. If you can't make up your mind between a couple of plausible alternatives, place a checkmark at the side and leave the question until you have worked the easier problems.

Answering Matching Questions

You can apply similar strategies to matching questions. Read all the items to be matched so that you know all the possibilities. Then take the first item on the left and read down the items on the right until you find the one that you're sure is the best match. If you are not certain, leave the item and go on to the next one. Fill in only those you are certain about. That way you will reduce the number of possibilities for difficult matches.

Some matching questions consist only of words and brief phrases to be matched. Others contain whole clauses, similar to those in true-false or multiple-choice statements. If that is the case, try to spot the key words.

Answering Completion Questions

One kind of question used fairly often in large classes is the completion question. Completion questions provide statements with key words or phrases left out. In answering this kind of question, choose your words carefully. The instructor probably has something very specific in mind. All things being equal, a single word is probably required, but if you think that more than one word is absolutely required, write them down. Try to recall the very best wording so that you will get full credit, not half. But if you can't think of the exact answer, write down something. Instructors seldom deduct for guessing in completion questions, and while you may look a bit silly to the grading assistant by giving some far-out answer, you just might have the right idea.

Finishing the Examination

We've told you to answer the easy questions first on an objective exam and then go back to the hard ones. Before you begin work on these harder questions, note how much time you have left and allocate it among the remaining questions. Leave some time for a final glance over the exam. You may spot some careless mistakes.

When you reread your examination, you will be tempted to change some of your answers. If you feel strongly that an answer should be changed, do so. If, however, you have a hard time making up your mind between two answers, don't change the answer you wrote the first time. If you are guessing, your first guess is more likely to be the right one. Change your answer only if you are reasonably sure that your first answer is wrong.

TAKING ESSAY EXAMINATIONS

In essay exams your work consists of writing organized and precise answers to questions rather than reading the questions and trying to figure out the right answers. At the one extreme these questions will require you to write down something quite specific. At the other extreme they will ask you to "discuss" some general issue in order to indicate the amount of thought you have given to what you have studied. Most essay exams will be mixtures of these two types. Then too, there are short-answer questions. These require a slightly different strategy, and we will have a word to say about these shortly. First, however, we will give you some general principles that apply to all kinds of essay exams.

Planning Your Time

Planning and allocating time are even more important in essay exams than in objective exams. Students are likely to know more than they have time to write down, and it is easy to get carried away on a subject you know a lot about. If you're not careful, you will spend too much time on some questions and give others short shrift. That will probably lower your grade because the grading assistant or the instructor will likely give all questions equal weight.

Read through the whole exam first and decide how much time you can afford to spend on each question. If you have a choice of which questions to answer, choose all your questions at the beginning. That decision should depend on a number of things—how much you know about a particular topic, how hard the question is, and, above all, how much you would have to write.

Following Directions

The key words in essay exams are the instructions. They are such words as "list," "illustrate," "compare," "outline," "state," "discuss," etc. Usually an instructor chooses such words carefully, and she or he expects you to do what you're told. Students who aren't prepared as well as they should be are tempted to write around a subject—to tell everything they know about a subject whether relevant to the question or not. This is not only a waste of time, it tells the grader or the instructor that either you didn't really understand the question or you didn't know what you were writing about. Graders and instructors ignore what isn't relevant, and tough instructors may even deduct for evading the question. Stick as close to the directions as you can. If you're told to list, do that. Don't illustrate

Important Words in Essay Questions

Here are some of the words that provide the critical instructions for answering essay questions. We've provided a brief summary of what each tells you to do.

Compare

Look for similarities and differences between the things mentioned (e.g., "Compare the U.S. and Confederate Constitutions").

Contrast

Stress the dissimilarities.

Criticize

Make your judgment about the item in question. Stress the deficiencies (e.g., "Criticize Paul Valéry's views on the poet's language").

Define

Provide a concise and accurate definition of what is called for.

Describe

Mention the chief characteristics of a situation or retell the essential features of a story (e.g., "Describe France on the eve of the revolution," or "Describe Conrad's *Heart of Darkness*").

Diagram

Provide a drawing, chart, or plan.

Discuss

Be analytical. Give reasons pro and con.

Evaluate

Provide both positive and negative sides of the topic (e.g., "Evaluate the role of Disraeli in forming the modern Conservative Party").

Explain

Give reasons for what is asked for. Provide the causes (e.g., "Explain the reasons for the notion of penetrance in population genetics").

Illustrate

Use examples. Or, where appropriate, provide a diagram or figure.

Interpret

Translate, solve, or comment on a subject, usually giving your judgment about it.

Justify

Provide the reasons for your conclusions or for the statement made in the question (e.g., "Justify Henry Clay's interpretation of the Constitution").

List

Provide an itemized list. The items should be numbered.

Outline

Organize your answer into main points and subordinate points. While it is not necessary that your answer be in outline form, it helps to prepare it that way.

Prove

Provide factual evidence or, where appropriate, a logical or mathematical proof.

Relate

Show the connection between the things mentioned in the question. Note this does not mean to compare, so if you are asked to relate the American and French revolutions, you are not to compare them but to show how one influences the other.

Review

Provide a summary, usually a critical one. A review usually also implies commenting on important aspects of the question.

Summarize

Provide a summary, usually without comment or criticism.

Trace

Describe the progress of some historical event or, where appropriate, describe the causes of some event.

Organizing Essay Answers

Here are two examples of brief answers to an essay question. Read them to see what you think of them, and then compare your judgment with our comment at the end. The question is: "What were the important results of the (English) revolution of 1688?"

The first answer

I will summarize the most important results of the revolution under three headings:

1. *Parliament's victory.* The most direct result of the revolution of 1688 was the final victory of Parliament in the conflict between it and the crown that had gone on all during the 17th century. Parliament, by declaring the throne vacant because of James II's desertion to France, finally established that the king ruled by choice of the people and Parliament and not by divine right. Parliament established a Bill of Rights, which said that the king was not above the law but was himself subject to the law. In the early years of the reign of William and Mary, many additional acts were passed which curtailed the powers of the crown.

2. *The end of religious conflict.* The revolution itself did not entirely end the religious troubles of the 17th century, but Parliament passed a Toleration Act which brought an end to many of the difficulties of the Dissenters. The Catholics, however, were still subjected to many infringements of civil liberties.

3. *A new political class.* The important general result of the revolution and the victory of Parliament was the beginning of a long era during which political power in England was divided between the landed gentry and the merchant class.

The second answer

The revolution of 1688 was very important. It was so important that it is sometimes called the "glorious revolution." Parliament won, and it passed a lot of acts which were against the king, and it invited William and Mary to rule jointly in England. William and Mary still had to fight though, especially in Ireland where James II was finally defeated. William and Mary cooperated with Parliament so there wasn't so much trouble between the King and Parliament. James II was very unpopular because he was a Catholic, and Parliament made it so no Catholic could ever become king again, although parliament made things easier for the Dissenters. This was the end of the Divine Right of Kings in England, though at first the country was ruled mostly by the aristocracy and the rich merchants. Real democracy didn't come until much later, so the revolution of 1688 wasn't a completely democratic revolution.

Notice that these two answers differ more in organization than they do in content. The first answer is not perfect, but it is balanced, clear, and factual. The second is much poorer because it is vague, disorganized, and full of irrelevancies and loose statements.

or discuss. If you're told to compare, be sure you do that. On page 64 is a table that lists the key words in the instructions for essay exams and explains how to interpret them.

Organizing Your Answers

The significant difference between a good essay answer and a poor one is a matter of organization. The best way to make sure that your answer will be coherent and organized is to outline. When you're sure you understand what the question is about, decide what points you will make and sketch these out in outline form. Use this outline as a guide to writing the answer. After you are through, you can cross out your outline so that it won't be taken as part of your answer. Your grader isn't likely to mind if you do this; most graders are impressed by your attempt to organize things into a coherent whole. If you don't outline, you will get off the subject more easily, and in the rush of writing you may forget some important points.

You can even write some answers in an outline form. The fact that you are well enough organized to do so will generally impress the grader. Don't make your outline skimpy, however, and don't use incomplete sentences. Number the main points and even the secondary points. The main reason some instructors prefer essay exams to objective exams is that essay exams force you to organize information in your own mind. You are much more likely to get credit for what you know if you express it in a well-organized outline form. Look at the two examples of brief answers to an essay question on page 65, and see if you can tell why one answer is better than the other.

Choosing Your Words

Take care to choose your words carefully in answering an essay question. Instructors are not mind readers. They can't guess what you intended; they can only judge what you actually said. So say what you mean. Say it precisely. Give illustrations (if appropriate), and supply relevant details. Make it clear that you know what you're talking about. The two examples on page 65 of organized and disorganized answers illustrate the difference between precise, accurate statements and statements that, while they may be intended to say the same thing, don't say it in quite the right way.

Know the difference between padding your answer and elaborating your points. Bringing in extraneous points, repeating what you have already said, and being unnecessarily wordy are all padding. If you can't see the difference between the two examples in this respect, you may need some help in writing. Even though the poorly organized answer is shorter, it is full of padding. The other is not.

Writing Legibly and Correctly

Poor handwriting handicaps many students in essay exams. Instructors can't give you credit for something they can't read. Some instructors try hard to decipher illegible writing, but others have no patience with it and will mark down the illegible or barely legible paper. One study of the matter showed that an answer written in a poor hand was judged a whole point lower than the same answer written in a clear hand. And the graders in this study were told to ignore handwriting.

Take the trouble to put your answers in good English. Punctuate properly and spell correctly. Poor writing implies disorganized and confused thinking as well as inadequate command of the subject matter. Poor spelling, especially of important or technical words, suggests careless reading and study. It is only natural that mistakes of this sort will pull your grades down.

TAKE-HOME AND OPEN-BOOK EXAMS

Take-home and open-book exams are fairly common in college. They are most often to be found in courses in which there is an emphasis upon problem solving—courses in such different subjects as mathematics, statistics, philosophy, and organizational management. The purposes of take-home and open-book exams are slightly different, and each requires a slightly different approach.

Take-Home Exams

First of all, know the rules. Are you allowed to read the exam before you study for it? How much time are you allowed in taking the exam? Usually, you are told that you may consult any references you wish but that you may not talk to another student about the exam. It doesn't take much sense to realize that take-home exams are not going to emphasize factual information. They are not the sort of thing on which you can make a high grade just by copying out of the book. The whole purpose of take-home exams is to see how *you* think. More often than not they require you to solve a particular problem. In a take-home statistics exam, for example, you may be given some data and asked to treat those data the right way statistically. That will require you to understand the purpose of the data, to select the right statistical measure, and to apply that measure to the data correctly. In a philosophy exam, you may be asked to apply different sets of ethical principles to some problems of life.

If you are allowed to read the questions beforehand—and in most instances that will be the case—read them and decide what technical information you will need. Then read or review the books or your notes that cover the problem you are faced with. In some instances you will have to decide whether the problem on the exam is to be solved by one method or another. In short, you will have to make a decision about what to read or look up. That is a critical decision, for you could select the wrong method or the wrong set of principles. Here is where many students make their mistake. The decision must be informed, through a basic understanding of a subject. If, at the beginning of the semester, the instructor announces that the exams will be take-home, some students assume they won't have to study until they have the exam in hand. It may then be too late.

When you have decided what background you will need to solve the problem in a particular question and have done the necessary reading, plan your answer and plan it carefully. You might even outline the steps you need to go through to answer the question. Then go about solving the problem of synthesizing the information needed to answer the question. Work deliberately and carefully. Minor mistakes might squeak by on a regular exam, but they won't do on a take-home exam. If you have to do some calculations, double-check them (double-check, not just check), for once again, while you might at least get partial credit if you make arithmetical mistakes on a regular exam, you will not get credit for a wrong answer on a take-home exam.

After you finish the exam, put it away for a while. If you have the exam only overnight, you can only afford to put it away for a couple of hours at the most. But if you have several days, put it aside for a day or so. Then take it out and go through all the steps you went through originally. Decide what it is you need to answer the question or solve the problem. Be sure you consider alternatives. Make certain you have made the right choice. Then review the reading or your notes, and, finally, recheck your calculations or reread your answer and make whatever changes are necessary.

Open-Book Exams

Open-book exams are usually based on the same principle as take-home exams. They emphasize problem solving, thinking, and discovery. However, they require a slightly different approach because you will likely have only a limited time to complete them, and they must be taken in the classroom. You can't afford the time to review all the relevant material. Rather, at best, you can afford to check certain points in the textbook or your notes, look up equations, consult tables, and the like. Therefore, it is just as important as with an ordinary exam to do all your studying ahead of time. *You can't afford to study in the exam room.*

Check in your sources where necessary, but spend as much time as possible writing the exam. As with take-home exams, however, it is very important to plan your answers. A logical organization counts even more in open-book exams than in ordinary exams. Make sure you have picked the right technique or the right material with which to answer the question, plan or outline the answer, and then write it or do your calculations. Keep your work legible and easy to read. Show how you got intermediate answers if the problem is statistical, mathematical, or in the physical sciences.

Otherwise, all the strictures for essay exams apply. Allocate your time among all the questions carefully, write legibly, and use sensible English. Remember, however, you may have *less* time per question than you would in an ordinary essay exam because at certain points you might be expected to look something up or read some table or graph.

LEARNING FROM EXAMINATIONS

Most students think of examinations just in terms of grades. In fact, exams are more than that. The best "excuse" for examinations in education is to give you a chance to learn from them. You may not realize that, and, as a result, you may fail to use exams for their educational value. When you get your exam paper back, what you most likely do (quite properly) is count up the numbers assigned to the questions to see if the instructor made a mistake, or you may look over your answers for something to quibble over (graders are not perfect), but that is about it. You put the exam aside and forget about it.

If you think that you have been unfairly graded, discuss the matter with your instructor or the grading assistant. It is far more important, however, to read your exam over and ask yourself: "Did I really understand what was asked for?"

Try to find out what your mistakes were and how you lost credit. If the notations on your exam are not detailed enough to let you know, make an appointment with the instructor (preferably) or with the grading assistant to see where you went wrong. Don't be combative, just try to find out where you went wrong.

If you study your exam carefully and get some comments on it, you will achieve a deeper and better knowledge of the subject; you can uncover things in your study habits that you didn't know about and gaps in your understanding. Mistakes, when promptly corrected, provide one of the best tools for learning.

7
WRITING PAPERS

I SAID FOUR HUNDRED **WORDS,** WAYNE, NOT FOUR HUNDRED PAGES . . . .

Can you put your ideas into words? The most important thing most students get out of the whole of formal education is the ability to read difficult material and to write about difficult topics in a sensible and organized way. This chapter is about writing. It concentrates on writing papers in college courses as different as history, psychology, and marketing. The same steps are involved; the same writing techniques apply. What we have to say here is by way of showing you, through some specific examples, how to express ideas and how to put those ideas in such a way that other educated persons can understand them.

Most likely, you will be required to take a college-level course in English writing. Given half a chance, a course in writing can help you learn how to write accurately and clearly so that you can convey complicated ideas without getting hopelessly mixed up. In most of these courses you write some themes or compositions, and the instructor goes over these carefully enough to tell you what you are doing right and what you are doing wrong.

A lot of students hate writing. If you are one of them, the composition course will be a chore, and unless you are lucky enough to have a particularly good teacher, not very helpful. You may try to find easy topics and then write about them in a way so as to risk the least challenge by the instructor. Too bad. Even if you don't like your English writing course, you will have to face the challenge of writing in other courses. College instructors—good college instructors, that is—are sticklers about teaching you how to write well. So if you are in a college that aims to really educate you, you are going to have to learn how to write. We can't instruct you in writing—only someone who goes to the trouble of correcting what you write can do that—but we can provide you with some rules to make it easier for you to write well and to concentrate on learning how to write rather than just going through the motions.

Very few of you will become professional writers, but almost all of you will have jobs in which, from time to time, you will have to write clear direct prose. One of us knew an engineer who was a supervisor for a whole office of engineers working on a mammoth project. He was so offended by the inability of his engineering staff to write that he made the whole lot attend a class in writing every Friday afternoon. Writing is *the* basic skill for educated people. No matter what you do after college, there will be times when you will have to write well enough to communicate something to other people.

We've cast this chapter in such a way that it is mainly about writing term papers. We can't cover everything. You may find it useful to buy one of the many good handbooks of composition and manuals on writing that you can find in any college bookstore. We mention some of these later on. These books will go into greater depth than we do and they are worth the effort to read.

STEPS IN WRITING A PAPER

In this section we will tell you about the steps in writing a paper. Then we have a section on using the library and taking research notes. In the final section we'll give you a little advice about the mechanics of writing.

Choosing a Topic

Sometimes topics for a paper will be assigned to you, but usually you will have some freedom in picking your own topic. In the case of themes for English composition, you may be free to write about anything that interests you.

Most instructors will warn you against picking a topic that is too broad or too difficult, but you will also have problems if you pick a topic that is too narrow or one in which you have a lot of personal involvement. You may flounder around because you just "can't think of anything."

One way to find topics for a particular course is to thumb through the indexes of textbooks and scholarly books on the subject. Suppose, for example, you are taking a course on American political parties. You may find an entry in your textbook index: "Conventions, beginnings of." You turn to the pages indicated and you find three or four paragraphs on the matter. You read that, at first, Presidential candidates were nominated in secret by caucuses of Congressional representatives, but by the 1830s this system was replaced by open nominating conventions. How this came about might interest you, and so you tentatively pick the topic: "The rise of nominating conventions." By way of practice, pick up a textbook and see how many topics you can identify that might be suitable for a term paper.

Lecture notes are another source of topics. Make special note of things that come up in lectures that might interest you. Look for topics that relate to your major or potential major. If you are a major in speech pathology taking a course in the psychology of language, you might find the instructor alluding to problems of language development in the deaf. That could provide a topic for you.

For some kinds of papers you have to look for other ways to find topics. In one engineering course, for example, students are required to do a project on the design of common household articles. The student must select something such as a stove, a vacuum cleaner, or even a broom and tell what is wrong with its design and how to improve it. Here the trick is to pick something that allows you to show some ingenuity and originality.

Many of your courses will ask for papers based on your daily experience. Most of us write best when we write about things we know about and are interested in. If you are taking a course in social organization, for example, you might want to write a paper about the role of the hometown high school basketball team in the social structure of the town.

Other good topics come from relations between courses. You may be taking a course in United States history and one in twentieth-century American literature. For the literature course you may have read and liked one of the novels of Sinclair Lewis. For the history course you could write a paper on the social changes of the 1920s depicted in three Lewis novels—*Main Street, Babbitt,* and *Elmer Gantry.*

Choosing a topic that is likely to interest the instructor is, by the way, a good rule. This isn't as crass as it sounds. Good writers take into account their potential audience, and your main audience for a term paper is the instructor and the grader. If you don't know what the instructor would be interested in, choose an important topic, one that would likely interest a number of people.

But even more important is choosing a topic that interests you. To do a good job you will have to spend a fair amount of time working on the topic, so it should be something that you want to learn more about or some idea or experience that you want to understand better.

Gathering the Data

Where and how you gather the material for your paper depend upon the subject you are writing about, the type of paper required, and its length and complexity. Sometimes you will have to do little reading and instead write an informal essay on something of personal interest. More often, however, you will have to learn something new. In this case you will probably make heavy use of the library and you will have to take research notes.

To get started, you should do some background reading. Your textbook or other books you have read in the course usually can supply some background. If you get stuck, talk to your instructor. He or she can help you clarify or limit a topic and perhaps supply some sources for background reading. In many cases, these background sources will furnish a bibliography that will lead you to other materials. In other cases, you will have to go to abstracts, cumulative indexes, or special bibliographic sources to compile a list of things you should read. And, of course, once you begin reading in earnest you will find additional references.

As you consult your references, you will prepare a working bibliography. Unless you're a real computer jockey with access to some good indexing programs, you'll keep your working bibliography on 3 × 5 or 4 × 6 cards. Later if you wish, you can transfer your file card notes to a computer disk, but the cards are best. Something we will talk about later are the various computer programs for retrieving books from the catalog. If your library has one of these you can use a cut-and-paste approach to making out cards for books, but generally it won't work for periodicals, so you will inevitably have to make some handwritten notes.

Let's assume you will use cards. For each book or article you consult, prepare a card which contains the following information: (1) the author(s) of the book or article (also the editor or translator of books where applicable); (2) the title and edition (if not the first) of the book, and, if available, the library call number. If you use the library's card catalog or printout program, all that information will come automatically, but if you work directly from the book, make sure that you get the information about the name of the book and the author from the title page and not from the spine. For books you will need (3) place of publication; (4) name of publisher; (5) copyright date. Most of the time you will find the latter on the back of the title page. For articles you will need (6) the volume number of the journal or magazine if given; (7) the year; (8) the page numbers of the article if the journal or magazine cumulates page numbers through the year; if page numbers are for just a single issue, you will need to note the month or date of issue as well as the page numbers.

Assign a number (1, 2, 3 . . .) to each bibliographic card and write it in the upper-right-hand corner.

As you read, take notes, either on the back of the cards or on separate cards, and code the notes to the bibliography cards. This will save you the trouble of duplicating all the information on the cards. Study the sample bibliography cards on pages 71 and 72. If you are careful and accurate in preparing your cards, you will save time and grief when you are ready to compile your final bibliography.

Notes for a paper based upon library research are not like the notes you take from textbooks. Research notes are usually not outlines. Instead they are in the form of summaries or quotes. *Make sure you indicate very clearly when you are quoting.* Even famous scholars have been called to task for using other people's words without attribution. Doing that can mean deep trouble for students, and in institutions which have strong honor codes it can mean expulsion. A safe way to make sure you get a quote right is to photocopy the relevant pages from the source.

How lengthy or detailed your summary is depends upon the length of the reading, on what the instructor has suggested that you do, and your purpose in reading. You can make rough reading

Bibliography Cards

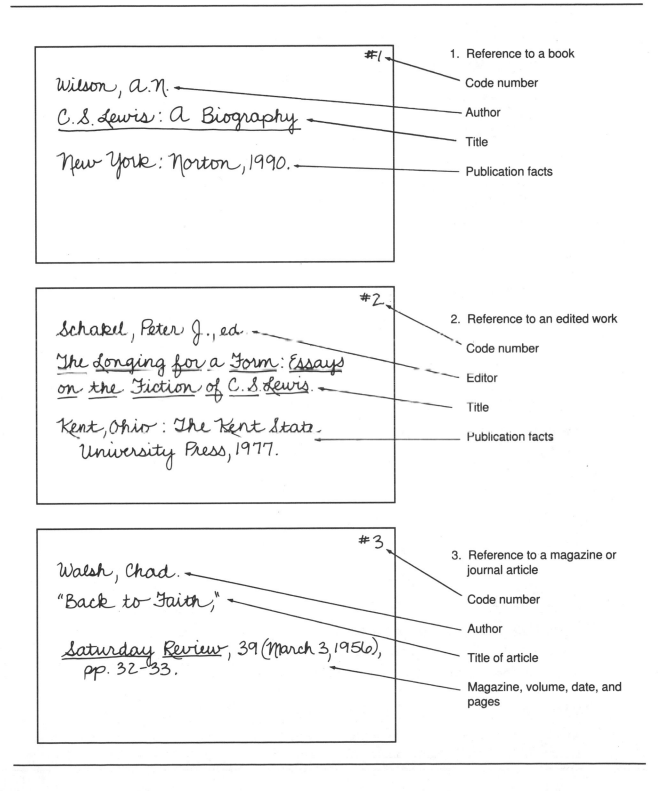

Note Card, Corresponding Bibliography Card, and Quote Card

Study the sample note card and its corresponding bibliography card.

Influence of Charles Williams on C.S. Lewis
    Williams was a great friend of Lewis and given a warm welcome when he arrived in Oxford. He became a regular member of the Inklings. Though Lewis denied being consciously influenced by Williams in his work, Green believes that the unconscious influence of Williams made the war years productive for Lewis.
                                    p. 184

— Code number

— Topic heading

— Note

— Page reference

Green, Roger L. and Hooper, Walter.

C. S. Lewis – A Biography

New York & London : Harcourt, Brace Jovanovich (Harvest Books), 1974.

The code number on both the note card and the bibliography card tells you the source of the note.

Suppose you had decided not to code your references. Another note card in this example would then be in the following form:

Green & Hooper
C.S. Lewis–A Biography

Lewis – Early Childhood
    "I am a product of long corridors, empty sunlit rooms, upstair indoor silences, attics explored in solitude …"

Written by Lewis in his autobiography
                                    p. 20

— Abbreviated version of author and title

— Topic heading

— Note (a direct quotation)

— Use of ellipsis, indicating part of a sentence is missing

— Page

notes as you go, but when you have made a succinct summary you can discard your rough notes. Once again, be sure to distinguish between summaries and quotes from the author. If you quote, be sure to note the page of the quote.

Another thing about note taking for a research paper is that you don't know exactly how many notes you will use for your paper until you have finished reading almost all your materials. Your original topic may turn out to be too big, or some of the sources you consulted may prove to be irrelevant or unimportant. Neither do you know as you read just how you will organize your paper. That will usually come from the reading itself. And it is a sure thing that no matter how you organize your paper, you are not likely to use the notes in the order in which you took them. That is why it is useful to take notes on cards. For a large paper requiring a lot of cards, you will need a card box in which to file them. If you buy a thousand cards at a time (that isn't as expensive as it sounds) you will get a reasonably sturdy cardboard box with them. Otherwise you can buy a metal or plastic box at your college bookstore. Consider investing in alphabetic dividers. People who do a lot of writing of factual books and articles almost always do this.

You might want to index your cards by topics. If, for example, you are summarizing an article about smoking and heart disease, the topic heading on your card might be "Smoking—effects of nicotine on heart rate." Most summaries will fit on one card, but if you do need more than one card for a given topic, label the cards a, b, c, . . . Make sure that you code each card for its source.

When you copy an author directly, make sure you copy accurately. If you use only part of a direct quotation, use ellipses (three spaced period marks) to show that you have left something out. Once again, don't forget to write down the pages for the quote.

All this may seem to be complicated and cumbersome at first, but once you are used to the card system for taking research notes, you will find it easy. If you use a computer to store your research notes, you can put your summaries and quotes under each entry if you like, but that makes it difficult to print out a bibliography for your paper. Find a system that enables you to both store and retrieve information efficiently.

Constructing an Outline

About the time you are finished taking notes, you will want to begin to think about the form of your paper. Making an outline is not a bad idea. First read through your note cards and rearrange them according to the topic headings that are forming in your head. This will give you some idea about how your paper should be organized. If you construct an outline (which, once again, is a pretty good idea), arrange your main and subordinate headings in a good, logical order. If you haven't read what we had to say about the format of outlines (pages 52–53), look at it before you begin.

It depends a bit on how you work best, but for most people spending a few extra minutes on an outline is worth it. It will make your paper better organized and your writing job an easier one. After you begin writing you may want to revise your outline or just use it as a guide and reminder as to what yet needs to be said. An outline may also tell you that you have to do some more reading or that you may have to make a thin section into a substantial one.

Writing the First Draft

Very few people can get by with just one draft. There are a few famous authors who have managed it, but most careful writers go through several drafts. This book went through an outline and at least three drafts (it was hard to count because two of us worked on it). Two drafts should do for most term papers, but something as important as a senior thesis may require more.

If you've made an outline, rearrange your notes in the order of your outline. Then write. For writing, allow yourself a large block of time during which you can work without interruption. Writing a long paper all in one session is a big undertaking, but a lot of students find they can do it, particularly if the paper is less than ten typewritten pages. For a first draft, don't worry too much about getting everything just right. Some writers just leave a space when they know they can come back later and fill in something that is not essential to the organization of the paper. Once you get your essential ideas down, you can correct things easily enough.

Leave plenty of room for corrections and alterations. *Never, never* single-space a first draft, even if the final version is going to be single-spaced. If you are working on a word processor, you can single-space as you enter the information, but double-space the first printout, even if you have made corrections on the screen.

When you have completed the first draft, go over it for obvious changes. This step applies to computer produced copy as well; you can make the changes on the screen. But if you are like one of us and are liable to wipe out a whole section by trying to move a paragraph, do it by hand. Nobody is going to look at your first draft but you.

If possible, allow as much time as possible between the first draft and a revision. You will have a fresh perspective, and it will be easier for you to detect mistakes and lapses in grammar and writing if you do.

Revising the Paper

After you have put your work aside for a time, revise. *Check first the coverage.* Did you get everything in that you should? Is there anything that slipped by the first draft? Did you not explain certain topics sufficiently? You may need to go back to your notes for something that you left out or something you think you might not have gotten quite right. You may even have to go back to the library to check on something or dig up additional material. If you want to write a really good paper, it is worth the effort.

Then check the organization of your paper. Does it hang together? Be critical, because if you aren't, the instructor will be. Are the headings and subheadings, if you use them, in the right places and clearly indicated as to their relative weight? Are the transitions between sections smooth? Should you have a summary and a conclusion? If you're not satisfied with your organization, change it. That may mean simply a cut-and-paste job or moving paragraphs on the computer. Or it may mean rewriting sentences and even whole paragraphs.

Finally, check the mechanics. Are your sentences grammatical and understandable? Do you have some wordy and awkward constructions? Look at your verbs. Do you overuse all-purpose but sometimes meaningless verbs such as "involve"? Do you use the passive voice monotonously? If you don't know what the passive voice is, stop now and look it up. You will, of course, have a good diction-ary handy, but in addition, refresh your understanding of what is good style by glancing at a concise handbook such as *The Elements of Style* by William Strunk, Jr., and E. B. White. We'll have more to say about this later.

Documenting the Paper

When you write a paper using other people's ideas, you must give credit to your sources. Using someone else's ideas or the discoveries reported by other people without acknowledging your debt is described by a single word. The word is "plagiarism." This is a serious offense. As we told you earlier, in many colleges and universities detected plagiarism is grounds for dismissal.

In a research paper, documentation may be given in the text by footnotes keyed to a bibliography. The footnote can give the full reference, the author, and title, or merely the author and date. If the reference is well known and short you can acknowledge it in the text (not as a footnote) and not enter the source in the bibliography. A Biblical reference is an example. "When I was a child, I spoke like a child. . . ." (I Corinthians 13:11) (Exception: If you use a new or not well-known translation of the Bible, you should refer to it by footnote.) Other examples of references which do not need footnotes include well-known quotes from literature: "Good night, sweet prince, and flights of angels sing they to thy rest." (*Hamlet*, v. ii 59) Well-known sayings do not need to be footnoted. You might write: As Harry Truman said, "If you can't stand the heat, get out of the kitchen."

Footnotes belong either at the bottom of the page, numbered consecutively, or in a list at the end of the paper (technically, in the latter case they are called endnotes). The number of the footnote appears as a superscript in the appropriate place in the text. Sources that you use merely for background material and that you do not directly draw upon can simply be cited in your bibliography. The endnotes do not constitute a bibliography. You must have a complete listing of your source material.

There are several ways to do footnotes. Consult a style manual, such as *The MLA Style Sheet*, published by the Modern Languages Association. There are dozens of others. Some instructors have a preference for a particular style. If so, find out what it is and *follow it*. Most of these sources give you forms of citation and keys to standard abbreviations (op. cit., ibid., etc.). Whatever form you choose, be consistent in your use.

In the social sciences and to a degree in the natural sciences, each discipline has its own form for citation. For example, in a psychology course you might say in a paper: "It is well known that autonomic responses may be influenced by cognitive activity (Jones, 1988)." Or, alternatively, "Jones (1988) argues that autonomic responses are influenced by cognitive activity." If there are two or more references in the same year by the same author, add letters to the year: "(Jones, 1988a; Jones, 1988b)." Be sure to find out whether or not your instructor wants you to use this form. But also be sure *not* to use it where it would be inappropriate. If you are a psychology major this form probably comes naturally, but don't spring it on your English instructor.

There is an art to knowing what information needs to be acknowledged by a citation and what information is general knowledge. If you are going to err, err on the side of too much documentation rather than too little. When in doubt, acknowledge your source.

Your final bibliography will consist of all the works you consulted in your paper, even if you do not refer to them directly in a footnote. Since you already have your working bibliography on cards or on a disk, all you need to do is to go through the cards and eliminate the references which you did not use and prepare a list alphabetized according to the authors' last names. (In footnotes, authors' first names come first.) If you cite more than one work by the same author, list these in alphabetical order by title. Caution: In some disciplines you are expected to list multiple works by the same author according to date. Also, in the social and natural sciences you usually do not list works which you have read but have not actually cited.

Preparing the Final Draft

By this time you will probably feel that your job is finished and that you will want to get the final version typed as soon as possible. But if you can, set the paper aside for a day or two. You will likely want to make a few more corrections before you prepare the final version. This is particularly true if this is a major paper. We know that students like to stay up all night working on a paper that is due the next day, but if the paper is important to you, or if your entire grade hinges on it, our advice is to give it time to rest before you have to turn it in.

A term paper should be typed. We've both accepted term papers handwritten, but we can say from experience that it is very hard to avoid being prejudiced against such papers. If you don't type well enough yourself, get someone else to do it. Use a good grade of paper (but not the "erasable" kind), standard size (eight and one-half by eleven inches), and *double space*. Never turn a paper in that is single-spaced unless that is specifically required. If you use a dot matrix printer that requires special paper, it may be worth the effort to photocopy the paper and turn in an enhanced photocopy. If you place your footnotes at the bottom of the page, they can be single-spaced and set off from the text by a line extending across the paper. You will find a sample page with this form of citation on page 76. Number every page except the title page in the upper-right-hand corner. We emphasize this because students who prepare papers on the computer do not always include page numbers. If you have to, put the page number in by hand.

If you *must* write the paper by hand, use lined paper and skip lines between each line of text. This will make room for your instructor to write comments and corrections. When you prepare the bibliography, double-space between each entry, but you can single-space lines within each entry (see the example on page 77).

When the paper has been typed or copied in its final form, proofread it carefully. We all make mistakes. *Make sure you have a duplicate copy before you turn the paper in.*

USING THE LIBRARY

The library is the heart of any college or university. If you don't use your library, you are missing the most important intellectual treat your college or university has to offer. You go there to gather material for the papers you write, to find the required or supplementary reading, to study when your dormitory or home is too noisy, and, yes, just to enjoy the best works that your civilization has to offer you.

Page with Footnotes

The following is a page from a term paper on Margaret Fuller, a nineteenth-century feminist. This excerpt illustrates the use and form of footnotes in term papers.

In Mount Auburn cemetery in Cambridge, Massachusetts, is a memorial stone raised following the death by shipwreck in 1850 of Margaret Fuller, Marchesa Ossoli. The inscription on this stone reads in part: "By birth a child of New England, By adoption a citizen of Rome. . . . In youth . . . seeking the highest culture. . . . In maturer years, earnest reformer in America and Europe."[1]

If a few words carved on a gravestone can sum up the span of a life, these words do so for Sarah Margaret Fuller. This paper explores briefly her passage from the rarefied culture of New England Transcendentalism to the European revolutionary movement of 1848. For, although Margaret Fuller was formed by the New England of the early nineteenth century and molded in its image, she left the peace of Concord, the familiar intellectual world of Cambridge, for the bustle of New York, and then, beckoned by her long cherished dream of Italy, she arrived finally at Rome where she found her spiritual home.[2] From a youth devoted to culture of self she moved to reform and finally to participation in the Roman revolution of 1848.

The young Margaret's worship of genius and power and her disdain for the "vulger herd"[3] became the faith of the mature woman in the unspoiled nature of the people.[4] Her early desire to remain aloof from such experiments in . . . .

1. Mason Wade, *Margaret Fuller: Whetstone of Genius*, Viking, New York, 1940, pp. 271–272.
2. R. W. Emerson et al., *Memoirs of Margaret Fuller Ossoli*, v. 2, Phillips, Samuels & Co., Boston, 1852, p. 216.
3. Ibid., v. 1, p. 134.
4. Ibid., v. 2, p. 225.

You may not know all the things that the library, even a small library, can do for you. One of us went to a small college with a very limited library, the other to a big university with access to the best library resources in the nation. Both of us, however, realize how important knowing how to use a library is. In particular, if you are in a big school, don't let the size of the library defeat you. Libraries are organized on logical principles, and librarians are there to help you.

Layout of the Library

Learn how your library or libraries are organized. Big institutions usually have several libraries (in fact, in the biggest, individual departments have their own libraries). In most research universities there is both an undergraduate library and a research library. In some institutions the research library is open to anyone—if so, browse in it. In others, you need special status—usually being a faculty member or graduate student—to use it. Don't let that discourage you. Even if you can't enter the stacks, you can check materials out. In rare book collections you may have to have someone photocopy material in order to use it. Persist; you can always get access to what you need if you try hard enough.

During orientation or as soon as possible after you start classes, go to the library (or libraries, if your institution has a library specifically for undergraduates) and look around. At many places, the library staff will provide orientation meetings for students. If so, take the time to go to one. Most larger libraries have directories posted at various points to guide you. Some libraries publish manuals that list and describe the services they offer. In any event, take advantage of whatever your institution offers by way of an introduction to library services. But it is absolutely essential that you know where to find the following:

1. Card catalogs and computerized retrieval systems. The card catalog tells you what is in the library, and by a coding system (in most institutions the Library of Congress system), how to find what you want. In the traditional card catalog

Sample Bibliography

Here is a sample bibliography for a term paper on "Gender in Contemporary Higher Education."

Archer, J., & Lloyd, B. B. (1985). *Sex and gender.* Cambridge: Cambridge University Press.

Astin, A. W. (1977). *Four critical years.* San Francisco: Jossey-Bass.

Astin, A. W., Green, K. C., Korn, W. S. & Schalit, M. (1986). *The American freshman: National norms for fall 1986.* Los Angeles: Cooperative Institutional Research Program, Graduate School of Education, University of California.

Bernard, J. (1972) *The sex game.* New York: Atheneum.

Chickering, A. W., et al. (Eds.) (1981). *The modern American college.* San Francisco: Jossey-Bass.

El-Khawas, E. H. (1988). *Community college fact book.* New York: Macmillan.

Gerson, J. M. Women returning to school: The consequences of multiple roles. *Sex roles, 13,* 1–2, 77–92.

Harding, S. G. (1986). *The science question in feminism.* Ithaca, New York: Cornell University Press.

Henley, N. & Barrie, T. (Eds.) (1975). *Language and sex: Difference and dominance.* Rowley, Massachusetts: Newbury House.

Mendelsohn, P. (1986). *Happier by degrees.* Berkeley, California: Ten Speed Press.

Springer, M. (1988). Women and power in higher education: Saving the Libra in a Scorpio world. In S. S. Brehm (Ed.), *Seeing female: social roles and personal lives* (pp. 145–156). New York: Greenwood Press.

there are usually cards in three categories—author, title, and subject. These three types of cards are illustrated on page 81.

In bigger libraries card catalogs are being phased out in favor of computerized retrieval programs. These differ slightly from institution to institution (they even have different names—at the University of Virginia it is called Virgo; at Georgetown it is called George). These systems are user-friendly, but even so, learn how to use them as soon as possible. Most of them provide printouts of what you call for (see samples of retrieval printouts on page 82), and you can use these printouts for your sources (remember we said that you can use them on a cut-and-paste basis to make your bibliography cards).

2. Reading rooms. Large libraries usually have several reading rooms, one for each of several functions or subjects. For example, there may be a reference reading room and one for periodicals. Smaller libraries may have one general reading room. Check them out. In some of the newer libraries, often called learning or media centers, there may be no specific reading rooms, but, instead, comfortable chairs and tables scattered throughout the stacks or wherever the books are located.

3. Computer facilities. Modern campuses abound with computer facilities, but the ones intended for the typical undergraduate usually will be located in the library. Find out about these and go to whatever orientation session is offered to tell you how to use them. Many of these facilities are open on a round-the-clock basis (we've heard undergraduates say that their paper was late or badly edited because they could not get access to a computer terminal until three a.m.). Find out where *all* of your computer facilities are located, but the library is bound to be one of them.

4. *Reference facilities.* Reference works are kept separate from general books and periodicals. They are sometimes to be found in a separate reference room. These rooms include encyclopedias, biographical dictionaries, yearbooks, and other valuable resources. These reference works can't be taken out of the library, but you can usually make a photocopy of what you want. Something students don't know is that there is nearly always a librarian who specializes in reference. If you are in despair because you don't know where to look in the reference section (you may even want to know the address of a writer who lives in Malibu!), consult the reference librarian.

5. *Current periodicals.* Current periodicals are usually shelved in a periodical room or in a separate section of the main reading room. Back issues are bound and shelved along with books by subject matter. Occasionally, however, they are shelved separately, particularly in smaller departmental or branch libraries. If you need a periodical from the last year or two and can't find it on the periodical shelves, ask the librarian about it. It may be out being bound, or it may be missing. In any event, you will be doing a service by asking about it.

6. *Stacks.* "Stacks" is the word for a series of shelves on which books are arranged for compact storage. The shelves are spaced just far enough apart to let you get between them. The stacks in big university libraries may cover many floors of a large building. Stacks are either *open* or *closed.* Open stacks are available to all users of the library. They are usually found in smaller, undergraduate institutions, though some of the largest and best research universities pride themselves on maintaining open stacks for everybody. Closed stacks require a special permit for entry. They are usually restricted to faculty and graduate students. If your library has open stacks, you may go directly to the shelves to find the books you want (and better yet, you can freely browse through the stacks). If it has closed stacks, you will have to fill out a card requesting the book or books you want and wait for a library staff member to get it for you. Big research universities which have closed stacks also usually have undergraduate libraries with open access. If you can't find what you want in the undergraduate library, *do not hesitate to go to the research library.* Except in the most benighted of institutions, you will be welcome. As we pointed out earlier, even if you aren't given free access, you can probably get use through persistence.

7. *Reserve shelves.* Almost every college library has a separate section of reserve shelves. Even the smallest departmental libraries have them. Here the books are shelved according to the *courses* in which they are used. (Make sure you know your course number, for more often than not these books are shelved by course number, or instructor's name, rather than by course title.) The idea behind reserve shelves is a good one; it is to make sure that everybody in the course has access to the required or supplementary reading. These books sometimes do not circulate; they can be used only in the library. If they do circulate, it is usually for a short period, perhaps overnight. Penalties for late return of circulating reserve books are steep, so make sure that you know what the time limits are and observe them.

8. *Special collections and facilities.* Most libraries, even those with open stacks, have some material, often valuable or rare books and manuscripts, kept in special rooms. To save space, many periodicals and some rare books are on microfilm or microfiche to be read with the aid of a special reading device. Make sure you know how to get access to machines necessary to read microfilm, etc. The library will also have record and tape collections for foreign languages, music, poetry, and drama. More and more libraries have videotapes and filmstrips. Find out where these collections are and know how to use the equipment.

If a book you need is not in your library, it can usually be obtained for you by loan from another library. Check with a librarian before you decide that you can't use something because it isn't available.

Most large libraries provide daily computer printouts which list the books currently checked out. If the book you want is not on the shelf, check the printout and ask the librarian to request that it be returned. If the book is neither on the shelf nor circulating, have the librarian put out a search for it.

Classification

Everything in the library is classified according to some system. The almost universal system now is the Library of Congress Classification System, though a few institutions still use the simpler Dewey Decimal Classification System. The Library of Congress system uses letters of the alphabet for its general subject divisions and numerals for finer distinctions. Within each subject class a letter stands for the author's name, followed by a serial number to distinguish among books in this category. For example, *Wealth and Poverty* by George Gilder has the number HB501.G46. HB is the code for economics (H by itself stands for the social sciences generally); the number 501 stands for a particular subject matter in economics. The G46 is the specific number for the book (G is the first letter of the author's last name). This group of letter and number combinations constitute the call number, or location symbol, for the book. It tells you or the library clerk where to find the book.

The Dewey system is usually to be found in smaller libraries, though until quite recently there were some very large libraries that used it. Numerals rather than letters indicate the subject classes. Each subject class is subdivided into ten parts, and each of these, in turn, includes ten smaller parts. By the use of decimal places, additional subdivisions can be carried out indefinitely.

By the way, you can't rely on any classification system to lead you infallibly to the right books. Classification is always a matter of judgment, and there are always gray areas. You may want something falling between linguistics and anthropology or between psychology and biology, so watch for the topics you want and not the classification numbers.

Card Catalogs and Computerized Retrieval Systems

As noted earlier, books in libraries are classified three ways: by *author*, by *title*, and by *subject*.

Some libraries file all cards in a single alphabetical arrangement, but others, particularly big libraries, use a *divided catalog system*. In these systems, one card catalog contains cards alphabetized by author and title, while the other contains the subject cards. Where computerized retrieval systems exist, you generally don't need to worry about such matters. You can call up entries by author, by title, and by subject.

The subject catalog, whether in a computerized retrieval system or in a traditional card catalog, is particularly useful in the early stages of doing research for a paper. You can look up a particular subject and thumb through the cards or scan the computer screen for items that appear to be usual or interesting. Later, when you know what author or title you are after, you can use the author and title entries to locate particular books. In some computerized systems the subject listing goes by the name "key word."

Here are some rules you should know in order to make efficient use of the catalog:

1. Cards and entries are alphabetized according to the first word of the entry. This will vary depending on whether this word is the author, title, or subject. In book titles, articles such as "the," "a," and "an" are neglected. *The Politics of Jacksonian Finance* by John M. McFaul would be filed under the P's by title (the article "the" is neglected), under the M's by author, and under the U's by subject (United States—Politics and Government 1815–1861).

2. Headings containing abbreviations such as St. (Saint) and Mt. (Mount) are alphabetized as if they were spelled out in full. Names beginning with Mc or Mac are alphabetized as if they were all spelled Mac. Thus:

MacAdams, Alta.
McAdams, David.
McGuire, J.
Machado, A.

3. Most libraries alphabetize titles and subjects consisting of more than one word in a word-by-word filing. Thus the order would be New York, Newark. Some libraries, however, use a letter-by-letter system without regard to spacing between words; here Newark would come first and New York second.

4. The titles of books that begin with numbers are alphabetized as if the numbers were spelled out. *20,000 Leagues Under the Sea* would be filed by title under the T's.

5. Subdivisions of historical subjects are usually arranged chronologically as in the following:

> United States—Politics and Government 1783–1814.
> United States—Politics and Government 1815–1861.

6. Subdivisions of other subjects are usually alphabetical as in the following:

> France—Art.
> France—Geography.
> France—Government.
> France—Music.

7. People are listed before places, places before subjects, and subjects before titles as in the following two listings:

> Jefferson, Thomas.
> Jefferson City, Missouri.
> *Jefferson*, by A. J. Nock.

> Mineral, Virginia.
> Mineral.
> *Mineral Deposits*, by W. Lindgren.

8. Books *by* a person are listed before books *about* a person as in:

> Sinclair, Upton, *World's End*.
> Sinclair, Upton, *Upton Sinclair, American Rebel*, by Leon Harris.

If you know how to use a computerized retrieval system or the card catalog, you can tell a good bit about a book before you see it. Study the sample author, title, and subject cards on page 81 and look at the sample retrieval printout on page 82.

Periodical Indexes

Although card catalogs and most computerized retrieval systems will give you the titles of periodicals in particular subjects, they usually do not index individual articles in periodicals. We suspect that the day is coming when retrieval systems will give you at least the title of articles of the last few years, but that day has not arrived except for a few specialized research libraries. Since much of your paper writing, especially in advanced courses, will require you to get information from articles, you will want to consult one of the many indexes to the periodical literature. For current events and news stories, the *Readers' Guide to Periodical Literature* is the most useful index. It lists articles appearing in popular magazines and less-technical journals. For more scholarly articles, particularly in the humanities, arts, and to a lesser degree in the social sciences, the *International Index of Periodicals* is the source to use. But almost every discipline has its own abstract or index publication. One of the most helpful things you can do when you choose your major is find out what the basic abstract or index system is in your discipline. We need to say a word more about abstracts.

Abstracts

Abstracts go beyond merely indexing the literature in a particular field. They summarize the articles so that readers can determine which ones will be useful. Wherever abstracts are available, consult them—they can be of great help in putting your bibliography together. The best-known examples of such abstracts are *Chemical Abstracts*, *Biological Abstracts*, *Psychological Abstracts*, and *Educational Abstracts*. These all put out indexes at annual or semiannual intervals. So, to find articles in these fields, go to the index for the year (if the abstracts are not yet bound for that year they will be in a separate issue), jot down the abstract number, and scan the abstract to see if the article will be helpful. If it looks promising, write down the whole entry, look up the journal in the catalog to find its call number, and then request the journal so that you can read the original article.

Newspaper Indexes

If you need current newspaper articles, your best bet is *The New York Times Index*, which covers all the important articles published in that newspaper. Despite its name, *The New York Times* is the closest thing we have to a national newspaper or newspaper of record in the United States. Nearly every college library subscribes to the paper itself, to its *Index*, and usually to the microfilm edition. Even if you intend to go to other newspapers, *The New York Times* is the place to start. The *Index* dates events precisely enough for you to look them up in other newspapers or magazines.

Catalog Cards by Subject, Author, and Title

Subject

```
                    MOGUL EMPIRE—HISTORY
    DS
    461     Hansen, Waldemar.
    .H33        The Peacock Throne : the drama of
    1981    Mogul India / Waldemar Hansen. — Delhi
            :  Motilal Banarsidass, 1981.
                xi, 560 p. : ill. ; 25 cm.
                Bibliography: p. 533-545.
                First Indian reprint of the 1972 edition.
                Includes index.

                1. Mogul Empire—History.   2. India—
            History—1500-1765.   3. Taj Mahal—
            History.   4. Shahjahan, Emperor of
            India, ca. 1592-1666.   I. Title.
```

Author

```
            Gilder, George F., 1939-
    HB          Wealth and poverty / George Gilder.—New York : Basic
    501     Books, c1981.
    .G46
                xii, 306 p. ; 24 cm.

                Bibliography: p. 280 205.
                Includes index.
                ISBN 0-465-09105-9 : $16.95

                1. Capitalism.   2. Wealth   3. United States — Economic
            conditions—1945-.   4. United States—Economic policy.   I. Title
            HB501.G46                330.12′2—dc19           80-50556

            Library of Congress
```

Title

```
                Computers in video production
    PN
    1992    McQuillin, Lon B.
    .75         Computers in video production / by Lon McQuillin.—White
    M36     Plains, NY : Knowledge Industry Publications, c1986.

                x, 186 p. : ill. ; 29 cm.—(video bookshelf)

                Bibliography: p. 167-170.
                Includes index.
                ISBN 0-86729-182-6 : $39.95

                1. Television—Production and direction—Data processing.
            I. Title.   II. Series
            PN1992.75.M36      1986

            Library of Copngress
```

Sample Retrieval Printout

```
VCAT SEARCH REQUEST: A=DEESE JAMES
BIBLIOGRAPHIC RECORD -- NO. 6 OF 16 ENTRIES FOUND

Morgan, Clifford Thomas.
  How to study : Morgan and Deese's classic handbook for students. --
3d ed.  rev. / by James Deese, Ellin K. Deese. -- New York :
McGraw-Hill, 1979.
  vi, 118 p. : ill. ; 26 cm. -- (McGraw-Hill paperbacks)
  Includes index.
  SUBJECT HEADINGS (Library of Congress; use s= ):
   Study, Method of.

LOCATION: EDUCATION LIBRARY
CALL NUMBER: LB1049 .M68 1979
   Not charged out.




TYPE n FOR NEXT RECORD. TYPE i FOR INDEX.
TYPE r TO REVISE SEARCH, h FOR HELP, e FOR INTRO TO VCAT.
TYPE COMMAND AND PRESS ENTER==>




  VCAT SEARCH REQUEST: K=SHAKESPEARE AND MIDSUMMER
  BIBLIOGRAPHIC RECORD -- NO. 13 OF 143 ENTRIES FOUND

Lynch, Ina Celeste.
  The creation of the role of Helena in A midsummer night's dream / Ina
Celeste Lynch. -- 1985.
   36 leaves, [1],[8] leaves of plates : ill. (some mounted, some col.)
 ; 29 cm. Thesis (M.F.A.)--University of Virginia, 1985.
  Bibliography: leaf [37].
SUBJECT HEADINGS (Library of Congress; use s= ):
  Shakespeare, William, 1564-1616. Midsummer night's dream.
  Shakespeare, William, 1564-1616--Characters--Helena.
  Acting-Study and teaching--Virginia.

LOCATION: FINE ARTS Theses
CALL NUMBER: Masters Drama 1985 .L96
  Not charged out.



     FOR ANOTHER COPY AT THIS OR ANOTHER LOCATION, press ENTER

TYPE n FOR NEXT RECORD. TYPE i FOR INDEX.
TYPE r TO REVISE SEARCH, h FOR HELP, e FOR INTRO TO VCAT.
TYPE COMMAND AND PRESS ENTER==>
```

Note: The unpublished thesis by Lynch does not have a Library of Congress call number. In general all unpublished items do not.

Reference Books

Reference books are useful not only for digging out materials for research papers but also for answering questions that may interest you. There are a lot of them: encyclopedias, yearbooks, dictionaries, atlases and gazetteers, books of quotations, etc.

Encyclopedias. If you want to look up a particular topic such as mathematics in ancient Greece, a general encyclopedia is the best place to start. The most commonly used encyclopedia in America, despite its name, is the *Encyclopaedia Britannica*, but for many purposes there are others, including the *Encyclopedia Americana*, which are as good or better. If your library is a large one it will contain many encyclopedias, including such specialized works as the *McGraw-Hill Encyclopedia of Science & Technology* and the *International Encyclopedia of the Social Sciences*. There are others in such fields as music and art. *Grove's Dictionary of Music and Musicians*, despite its title, is really an encyclopedia about music.

Yearbooks (Annuals). To find out what happened in a particular year, consult one of the yearbooks. *The American Annual* (1923–) is the annual supplement to the *Encyclopedia Americana*, and the *Britannica Book of the Year* (1938–) is a similar supplement to the *Encyclopedia Britannica*. Both contain articles covering events or important developments in the year named.

Other yearbooks and almanacs contain statistical information, miscellaneous facts, and brief summaries of events. They give you almost any conceivable kind of statistical fact. Among them are the following:

The World Almanac and Book of Facts (1868–) is a stupendous compendium of facts, mostly about the United States. Here you can find everything from the population of some remote hamlet in Kansas to the birth dates of movie stars.

Information Please Almanac (1947–) is a similar compendium with fewer statistics and more articles.

Whitaker's Almanack (1869–) is a British publication similar to the *World Almanac*.

The Statesman's Yearbook (1864–) contains information about world governments.

Statistical Abstract of the United States (1878–) is a government publication containing statistical information about industrial, social, political, and economic aspects of the United States.

Dictionaries. A dictionary, as we usually think about it, is a book of words, alphabetically arranged, which you consult to find proper spellings, meanings, usages, and derivations. However, as we've already said, some specialized encyclopedias are called dictionaries. In addition, there are two other kinds of dictionaries you will find in the library: dictionaries of languages and biographical dictionaries. You will also find specialized dictionaries that deal with special topics, such as medicine, biology, or physics.

Libraries will have large unabridged dictionaries of the English language that are generally too expensive and unwieldy for home (or dormitory) use. Among these are *Webster's Third New International Dictionary* (commonly referred to as *Webster's Third*) published by the Merriam-Webster Company; *Funk & Wagnalls New Standard Dictionary*; and the biggest of them all, the *Oxford English Dictionary*, or OED (also known as the *New English Dictionary* or NED, its name when first published). For most students these are sources to consult when you need to know something about the history of words, or about some unusual, perhaps obsolete, usage of a familiar word.

If you are bogged down in the technical lingo of some specialized subject such as chemistry, psychology, medicine, or biology, you can consult dictionaries restricted to these disciplines. While few of you will want to own one or more of these books (they are expensive), make use of them in the library (there's another good reason for studying in the library).

When you want information about people, use a biographical dictionary. For Americans no longer living who were influential during their time, there is the *Dictionary of American Biography*. For important people in Great Britain, there is a reference series called the *Dictionary of National Biography*. For people who are still living there are the various *Who's Who* volumes. *Who's Who* itself contains information mainly about people in Great Britain. *Who's Who in America* is the most general biographical reference work for living Americans. But there are a host of such publications. The trick is in finding just the right one. The U.S. government through the Government Printing Office (GPO) issues valuable pamphlets and official publications. There are clipping services (to which your library may subscribe for items of local interest), and there are, in your library, a whole host of audiovisual materials.

Reference Librarians

Most libraries, particularly large ones, have librarians whose chief function is to help you with references. Faculty members consult them all the time (one of the reference librarians at the University of Virginia can recognize our voices on the telephone), but they really like to help students. If you are in doubt about where to look up something, go to the reference desk. The chances are you can be helped.

In General

The number of books and articles published each year is almost beyond comprehension. Nevertheless, by using reference books, abstracts, indexes, and the like, you can track down one particular fact about the most obscure topic imaginable from the whole mass of material the library contains. The ability to use these resources puts the whole world of printed (and computer-based) information at your disposal. It is one of the best things a college education can give you. The future belongs to the information explosion, and if you are going to be there to grasp what belongs to you, there is no better place to start than in college and in the college library.

IMPROVING WRITING SKILLS

The ability to write well comes mainly through practice. Oh, yes, there are a few people who know how to write from the day they first take pencil (or crayon) to paper, but for most of us, we have to learn the skill. Even if you have mastered the rules of composition, grammar, and punctuation, you still need to think about your use of the language. Learning how to write well takes time and a certain amount of self-examination. It is mainly to help you in your self-examination that the following guidelines are offered.

Aids to Writing

Certain things you ought to have on your desk. An absolute minimum is a good dictionary. A close second is a book on English style; a third, perhaps, is a good thesaurus. To these you can add various works related to your course of study.

The Dictionary. The best dictionary is one that is up to date and complete enough to include all the nontechnical words you are likely to want to understand, use, or spell. We've already listed a few of the dictionaries that are useful to have (these are often called "desk dictionaries" for good reason).

No matter which one you choose, it will not help you much unless you get into the habit of using it. Before the days of hand-held computer spellers and spell-check programs on computers, students made the most use of their dictionaries to check spelling. You still need a good dictionary for that purpose. But a far more important use of the dictionary is as a source of information about the meanings and usage of words. One of the best ways to educate yourself is to become a definition hunter. By looking up words you don't know or words that seem to be used in strange ways, you will greatly increase your ability in the most widely used intellectual commodity of our time, the ability to read and to write.

Style Guides. Besides the dictionary, you probably ought to have a handy reference on grammar, usage, and punctuation. There are a legion of these. One of the best is *The Elements of Style* by William Strunk, Jr., and E. B. White, which we referred to earlier in this chapter (page 74). This little book, less than one hundred pages in length, summarizes the basic rules of usage, the main principles of composition, some rules of form, and ways to improve style. It will answer a lot of your basic questions about composition, and it will help you avoid the common mistakes college students make in writing.

Other useful handbooks are Perrin's *The Writer's Guide* and the *Harbrace College Handbook*. A book we both like is the Evans and Evans *Dictionary of American English Usage*. We recommend it because of its fascinating account of usage in American English. A more practical guide is T. M. Bernstein's *The Careful Writer, A Guide to English*

Usage. If you are concerned about organization in your writing, there is nothing better than Christensen and Christensen's *A New Rhetoric.* If you really want to be correct and proper, you ought to know about Fowler's *A Dictionary of Modern English Usage.*

The Thesaurus. Peter Mark Roget was a nineteenth-century physician who loved words. He compiled *A Thesaurus of the English Language,* based on a system that he invented for classifying the totality of human knowledge. Like Webster's *Dictionary,* his work has long been copied by others, sometimes well done and sometimes not. But in nearly all of these thesauruses, the most useful section gives a comprehensive listing of synonyms—words with similar meanings—and antonyms—words with opposite meanings. Referring to these listings may help you pick just the right word when that is a critical matter. Many writers swear by it. A similar work built on different principles is *Webster's Dictionary of Synonyms.*

How far you go in building a personal collection of aids to writing will depend partly on how much money you have to spend and partly on your interests. If you are going to be majoring in a subject in the humanities or in the social sciences where you will be required to write more papers than you would if you were in the natural sciences, you will probably want at least some of the basic references we have mentioned. But whatever you acquire, use them.

Basic Aids. If you find reading this book difficult, then you need more help than the above suggestions provide. But more to the point, you probably need personal help. You may have a unique problem with written language that only a one-on-one diagnosis and tutoring can solve.

Developing Good Writing

The main difference between good writing and bad writing is that good writing says exactly what the writer intends. Some writing, of course, has a literary as well as an informative purpose. But for most of us, writing informative prose clearly, accurately, and simply is enough.

Sentences. Good writing consists of clear sentences arranged in orderly paragraphs. With this in mind, look carefully and critically at your first draft. You will want to ask yourself: "Have I said exactly what I intended to say? Have I said it in the simplest and most direct way?" Then you will want to examine your draft for faults. Here are some of the most common faults in sentences.

1. The sentence fragment. "High school and college are very different. First the demands that college makes." The second "sentence" is not a sentence but a fragment. It has both a subject and a verb, but it is not a complete sentence because it is cast in the form of a subordinate clause. We don't know whether the writer intended "Here are the demands that college makes," or "The demands that college makes are greater." Sentence fragments can be used effectively (Mark Twain was a master of them), but you must know what you are doing. Most of the time, for most of us, they are to be avoided.

2. The run-on sentence. "The party was a roaring success, empty cans and paper plates were scattered everywhere." Here, two complete sentences are incorrectly spliced together by a comma. There are a number of ways to correct this sentence, depending upon what the writer meant. He might have meant, "The party was a roaring success, *but* empty cans and paper plates were scattered everywhere," in which case the separate clauses of a compound sentence are joined by a coordinating conjunction ("but"). Or possibly the writer simply meant to set down two sentences more or less unrelated to one another. In that case he should have written, "The party was a roaring success. Empty cans and paper plates were scattered everywhere." Or he might have meant to convert his run-on-sentence into a complex sentence by making one of the clauses subordinate to the other: *"Because* the party was *such* a success, empty cans and paper plates were scattered everywhere."

3. Lack of agreement between subject and verb. "Each of us plan to go." The simple subject of that sentence, "each," is singular, so the verb should be in the singular form: "Each of us *plans* to go." People commonly commit this error when the subject phrase contains both singular and plural nouns. In that case, you need to find the simple subject of the sentence (what the sentence is really about) and see whether it is singular or plural.

Incidentally, the word "none" as a simple subject generally takes a singular verb.

4. Lack of agreement between pronoun and antecedent. "Each person on the team did their best." The use of "their" to replace the awkward location "he or she" has become common. You hear it from TV commentators, and you read it in the newspapers. But it is still an error. It is better to reword the construction to avoid the lack of agreement.

5. Dangling or misplaced modifiers. A typical case of a dangling modifier is one in which the modifier or participle modifies the wrong noun as in "Having finally found our seats, the game had already started." The sentence implies that it was the game that found the seats. Clearly the author of this sentence meant something like: "The game had already started when we finally found our seats."

Another error similar in nature is one in which an elliptical construction (an elliptical construction is one with an element implied rather than actually stated in the sentence) results in a dangling modifier. For example: "While still rehearsing, Nancy arrived." The author meant, "While we were still rehearsing, Nancy arrived." Elliptical constructions are useful, but you must be careful to make your meaning clear.

6. Trivial errors. There are a lot of mistakes that are not important in themselves (because they seldom distort meaning), but they identify you as an uneducated person. The confusion between "there" and "their" is an example. Most of you know better, but sometimes in the pressure of completing an exam, you will let something like this slip. Give yourself time to check your exam answers.

While we are at it, we should point out that the words "data" and "phenomena" are plural nouns. The singular in each case is "datum" and "phenomenon." The data/datum error has been around a long time, and one hears highly educated persons say "this data." The phenomena/phenomenon confusion is fairly new, but it has become widespread enough so that you can hear it from TV commentators.

Most errors can be detected by paying careful attention to the logic of the sentences you write.

But in addition to correcting such errors, you can improve your style by avoiding the passive voice where the active voice would do, by varying the kinds of sentences you write, and by eliminating wordy and awkward constructions.

Paragraphs. A paragraph joins sentences that are related but separate. Every paragraph should have a *topic sentence*. That sentence contains the main idea of the paragraph. Everything else in that paragraph should develop, explain, or modify that main idea, or be a transitional sentence to the next paragraph. Most of the time the topic sentence comes first. That makes sense, because then the reader knows what the paragraph is about from the beginning. Sometimes, for reasons of rhetoric, the writer will delay the main idea until the end of the paragraph. If you want to do that, make sure you are in control—your readers may get the wrong idea about what you are trying to say.

Sometimes you will want to pull together everything you have said in a paragraph in a *summary sentence*. You can often use such a summary statement as a transition to the next paragraph. By tying together the beginning and the end of a paragraph and relating it to the next paragraph you can make your writing clear and easy to follow.

What we have said about paragraphs applies to larger segments of your writing. For example, when you write a paper, the first paragraph can serve as a topic statement of what the paper is about, and the paragraph at the beginning of a section can tell what that section is about.

Writing good paragraphs calls for order and logic. That is why outlining is useful. It helps you organize your paper into tight, well-constructed units that carry your readers along smoothly and enable them to grasp your meaning.

If you make writing good paragraphs second nature, you can concentrate on other aspects of writing—style and rhetoric. To help you appreciate what well-organized paragraphs are like, we have provided an analysis of two sample paragraphs on page 87.

Grammar and Usage. Good writing is based upon a sense for the grammar of the language, and the rules for grammar come from good writing (and speaking). Moreover, grammar is appropriate to the occasion. There are different levels of grammatical usage. A sentence such as "It sure ain't a

Two Sample Paragraphs and Their Analysis

(From an essay on Sinclair Lewis)

This mastery of the art of description is evident in *Main Street,* which portrays a small, provincial town in minute detail. Lewis was an acute observer of people and places, with a keen ear for the vernacular of the Middle West. He drew heavily on his own background: Will Kennicott's office in Gopher Prairie was a replica of Dr. E. J. Lewis' office in Sauk Centre, the social work of the Thanatopsis Club—establishing the rest room for farmers' wives, the anti-fly campaign, tree planting—was drawn from the activities of Lewis' stepmother, an active club-woman. The character of Carol and her reaction to Gopher Prairie is in many ways modeled on that of Lewis' first wife, Grace Hegger, and her view of Sauk Centre.

— Transitional sentence
— Topic sentence
Explanation and elaboration

(From an essay on the Missouri Compromise)

If New England opposition to slave representation was the major irritant in the growth of the sectional hostility which broke out in 1819–1821, there were others as well. Over the years there had grown up in the South a distinct anti-Yankee sentiment, in part aggravated by the trading practices of Yankee peddlers in the Southern states. This sentiment was given sharp utterance when the disastrous effects of the Panic of 1819 were felt south of the Potomac. In searching for reasons for their distress it was easy for Southerners to find in such measures as the Tariff of 1816, internal improvement schemes, and the Second Bank of the United States a convenient scapegoat. The exuberant nationalism which had followed the close of the war and had caused the Southerners to support these measures was forgotten, and a sober second thought convinced most of the South that the North was being favored at its expense.

— Topic sentence
Examples and elaboration

---

real friendly dog" is clear and easy to understand. It would not, however, be appropriate in formal standard English. Most educated people can use their language at different levels. They can speak colloquially when the occasion demands, and they can speak formally as well. They can also vary their writing, though probably not quite so easily. This ability to move back and forth between the most colloquial style and formal language is one of the marks of an educated person.

Standard English varies in level. *Informal English* is more often used in speaking than in writing. It is the way educated people talk in informal situations, where slang, local expressions, and well-controlled deviations from the grammar of standard English are appropriate. *General English* is the kind of language educated people use in more formal conversations, in business letters, and in talks or in articles for general audiences. *Formal English* is more often written than spoken, and it is what you will find in technical writing and academic books.

Most of your writing should be in general standard English. Avoid a formal style for the most part. It sounds stilted, and unless you are an unusually good rhetorician, it is hard to write clearly and accurately. Be sure you know the main rules of the standard grammar of English and how to use them in a sensible way. If you ignore the basic rules of English, you make your writing illogical and hard to read. What is more, you will appear to be ignorant.

What are these basic rules? We can't take the space here to go over them, but we can present you with some questions to test your grasp of grammar. If you have a hard time answering them, you owe yourself a review of the fundamentals.

The questions are these: Can you identify the subject of a sentence? Do you know the difference between the phrase containing the subject and the simple subject? Do you know what a direct object is? A prepositional phrase? Can you identify the nominative, objective, and possessive cases of pronouns? Do you know what "the principal parts of a verb" means, and can you identify them for regular and irregular verbs?

Do you fall into some of the common traps awaiting you in the language? One of these is the use of the irregular verbs "lay" and "lie." If you were to write "He laid there for some time," you would be showing your confusion, for "laid" is the past tense of the verb "to lay" and not the past tense of the verb "to lie." (If you don't know that difference between these two verbs, look them up in a dictionary or handbook.) The past tense of the verb "lie" is "lay," so the sentence should read, "He lay there for some time."

Mistakes such as this one are not terribly important by themselves, and they seldom interfere with your ability to say what you mean. Nevertheless, they show that you do not understand the English language as well as an educated person should. The real purpose of studying grammar is not to avoid trivial mistakes but to help you write good standard English. Trivial errors, however, are often symptomatic of your level of ability in using the language. If you make them, the chances are that you can't identify such important things as the subject of a sentence, the direct object, the object of a preposition, the indirect object, and verbal auxiliaries. Even more important, the chances are that you do not know how to correct a mistake once you have made one.

Get in the habit of carefully reading what you write so that you correct your own mistakes. When your instructor corrects something on your paper, make sure you know what the correct form is and why you made the error. If you don't know why you made a mistake or why you were corrected, find out. Once more, the little book by Strunk and White, *The Elements of Style,* will help you do this.

Punctuation. Good punctuation is essential to clear writing. You can punctuate properly just by knowing a few rules and applying common sense. The purpose of periods and commas is to set ideas apart. They help readers keep things straight.

Periods

The period is the basic punctuation mark. You use it to show that an idea together with its modifiers or coordinate ideas is complete. A complete idea is expressed by the one-word sentence, "Stop." In writing you would set this one word off by a period.

How do you know when you have written a complete idea? Think about how you talk. Your intonation changes, and very likely you will pause at the end of a sentence. That is like putting in a period, and yet you don't have to think about it, nor does anyone have to tell you how to do it.

Most of the time a complete idea will relate a subject and a phrase that contains a verb. That's true even in a one-word sentence. The sentence, "Stop," implies a subject. It is usually an order, and if it is addressed to you, what it means is, "You stop doing whatever it is you are doing." Sometimes verb phrases are complicated, and sometimes one idea modifies another within the same sentence, so that *complex sentences* contain two or more ideas. But whenever that happens, one idea is the main one which the others modify or elaborate.

Commas

Commas are used to separate ideas that are related. The following elements are separated by commas:

1. *An idea that depends upon another.* "If it rains, the picnic will be postponed." The first idea, which is a dependent or subordinate clause, is separated from the main idea by a comma.

2. *Two main ideas connected by a conjunction.* The comma goes before the conjunction, as in: "Jerry got a new stereo, but he left it at home."

3. *Items listed in a series.* "I'm taking economics, psychology, French, and physics."

4. *A main clause and parenthetical expressions.* "No one, you will be happy to know, flunked the exam."

5. *Noun phrases and their nonrestrictive appositives.* "Bill, my oldest brother, is getting married in the fall."

6. *The parts of dates.* For example, "December 25, 1991," or "May to December, 1938," or "Monday, January 20, 1906."

7. *Titles or names in direct address.* "I'm calling, Sue, to invite you to my birthday party." "Excuse me, professor, but I think you are wrong."

8. *Nonrestrictive relative clauses.* "John, who was the last to leave, got stuck with the bill." Restrictive clauses are not set off by commas as in: "The person who was the last to leave got stuck with the bill." Notice that in the latter case, the relative clause identifies the person—it is essential to the meaning of the sentence—while in the former case, the relative clause just tells you something incidental about John—that he was the last to leave. The main idea in the first sentence tells us that John got stuck with the bill, and the main idea in the second sentence says that whoever was the last to leave paid the bill.

This list doesn't exhaust the uses of commas, but it does give you some of the more important and common ones. Furthermore, there are minor differences among style manuals about some uses of commas. Finally, we have said nothing about colons, semicolons, question marks, and exclamation points. If you think you need some straightening out on these matters, consult one of the handbooks on English usage or the section on punctuation in a good collegiate dictionary.

Spelling. As a college student, you are expected to spell correctly *all* the words you write. Here are some ways to ensure that you do:

1. Be careful. Many misspellings are the result of haste and carelessness. Proofread. Do everything you can to make sure that mistakes in spelling are just not the result of misplaced fingers on the keyboard.

2. Pay attention to the spelling of new words and names. If you are not the kind of person who can look at a new word and be able to spell it immediately, practice writing or imagining how you would write new words.

3. Use the dictionary.

4. Get to know a few simple spelling rules ("*i* before *e* except after *c*"). Look for special endings. Find rules for spelling English in grammar books and dictionaries. Don't be guided by your dialect. One of us grew up in California when the prevailing dialect had "separate" (the verb) pronounced as *sePERate*. It took a long time to undo the effects of that pronunciation on learning to spell the word correctly.

Most instructors resent poor spelling. It makes them think either that you are illiterate or that you haven't taken the trouble to be careful with your writing. If you are weak in spelling, invest in something that will enable you to spell properly. As we mentioned earlier, many computers have automatic programs for correcting spelling errors (but

be careful; if you intend to write "make" but you write "mark," your computer isn't going to know that you made a mistake). Or use a hand-held spelling device. But better yet, be alert to your language. In English you can't always go by the sounds of words. Know that I *choose* my team well but I may *lose* the game anyway. Above all, have a good dictionary handy.

Vocabulary. A typical college student "knows" about 160,000 words. That is to say, he or she can understand in context (though may not be able to define precisely) that many words. Of course, the typical student uses fewer words. If your vocabulary is too small to express your ideas without causing the grading assistant to smirk, you need to improve your vocabulary.

Being in the habit of using the dictionary regularly is a big help. But learning the dictionary definitions, or *denotations*, of words will not necessarily help you understand their *connotations*. The connotation of a word is the meaning it suggests in addition to its literal meaning. For example, using the word "slender" to describe someone connotes approval, whereas "skinny" connotes disapproval, and "scrawny" even more strongly has a negative connotation. "Assertive" is a neutral word most of the time (but think about "assertive woman"); "pushy" is always negative. The more aware you are of the connotations of words, the more precisely you will be able to convey your own attitudes toward what you write about. And the best way to learn the connotations of words is to read widely.

One of the most common faults in students' writing is the use of big words when simple ones would be better. Why say, "The methodology employed in this investigation is factor analysis," when you could say, "We used the method of factor analysis."

Avoid jargon words such as "finalize"; use "complete" instead. The word "parameters" is often misused (most often to mean "limits"). Avoid it unless you mean it in its precise mathematical sense. Avoid euphemisms such as "passed away" for "died" and "intoxicated" for "drunk." Above all, be careful about using all-purpose and often meaningless verbs such as "involve."

Another fault is wordiness—using several words where one or two would do. Instead of saying, "In spite of the fact that it snowed, we went ahead with the party anyway," say "We went ahead with the party, despite the snow." Or instead of "He did his work in a careless manner," say "He worked carelessly." "She is a person who likes everyone" is better as "She likes everyone." When you revise your compositions, simplify wordy constructions when you see them.

Reading a lot is a good way to improve your vocabulary. Make an effort to read things that are well written. Ask yourself why this is good writing and something else is bad writing. Walter Lippman once said that he never read a single page of H. L. Mencken that bored him. That is high praise indeed.

Try your hand at editing someone else's writing. Many of the things you read could be better written. Textbooks are often written by people who know a great deal about their subject but could learn something about writing. Introductory textbooks, by and large, are well written (generally because they are carefully edited by copy editors), but advanced texts and treatises, particularly in the natural and social sciences, are often full of clumsy writing. Everyone knows how bad government documents can be. See if you can improve the sentences you find in sources such as these. You may never be one of the great stylists of the English language, but if you learn to write a technical report, a stockholder's statement, or a new government regulation so that it can be easily understood by literate people, you will have achieved one of the main purposes of your education.

8
STUDYING
A FOREIGN
LANGUAGE

JAZDAD TRXWJL!

TLPTHLK WAT XBARTIJ!

TAXI

Two subjects seem to divide students into two groups: those who can and those who can't. They are foreign languages and mathematics. The problem with both foreign languages and mathematics is that you have to put a lot of concentrated work into them. You can't go about working at them in the way in which you work at other subjects. They are, however, very different in their demands, and so that is why we have separate chapters for each of them. Learning a foreign language takes practice and, for most people, a fair amount of rote memory work.

There are a few people who have no trouble learning foreign languages. There are famous scholars who have *taught themselves* twenty or thirty different foreign languages. But nearly all of the rest of us have some trouble learning a foreign language. That is because learning a new language draws upon so many different skills. If you find reading a new language to be easy, you may have trouble understanding the spoken language. A lot of people who read and write other languages reasonably well have a tin ear and just can't hear—much less speak—the unfamiliar vowels of German, French, or Swedish. Even if you get through the hurdles provided by grammar and drill, you may find that you just can't think in Italian. Or you may be able to understand sentences in Russian but just can't find the right way to put them into English. Find out for yourself just what comes easily to you and what gives you trouble. If you identify those things you can do well, you can use them to get you over the rough spots. Or if you are a real clod and can't seem to get a hold anywhere in a foreign language, you will have to work extra hard. The purpose of this chapter is to give you some ideas for making your study of foreign languages as efficient and pleasant as possible.

A word of caution. There are a few people who cannot master even the elements of a foreign language. It is as if they have a specific disability for learning languages. But don't assume you are one of these unless you have tried your best, particularly if you are on a campus which requires a certain amount of foreign language study. One of us had a student who had taken elementary Spanish three times and flunked each time. She finally was exempted from the University's foreign language requirement. But once again, there are a few—very few of you—who, despite heroic efforts, can't manage a new language. Don't give up unless you absolutely have to.

BASIC RULES FOR LANGUAGE LEARNING

Keep Up with the Work

Steve runs on the varsity cross-country team. Every day, rain or shine, warm or cold, he runs at least seven miles. He wouldn't think of missing a day's practice. Even a bad cold can't keep him off the course, and once he ran ten miles with an infected splinter in his foot.

Steve also takes elementary French. He approaches French with less dedication. Twice he overslept and missed his class. Once he cut class to go to a track meet elsewhere. The week he had a cold, he felt too rotten to go to class. French is his least favorite subject, so he puts off studying it until the last possible moment. The result is that he squeaks by with a marginal D. Even if he passes, the chances are he will have to repeat it before he is ready to go on to the next level.

It has never occurred to Steve that the attitudes and habits that make him a good long-distance runner would also make him a good French student if he gave it half a chance. If he went after French the way he goes after running, he could be an A student.

You can fall behind in economics, history, literature, or even chemistry and catch up—though we don't recommend it. If you fall behind in a foreign language, however, you've had it. Regular attendance and regular daily preparations

are not just desirable, they are absolutely necessary in learning a foreign language.

Learning a language is cumulative. Everything you learn later depends upon what you have learned already. You have to know the meanings of words before you can put them together in phrases. You have to know how to pronounce the sounds and hear them accurately before you can talk to and understand a native speaker. You have to know about word order in the new language before you can understand anything but the simplest of sentences. You have to know how verbs are conjugated and how nouns and adjectives are declined before you can make sense out of the simplest of stories.

It takes dedicated practice. You know that if you work out at tennis one day a week you will never make the tennis team. With a foreign language you must practice regularly to be even moderately successful at learning that language. You must learn the simple things well enough that you can use them in understanding the complicated things.

Spend Lots of Time in Recitation

Recitation both in class and in study is basic to learning a new language. The easiest way to fail a foreign language course is never to recite. At least eighty percent of your study time, particularly in the early stages of language learning, should be spent in recitation. What is more, you need to recite on a daily basis—every day, not just three days a week just before class.

There are three skills you learn in acquiring a new language. First, you must learn to read it. Second, you should learn to understand it when you hear it. Third, you should learn to speak it. Americans are notoriously bad about speaking other languages. But we are going to have to learn. We have a large body of French speakers to the north of us growing in importance. And if you are thinking about running for Congress in the Southwest, you had better speak Spanish or you are lost before you start. If the only language you know is English, you are the poorer for it, and learning a foreign language is worth at least as much effort as goes into being a passable golfer, tennis player, or pianist. Like these things, learning a new language is learning a *skill*. Even if you only want to learn to read, you have to practice. And practice means recitation and translation as the most important step. But in order to recite and translate, you need to master the grammar and acquire a vocabulary.

Master the Grammar

Most American college courses in foreign language at the beginner's level stress grammar. Language teachers want you to learn the structure of the language you are studying. If you know the rules of grammar in a language, you can construct sentences of your own in that language, and you can understand what people say to you.

One problem with teaching from grammar is that many students have either forgotten or never learned the rudiments of English grammar. When they hear about tense, mood, gerunds, participles, and cases in Spanish, French, or Russian, they have no idea what the teacher is talking about. If you find yourself in this spot, try to make up your deficiencies as you go along. You can do this with the help of a handbook of English grammar. Another way is to "translate back" into English. See what the equivalent of the Latin or Russian nominative is in English. In fact, many people report that learning a foreign language this way—mastering the grammar of the language—is an important way to come to a deep understanding of English grammar.

Few students of English grammar, as a matter of fact, will have encountered expressions such as "a noun in the dative case" or "an accusative pronoun." The reason is that among European languages, English is unusual. It depends much more upon word order to express grammatical meaning than upon other things such as word endings. In most other European languages the endings do what word order does in English. In Latin, for example, the word for girl is *"puella."* Thus you would say *"puella puerum amat"* ("The girl loves the boy"). But if you wanted to say, "The boy loves the girl," you would change the *"-a"* ending in *"puella"* to *"-am."* You would most likely say, *"puer puellam amat."* You would change the ending because "girl" is now in the accusative case rather than in the nominative. Because of the dependence upon word endings, most Latin sentences can be written in different orders (though typically in simple sentences the verb is last). In English, order is all-important. (Think about "The boy loves the girl" and "The girl loves the boy.")

Whenever you come across an unfamiliar grammatical term in studying a foreign language, make sure you understand it. If it has an equivalent in English or a near equivalent, make sure you know what the comparable English construction would be. Some grammatical terms, such as "aspect," are rarely used in English (though English does have an aspect), but don't just throw up your hands when you read or hear about aspect in Russian. Find out what it means.

When you become skilled in the language, you will realize that the grammatical categories in that language have a meaning all their own, and you won't need English as a crutch. If you are studying German you should be able not only to rattle off the declensions of German nouns—nominative, *"das Haus"*; accusative, *"das Haus"*; genitive, *"das Hauses"*; dative, *"dem Hause"*—but also to understand how they are used in German sentences.

All languages are full of irregularities—exceptions to general rules and bafflingly contrary rules covering only a few words. These have to be learned by brute force. Although grammarians try to discover rules that will apply as broadly as possible, there are always exceptions. If you think French, German, or Russian is maddeningly irregular, consider your blessings—you don't have to learn English as a second language. It is far and away the most irregular of all of the familiar European languages.

In all languages the words that are most frequently used tend to be irregular or retain ancient forms. Consider conjugating the verb "to be." The simple present and past tenses of this verb are I am, you are, he/she/it is, we are, you are, they are, I was, you were, he/she/it was, we were, you were, they were. Contrast that with I walk, you walk, he/she/it walks, we walk, you walk, they walk, I walked, you walked, he/she/it walked, we walked, you walked, they walked. There are only two rules for walk: add "-s" to form the third person singular (she walks) and add "-ed" to form the past tense. For the most part, the only thing you can do with irregular verbs is to memorize them, recite them, and use them in the context of simple sentences. They have to become as second nature as putting one foot before the next in walking.

Language teachers stress grammar because it is the main tool we have for mastering a language when we have a lot of other things to do. You didn't learn to speak English (or whatever your native language is) by learning the rules of grammar. Most people learn the basics of their native tongue between the ages of one and five. They don't learn it by going to class three or four hours a week and practicing it for another eight or ten; they learn it by being immersed in it all their waking hours. And even then, a five-year-old still has a long way to go in using his or her native language like an adult. If you are a college freshman, it took you about eighteen years to achieve the mastery of English you have today. If you don't have all that time to practice, the most efficient way to learn a language is to learn grammatical rules, along with getting as much practice as you can in reading, listening, and speaking.

Learning Unusual Languages. The world has expanded, and while most of you will choose a familiar European language as a second language, some of you will want to tackle such languages as Thai, Arabic, Classical Greek, and Chinese. Most of these languages will not use the alphabet that you are familiar with—the Roman alphabet. Greek and Russian use a different alphabet, as does Arabic. Some languages, such as Chinese and Japanese, do not use an alphabet at all. If you are studying one of these languages, the most important step is to learn the code—the notation. If you can't decode the printed symbols you will be lost, even if you have a good ear for the sounds of the language.

Then too, many of these languages have an exotic grammar. English is exotic, but it is at least close enough to the more familiar European languages for us to latch on to grammatical landmarks in learning the new language. But Chinese and, to a lesser degree, Japanese are so different grammatically that most of the familiar landmarks are gone. In learning Chinese, you will have to work harder than your classmates studying French or German to master the equivalent level. Get used to the idea that you are going to be much more on your own—like a child simply thrown into the water and told to swim.

Learn to Think in the Language

You know that you have really mastered another language when you can think in that language. To think in a language means not only that you are fluent in it, but also that you don't have to trans-

late. You don't read English by translating; that is, you don't turn words into other words in order to understand. You know directly what each word means. You don't have to think about it. That is the goal you need to work toward in studying another language. Right from the beginning, you should try to associate foreign words not with their English equivalents, but directly with the objects, events, and qualities they name. As you become more skillful in your new language, you will find that you think in it without having to refer to the English equivalents.

LEARNING TO READ THE LANGUAGE

At first you will be tempted to translate. Resist that temptation. Learning to think in a new language is a gradual process, but you won't give it a chance if you don't try to think in the new language from the outset. As you go from one level to the next, you may find some of the following hints useful.

Studying by Phrases and Sentences

Whatever you do, don't try word-by-word translation. That will get you in trouble right from the start, and as the material gets more complicated it becomes a hopeless task. This is especially true with languages such as Latin and German in which the word order is different from that in English. Second-year students in German will easily get lost if they try to find their way through a sentence word by word, for German is so different that it doesn't make sense if it is translated literally in a word-by-word way. For instance, it has separable verbs, and they really provide traps for word-by-word translators. In separable verbs, the prefix to the verb can be detached from the verb and moved to the end of the sentence. If you try to translate the stem of the verb without its prefix, you will be translating the wrong word. But even in languages such as French, in which word order is very much like that of English, you will find it much better to try to grasp the meaning of a whole phrase or whole sentence. It will seem strange and unnatural at first, but once you get used to it, it will be the only way you will attack new sentences in a strange language.

If, after a semester or so of a foreign language, you are still translating word by word, you need help. You might discuss the problem with your instructor. It may be that you haven't memorized the basic elements of the vocabulary such as relative pronouns or irregular verbs. These together with verbal auxiliaries and certain other elements (such as prepositions, particularly in German) have to be second nature to you. You have to recognize them instantly when you see them in a sentence, and you have to know immediately what they mean.

Perhaps you don't know the syntax or word order well enough to be able to tell where you are in a sentence. For example, take the German sentence: *"Haben sie den Bauer gesehen, der auf dem Wagen sass?"* ("Have you seen the farmer who sat on the wagon?"). A badly confused student may try to translate *"der"* as a definite article ("the") rather than as a relative pronoun ("who"). This mistake would result from translating the sentence word by word rather than trying to see the pattern that the syntax makes. A parallel problem in French is illustrated by the sentence *"Elle a reçu les fleurs que lui ont envoyées des amies"* ("She received the flowers that friends sent her"), where the unobservant student may read the objective pronoun *"que"* ("that") as the nominative pronoun *"qui"* ("who"), thus making hash of the sense. If you look over the whole sentence and relate the words one to another, you will not make mistakes such as these.

Looking Up Words: Some Dos and Don'ts

The most common mistake students make in trying to translate is to look up too many words. There are two things wrong with this.

First, you may not have to look up the word if you read on and get the context in which the word is used. This is what we mainly do when we read something unfamiliar in English. Consulting a dictionary is only one way of learning the meaning of a word, and it is both time-consuming and sometimes ineffective, for it isolates the meaning from the context in which the word is used. Most of the words we know in English we learned from context. Context always limits the kinds of words that can appear in particular places in sentences. Because of this limitation, you can often guess the meaning of a word.

Second, you often find more than one meaning for a word in the dictionary. You will only know which meaning is the correct one by knowing the context in which the word occurs.

Thus, try to guess from context. If you are puzzled, consult a dictionary. Don't just stop when you get to a word you don't know; read the whole sentence and try to figure it out. Keep to a minimum the number of words you look up. Even if you make a wrong guess, something in the succeeding sentences will more than likely tell you that you have made a mistake.

If you do have to look up a word, mark it in some way so that you will know that it was a word that was unfamiliar to you. Then make sure you can place the word in the context of the sentence correctly.

Another thing: Always reread a passage soon after you have translated it for the first time. This way you can spot trouble and you become more familiar with the words that baffled you in the first place.

Dissecting Words

The time and place for paying attention to individual words is (1) when you have read a sentence and can't get its meaning because you're not sure about one or more words in it, and (2) when you want to build your vocabulary.

While learning a language, you are continuously adding to your store of usable words. You will save yourself a lot of work if you learn how to break words down into their elements. We have already said something about that in connection with building your English vocabulary (page 89), but this advice is perhaps even more significant in the study of another language.

Languages are put together in different ways, but most of them are like English in that they have root words or stems to which prefixes and suffixes may be attached. If you learn the general meaning of the prefixes and suffixes (collectively called "affixes"), you can often figure out a word you have never seen before just by dissecting it. In English, you know that the prefix "pre-" means before. Whenever you see "pre-" at the beginning of a word, you can tell that the word pertains to something going on before, as in premeditation, prelude, or premonition. It's much the same way in other languages, and even though there may seem to be a lot of affixes because of all the combinations they can produce, there are usually relatively few of them to be learned.

Some languages, such as German, have many

compound words. These are words in which the elements are not necessarily affixes and roots, but may be two or more whole words glued together. Thus, the German word *"Durchgangsgerechtigkeit"* means "right-of-way" or "thoroughfare," and it is compounded out of several separate words and affixes. If you study advanced German, you will have to learn how to dissect words, because many of the words you will run across will not be in the dictionary. The person who wrote them simply made them up by compounding existing words.

Using Cognates

Many words in other European languages resemble words in English with the same or similar meanings. That is because English has its roots in both the Germanic and Romance (French, Spanish, Italian, etc.) languages. Moreover, many English words were either directly borrowed from Latin and Greek or were coined by using Latin and Greek roots: for example, coaxial, fission, and interstellar from the Latin; economics, drama, biology, and cyclotron from the Greek. Some English words have even been borrowed from Hindi, Russian, and Yiddish.

Although the original form of a word carried over into English is likely to have been modified in the process, there is often a perceptible relation between the two, say, a word in French and one in English. If you learn to recognize such similar words, called "cognates," you will find translation to be easier. To get an idea of what we mean, take a pencil and a piece of paper and do the exercise that we have provided on the use of cognates on pages 98 and 99. (You don't have to know the languages other than English—in fact it is better if you don't.) You will find that you can guess with fair accuracy the meaning of many of the words in languages you have not studied.

You must be careful, however. Cognates can lead you astray, so you cannot rely blindly on similarities between foreign and English words. Sometimes strange things happen in the history of words that are borrowed from one language for use in another or words in two different languages that have a common heritage in a third. *"Le crayon"* does not mean crayon in French; it means pencil. The English word "black" is historically related to the French word *"blanc,"* which means white! Even when the meanings of cognate words are similar (as in *"crayon"* and "crayon"), there may be fine shades of difference between them that you can't easily detect. It is a good rule, therefore, to look up all such words at least once and check their meaning. But do this only after you have attempted a guess based upon their similarity to English. Identifying cognates helps make the study process an active one.

Using Cards

Studying a language takes a lot of memorizing. A good technique for making memorizing easier is to write a foreign word on one side of a card and its translation on the other. In fact, you can buy such cards on computer programs already prepared, though it is far better if you make your own (active participation again). You can test yourself by running through the foreign words while making translations of them. Whenever you're stumped or you're not sure, you can flip over the card for the correct answer.

Making up your own cards will help you with spelling foreign words as well as providing you with recitation. Keep your working stack of cards small. Make sure you have mastered your initial set before you add new cards. When you're absolutely sure of a word, take it out of the working stack.

When you begin to translate more difficult passages, it's a good idea to make a card for every word you have to look up. Run over these at set intervals, perhaps once a day. Each time you remember what the word means, put a checkmark on the card, and each time you don't, put a zero. When you have five checks in a row without any zeros, take the card out of the set.

Another way of using cards is to write down whole phrases, not just single words. These help you to think in larger units and to use words in their proper context. Then too, many phrases are idiomatic and cannot be translated literally on a word-for-word basis. The familiar French phrase *"Comment allez-vous?"* literally means "How do you go?" but the correct translation is "How are you?"

Many students write the English equivalent of foreign words in the margins or between the lines of passages they are translating. This is not as good as using cards. It sounds easier, but it has two disadvantages. First, it leaves the translation in full view and makes it almost impossible for you to recite without prompting. Second, focusing your attention on the translation keeps you thinking in English rather than in the new language. Since you eventually want to know the meanings of words without connecting them to English, the less you rely on English, the better.

Using Ponies and Trots

If you are in an advanced language class in which you are reading whole books or lengthy excerpts, you may be tempted to buy English translations known as "ponies" or "trots." Some ponies supply interlinear translations; the English words are printed between the lines of foreign print. Avoid these at all costs. Aside from distracting you, they keep you from figuring out the meaning of words, and they distort the foreign syntax. They deprive you of the ability to recite. Sometimes the translations are poor, so you may actually be misled. All in all, they are a real handicap in learning a new language.

In trots, the foreign text is on one page and the English equivalent is on the page opposite. This arrangement is useful if you want to read a book in a language you have never mastered. (One of us reads Latin very badly, and he has several copies of well-known books in Latin with translations on the opposite page.) However, it is a bad idea to use a trot as a *study aid*. It will slow down or even inhibit the learning process. In short, while there are times when it is profitable to read an English version of something you are going to translate, most times it is not. Something that is useful is to read something with which you are very familiar in English. Martin Luther's German version of the Bible is not only a great literary accomplishment, it is a good introduction to a clear and simple, if somewhat antique, German.

LEARNING TO SPEAK A FOREIGN LANGUAGE

Much of what we have said about learning to read a new language also applies to learning to speak one. In the early stages of learning, the two go together. Speaking the language helps you learn to read it. If you wish to gain speaking fluency as rapidly as possible, however, you will need to make use of some special techniques.

Total Immersion

You learned to speak English by hearing it spoken and by speaking it yourself. You learned by copying from others, inventing on your own, and being corrected, or being aware that you weren't saying things quite the same way other people were saying them. By the time you were ready to go to school and long before you could read or write, you had a better mastery of English than a person could acquire by studying it in college for a couple of years. All this happened without your knowing anything about grammar, reading, and writing.

Children are immersed in a world of language. That is how they learn it. Several of the crash programs for teaching people to comprehend and speak a new language in a short period of time—the Berlitz method, for example—make use of total immersion. However, total immersion is seldom possible for most college students. But even if you can't be a part of a total immersion program, you can practice the new language in a variety of situations and use it as much as you can to think with. Seek out native speakers of the language you are studying and get them to talk to you in their native tongue. Read foreign newspapers and magazines. Take out of the library foreign videotapes (preferably without subtitles) and listen to them.

In larger institutions there are generally houses or dining rooms devoted to a particular language. If you are studying French, for example, get into the habit of having lunch at the French House.

Imitating

To make a language habitual, you must practice it regularly. One important tool of practice is imitation. Here is where language laboratories are important. Almost every institution, however small, maintains language laboratories equipped with listening devices, recording devices, and tapes in at least the common European languages. You are probably required to log in a certain number of hours in such a lab. If so, exceed the number of hours. Listening to tapes of native speakers, recording your own speech, and correcting your errors all help you to master the spoken language. You learn the rhythm of native speech, and you can experiment with making unfamiliar vowel sounds.

Use of Cognates

Here are two translations of an earlier edition of How to Study, *one in French and one in Spanish. Even if you don't know French or Spanish, read through them and underline any word that resembles a word in English. Most of these words will be cognates; that is to say, they will be related to and will mean the same or similar things as English words. A few will be what the French call "false friends." These are words that resemble English words but mean different things. We have provided a list of words that resemble one another in English and French and in English and Spanish, together with the correct English*

Usage de fiches de vocabulaire

La technique qui suit s'est révélée efficace pour l'acquisition du vocabulaire. Lorsque vous rencontrez un mot moins familier, inscrivez-le au recto d'une fiche avec sa signification au verso; revisez ces fiches chaque jour, pointez-les chaque foi que vous vous souvenez du sens du mot et inscrivez un zéro chaque fois que vous devez regarder au verso pour vous rafraîchir la mémoire. Quand vous aurez pointé la fiche cinq fois sans aucun zéro, vous pourrez considérer que vous connaissez ce mot et vous jetterez la carte, évitant ainsi d'en accumuler un trop grand nombre. (page 74)

French Word	Similar English Word	English Translation
usage	usage	use
technique	technique	technique
suit	suit	follows
révélée	reveal	revealed, shown
efficace	efficacious	efficacious
pour	pour	for
acquisition	acquisition	acquisition
vocabulaire	vocabulary	vocabulary
rencontrez	encounter	meet with
familier	familiar	familiar
inscrivez	inscribe	inscribe, set down
signification	significance	significance
revisez	revise	revise
pointez	point	mark, check
souvenez	souvenir	remember, recall
sens	sense	meaning
zéro	zero	zero
regarder	regard	look at
refraîcher	refresh	refresh
mémoire	memory	memory
considérer	consider	consider
jetterez	jettison	throw away
carte	card	card
accumuler	accumulate	accumulate
grand	grand	large
nombre	number	number

translations. Check the words you underlined against the list, and be sure to note the correct translations. This exercise will show you how helpful hunting for similar words can be in understanding some of the familiar European languages.

The French translation, Comment Étudier, *was adapted from the English by André Roy and published in 1968 by McGraw-Hill Éditeurs, Montreal, Canada. The Spanish translation,* Como Estudiar, *was published in 1967 by Editorial Magisterio Español, S.A., Madrid, Spain.*

Uso de las fichas

Como ya hemos indicado, en el estudio de los idiomas hay que ejercitar mucho la memoria, y los estudiantes han probado un gran número de técnicas para hacerlo más fácil y eficaz. Una técnica muy empleada es escribir una palabra extranjera en la cara de una ficha y su traducción en la otra cara. (Desde luego, puedes comprar tales fichas ya impresas.) Puedes autoexaminarte mirando las palabras extranjeras y viendo las que sabes traducir. Cuando llegues a una cuyo significado no recuerdes, no tienes más que dar la vuelta a la ficha. Esta puede ser una práctica eficaz si se usa juiciosamente. (page 163)

Spanish Word	Similar English Word	English Translation
uso	use	use
indicado	indicate	appropriate, advisable
en	in	at, in, into, by, on
estudio	studio, study	study
idiomas	idioms	language, idiom
mucho	much	much, a lot of
memoria	memory	memory
estudiantes	students	students
probado	prove	test, try, prove
un	one	one, a
gran	grand	big, large, great
numéro	numeral	number
técnicas	technical	technique
empleada	employ	employ, use
escribir	inscribe	write
extranjera	extraneous	foreign
traducción	translation	translation
otra	other	other, another
comprar	compare	buy, purchase
tales	tales	such, such a
impresos	impress	printed
autoexaminarte	self-examination	self-examine
traducir	traduce	translate
significado	significant	meaning
no	no	not, no
eficaz	efficacy	efficacious, efficient
juiciosamente	judicious	judiciously
práctica	practice	method, skill

Memorizing

There is no way around it; you have to memorize in learning a foreign language as an adult. Imitating itself results in a kind of memorizing, but in addition to trying to duplicate what you hear, you must concentrate on remembering words and phrases. Rehearsing and reciting over and over again seems to be about the best way to do it. The object is to make certain things so habitual that you don't need to think about them. Then you can concentrate on what you want to say and on new combinations of words.

Studying Out Loud

Language labs are generally designed so that you can talk in response to what you hear. In cubicles more or less sound-insulated, you can respond to what the instructor says or what you hear on your tapes without embarrassment. But even when you are not in a language lab, read aloud as much as possible. As long as you read silently, you learn the language only visually. To be sure, reading aloud slows you down, but reading assignments, except in advanced courses, are generally short in language departments, so the lost time is worth the effort.

Spacing Studying Time Effectively

In learning something that requires repetitive practice—as learning a foreign language does—spacing the practice is essential for efficient learning. Don't make your study periods too long or too short. Divide an assignment into two parts and master each separately. Then allow time for re-reading and review. Provide for short rest or breaks. A half-hour is plenty of time if you are reciting out loud. If you break two hours of foreign language study into four half-hour periods separated by rest or by studying other subjects, you will learn more than if you work for two hours uninterruptedly on a foreign language.

IN GENERAL

Some courses emphasize reading the language, others speaking it. Some stress grammar, while others don't. Some require a very precise understanding of words, while others allow rather free translations and may even encourage it. More commonly in the past (when graduate schools required two foreign languages), larger institutions offered special courses in scientific French or German, so that students in the sciences could learn to read the technical literature in those languages. Nowadays, you are more likely to find such courses in Russian and Chinese. Whatever the emphasis of the course you are taking, your instructor will stress those techniques that are most suitable for the particular purpose of that course.

Many schools encourage students in foreign languages to study abroad. If you have the chance to spend a semester or a summer or even an entire year studying in another country, do so. There is no better way to become familiar with the way other people live and think than to live among them for a while.

We have had little to say about the special problems of learning languages that do not use the Roman alphabet—languages such as Greek, Arabic, and Hebrew—because, relatively speaking, few students take such languages. But the numbers are increasing, particularly for Japanese, Chinese, Russian, and Hebrew. If you have a talent for learning languages, treat yourself to some courses in one of these. Learning one of these languages, the organization of which is generally very different from English, can be one of the most valuable experiences of your college years.

Finally, we need to say an additional word about those people who have real difficulties with foreign languages. While there are differences in aptitudes for learning languages, most people who have trouble learning a language do so either because they do not study enough or because they study in the wrong way. Nowhere, except perhaps in studying mathematics, are good work habits more important than in learning foreign languages. Work habits are acquired, not built in, and you must make the effort to develop them if you are going to pass a foreign language. If you do have little aptitude for learning languages, you especially need to have good work habits, and you need to allow more time for studying a new language than most students. But remember, as Mark Twain remarked, even French babies learn to speak French.

9 COMPUTERS, MATHE-MATICS, AND SCIENCE

EITHER I'VE DISCOVERED A NEW GALAXY OR MARTIN FORGOT TO CLEAN THE LENS AGAIN.

We debated a long time before we decided to put the section on computers into this chapter, for though we usually think of computers as based in technology and mathematics, the truth of the matter is that most students use them as word processors (or to play games). But we finally decided that the math and science chapter is where the computer section belongs. What tipped our decision was our awareness of the phobias some students have for mathematics, science, and computers. Computer jockeys have difficulty believing this, but it is true. Most of what we have to say in this chapter is addressed to the student who, while perhaps not being phobic about the matter, tends to avoid computers, mathematics, and stiff courses in science.

If you have made a career out of avoiding science and mathematics and using computers, you have a lot of company. But even if you belong to a big club, it's one you shouldn't be in. Math or science phobia is one of the worst handicaps you can have in today's world. Not only do physics, engineering, chemistry, biology, and related fields require the tools of scientific thinking and mathematics, but social sciences such as economics, psychology, and sociology, as well as such practical fields as accounting and business administration, make use of them. Statistics, finite mathematics, linear algebra, and computer programming are all used in modern business management. Even if you are aiming for a major in literature or drama, you can't claim to be an educated person if you are nearly illiterate in mathematics, as some students are. The sooner you face up to deficiencies in science and mathematics, the better off you will be.

As for computers, many third graders and even

younger students know how to use them. The level of skill you acquire in mastering computers depends on your use for them, but some basic skill is absolutely required. Already, some visionaries are imagining all examinations being conducted through computers, and some colleges now routinely supply a computer and associated software for every student enrolled. In earlier editions of this book we stressed the importance of being able to touch-type. That is still important (particularly when you want to watch the computer screen as you compose), but being able to use computers for your homework, term papers, and course projects is now essential. Incidentally, touch-typing is not an altogether unmixed blessing when it comes to operating some compact computer keyboards.

Skim through this chapter. If what we say is obvious and elementary, you don't need to read the chapter in detail. The chances are you are a good student in science. But if you find something that is unfamiliar or that you recognize but need brushing up on, read and read in detail. If you find that you can't understand parts of this chapter, you are probably in serious trouble and need help. But whatever you do, don't give up and decide that you are a hopeless case. Sometimes deficiencies that prevent a student from understanding mathematics or doing well in science go all the way back to the early grades. If your deficiencies are this deep, you may need special tutoring.

If you think you can get by without understanding basic mathematics, consider the case of Anne. She graduated with a strong record and a major in English from one of the country's most prestigious colleges. All through her school and college career she concentrated on avoiding courses in mathematics and science. She barely got through ninth-grade algebra and quit doing any mathematics at all just as soon as she could. In college, she fulfilled her science requirement by taking a "rocks for jocks" course that made almost no demands upon scientific reasoning and none whatsoever upon mathematics. Two years after graduating from college, as the result of some job experience and other things, she decided that she wanted to take graduate work in psychology. She discovered that while some quite good graduate schools would be willing to take her without an undergraduate major in psychology, not one of them would let her get by without statistics. She

had no recourse but to go back and be tutored in the kinds of elementary mathematics and arithmetic operations that she had done so much to avoid. There is a postscript to this story: She eventually did so well in advanced statistics that she was asked, during her last year in graduate school, to be a teaching assistant in the computer-based statistics course in the institution's graduate school of business.

There is no time like the present to begin to correct your past mistakes. Use this chapter as a kind of test of how much you know and whether or not you are going about doing science and mathematics the right way. The chances are you can understand basic mathematics, even though you may never get into advanced mathematics or take something such as physics for engineers. If you can't understand a lot of the things we have to say, the sooner you realize this and do something about it, the better.

COMPUTERS

If, by some miracle, you managed to avoid having to operate a computer in high school, you need to correct this deficiency immediately. Learning to operate a computer, like learning how to drive, seems more difficult at the beginning than it really is. (Yes, there are some people who have a phobia about learning how to drive a car—the late writer H. L. Mencken tried and gave up after he ran into a lamp post.)

A computer keyboard may look like a typewriter keyboard, but it is not quite the same. For one thing a computer keyboard has a lot of keys that serve as "control" or "function" or "code" entries (the terminology varies according to the computer). Sometimes these keys enable you to do things that you can't do with a typewriter—such as move text around, enter new programs, and save what you have produced on disks. In some compact computers, such as lap-tops and "notebooks," certain of the regular keys double as function keys, so that when you press the control button and one of these keys you may find yourself in a different mode.

Kinds of Computers

There are so many variations in computers and computer hardware that we can only touch the surface. Your college or university may provide you with terminals that have access to the "main-frame" (the "big" computer located in the computer center). Sometimes student access to the mainframe is limited. In addition, some schools provide personal computers for general student use. There may be special rooms (usually in the library or the computer center) with banks of these instruments, complete with printers and sometimes other refinements. In many schools these rooms are open around the clock, and because they are less likely to be used at, say, two a.m., many students plan to do their homework or draft a term paper in the middle of the night.

Then there are computers that have limited functions (these are generally called "dedicated" computers). They can do word processing and sometimes things such as spreadsheets and database operations.

There are other means of expanding the usefulness of a computer. With the addition of a device called a "modem," you can use a telephone line to communicate with other computers.

Programs

Every computer requires a program in order to operate. For the computers that serve the main purposes in colleges and universities, a variety of programs are available. Some of them will do indexing for you. Others will perform elaborate statistical computations. (The latter use brings us to a caution. Don't use statistical programs blindly. They will compute on anything—nonsense, even. Sometimes students use them without understanding what they are doing, without any sense of the appropriateness, and, worse, sometimes just on a fishing expedition that will give them the results they want.)

There are programs for doing specialized accounting, programs that will give you interlingual translations (though you always have to clean these up), and programs for symbolic and numerical computations that mathematicians could only dream about as recently as twenty-five years ago.

Finally, you can learn to write your own programs. If you have a talent for this, particularly if you understand some particular field such as microbiology, psychology, or even literature, you have an advantage. There is a word of caution we need to add, however. Computer programmers are

sometimes like golfers—they become so absorbed in the process that they forget everything else. If you have an interest and a talent for programming, keep your enthusiasm from cutting short your actual study time.

Should You Buy a Computer?

One of the questions you may ask when you enter college is whether to buy a computer. Like many difficult questions, the answer is: "It all depends." Computers can be expensive, and like expensive stereos they are prime targets for thieves who specialize in student housing. On the other hand, if access to a college- or university-based computer system is difficult or awkward, having your own may be the best solution. Before you go out and buy a computer, though, check to see if the school you will be attending equips dormitory rooms with personal computers. A growing number of colleges and universities are doing so. Also, you might check with the school to find out if they offer special discounts to students for computers and software.

What Kind of Computer? Computers range in price and complexity. Some of the really good personal computers cost a thousand dollars or more, while dedicated computers—personal word processors—can be had for less than five hundred dollars. Here are some considerations that should go into your thinking if you decide to buy one.

1. Compatibility. All things equal you should have a computer that is compatible with the personal computers your school has available. Some schools have special arrangements with manufacturers, or they recommend a certain type of machine.

2. Portability. If you live away from home, you will want to have a computer that is easy to transport. By the time you put together all of the equipment needed for full operation of even a simple computer system—a screen, monitor, system unit, keyboard, disk drive, modem, and printer—you will have a lot of equipment to lug around. By the way, having a printer is essential, for that is the kind of thing that is likely to be most in use in your institution's computer lab. The cheapest are "dot-matrix" printers. If your professors are like us, they don't like them; their output is hard to read. But then many institution-based computer labs use them. The best printers (fast, easy to read, and of high quality) are laser printers, but they are expensive. Some students do their work on their own computer, then use the school's printer (if it's available) to generate nice looking copy.

3. *Your needs.* Consider how you use a computer. Do you use it almost exclusively to create and print text for papers and projects? If so, consider a personal word processor that is dedicated. These, however, have serious disadvantages. They have limited functions. You can use them to produce and edit text, but they won't do such things as index or alphabetize for you. Nor will they do arithmetic or mathematical calculations (but see below). A few of them will do spreadsheets, but that is about it. Many of them are not compatible with any of the "big" systems. Most of them let you store information on disks, but you can only use the disks on another machine of the same brand.

They are, however, portable and inexpensive. You can carry them around with you. They are not as versatile as lap-tops or notebooks, but they are a lot cheaper, and they do not require an auxiliary printer—the printer is built in.

4. *Lap-tops and notebooks.* The most compact and portable of the personal computers are lap-tops and the yet smaller versions, notebooks. They weigh only a few pounds, and they can operate on batteries for a few hours at a time. Many of them are compatible with the "big" systems (IBM, AT&T, etc.), but they are more expensive than the dedicated personal word processors. And how often do you want to use a computer on an airplane? Besides which they always require transferring via a disk to a printer.

5. *Hand-held calculators.* If your computer demands are modest besides producing term papers, you might want to consider the combination of a personal word processor and a hand-held calculator. You should have a hand-held calculator in any event. You can buy one that will do ordinary arithmetic for under ten dollars (solar powered—no batteries). For not a great deal more you can buy a specialized one that will calculate logarithms, find trigonometric functions, and carry special codes for going from British units

(the ones we use in the United States) to metric units.

If you buy a hand-held calculator, consider your needs. Some are meant for engineering work, others are specialized for statistical calculations, and still others are intended for typical business problems. After you have bought one, take the time to read the manual carefully and work through the sample problems. Some calculators are almost as complicated as a small computer (which is what many of them really are). Like computers, many of them have dual function keys. These make it possible to increase the number of operations without increasing the number of keys (so you can still hold the calculator in your hand), but be careful, for you must know what mode you are in. The more sophisticated hand-held calculators have memory registers. These enable you to store the solution to part of a problem while you work on the remainder. The most expensive calculators are programmable. That is to say, they are really miniature computers. You can work out your own problem-solving methods that can be used over and over again.

Best of all, hand-held calculators are genuinely portable. (Some are even wallet-size or smaller.) Many professors teaching courses for which examinations require calculations will have no objection to your bringing them into the examination room. We'll have more to say about hand-held calculators in the next section.

BASIC MATHEMATICAL SKILLS

Arithmetic

What is the heading Arithmetic doing in a book addressed to college students and students headed for college? Isn't that something that you learn to do in elementary school? Perhaps. But a lot of people forget how to do some of the less-familiar arithmetic operations when they don't use them every day, and a few people—otherwise intelligent and educated people—never learn how to do them properly. Hand-held calculators, of course, will do all the ordinary arithmetic operations for you. A few instructors, however, may insist that you do the arithmetic on examinations by hand. Be sure to find out ahead of time if that is the case so that you can practice doing the kinds of problems that may be required.

One of the things people easily forget because of disuse is how to deal with fractions. In certain courses in mathematics and science you may be forced to deal with fractions without converting them to decimals. If so, you may need a refresher on fractions. We have provided a summary of the rules for working with fractions on page 106.

Setting Up Problems

Every once in a while the newspapers will carry some story about how badly American students do with mathematics. It strikes us that the basic problem is not knowledge of the operations but how to set up the problem. Here's an example. Your college accepts sixty percent of all its applicants. You know that 360 students were accepted the year you came in. How large was the applicant pool from which your class was selected? To answer this problem you must first set it up properly. To do this, you will either mentally or on paper write out an equation. In writing an equation we let x or y stand for the answer. You must write the equation so that it corresponds exactly to the wording of the problem. Here is the equation for this problem:

$$0.6 \times x = 360$$

The quantity 0.6 stands for sixty percent. Why? Because sixty percent means 60 out of 100, which as a decimal fraction is written as 60/100 or 0.6. The total applicant pool is the unknown quantity, and so we represent it by x. We say 0.6 *times* x because whenever we say that something is a percentage of something else we are implicitly multiplying. Thus seventy percent of 200 is 140 (0.7 × 200).

But we cannot solve the problem the way it is now set up. That is because the unknown quantity, x, must be isolated on one side of the equation. Therefore, we rearrange the equation this way:

$$x = \frac{360}{0.6}$$

If you don't know how we did this or why we *divided* 360 by 0.6, you have forgotten algebra. You will find a brief account of some elementary rules of algebra in the next section. If this account doesn't ring a bell right away, the chances are that you need some remedial work before you can do even elementary college courses that require some mathematics.

The answer to the problem is 600 (360 divided by 0.6).

A Little Algebra

Most college students have had some algebra, but because the basic operations are often poorly learned or easily forgotten, many students have to refresh themselves when they take a course in elementary statistics, or some other course that demands a little algebra. Some students, like Anne, have to be tutored in the basics before they can tackle courses in statistics or business mathematics. But most of you who feel a little rusty can tutor yourselves.

First of all, numbers in algebra have signs; they are either positive or negative. If a number has a negative sign in front of it, it is negative. Thus, –8 is a negative eight. If a number has no sign or a plus sign in front of it, it is positive. Thus, 8 or +8 is positive eight. Sometimes students are confused, for the plus and minus signs are also used in algebra and arithmetic to indicate the *operations* of addition and subtraction. But if you keep in mind that the operations, addition and subtraction, and the signs of numbers are different, you won't be confused.

Everyone is acquainted with positive and negative numbers because that is the way we scale temperature. When we read that the temperature in Chicago yesterday was –2, we know that it means that it was two degrees below zero. There are lots of uses for negative numbers that are not quite so obvious. For example if I owe $15 more than I have, I might say that my assets are –$15.

You can think of negative and positive numbers as numbers that keep increasing from zero in opposite directions like this:

$$\overset{\displaystyle +\,+\,+\,+\,+\,+\,+\,+\,+\,+\,+}{-5\ -4\ -3\ -2\ -1\ \ 0\ +1\ +2\ +3\ +4\ +5}$$

Rules for Addition and Subtraction of Algebraic Numbers. The rules for algebraic addition and subtraction, or the addition and subtraction of negative *and* positive numbers, are simple, and they should cause you no trouble, if you are careful. Here they are:

1. If the numbers are either all positive or all negative, to add, find the sum of the numbers and give the sum the sign of the numbers. Thus, –2 plus –4 is –6.

Some Rules for Computing Fractions

Definitions

1. A fraction is one or more of the equal parts into which something can be divided. Examples are:

$$\frac{1}{2} \quad \frac{1}{3} \quad \frac{3}{4}$$

2. Fractions are written $\frac{1}{2}$ or ½.
3. The lower number is the *denominator.*
4. The upper number is the *numerator.*
5. *Mixed numbers* are whole numbers and fractions. Examples are:

$$3\frac{1}{2} \quad 2\frac{2}{3}$$

Adding fractions

1. To add fractions, the denominators must all be the same. Thus $\frac{1}{2}$ and $\frac{1}{3}$ cannot be added until the 2 and 3 are changed.
2. To make the denominators the same, find the *smallest* number (the lowest common denominator) that can be divided evenly by all the denominators. Examples are:

> For 2 and 3, it is 6.
> For 7 and 13, it is 91 ($7 \times 13 = 91$).
> For 2, 8, and 9, it is 72.

Note: For many cases, you will have difficulty finding the smallest number by inspection. Find the smallest number into which you can divide as many of the numbers as possible. Then multiply that number by the number you *cannot* divide into it. This will be the lowest common denominator. Take, for example, 2, 3, 6, 7, 8, 9. All but 7 can be evenly divided into 72. The lowest common denominator is therefore $72 \times 7 = 504$.

3. Multiply the numerator by the number of times the original denominator goes into the lowest common denominator. An example is:

$$\frac{1}{2} + \frac{1}{3} = \frac{1 \times 3}{6} + \frac{1 \times 2}{6} = \frac{3}{6} + \frac{2}{6}$$

4. Add the numerators and place the lowest common denominator as the denominator of the sum. An example is:

$$\frac{3}{6} + \frac{2}{6} = \frac{5}{6}$$

5. If the numerator is larger than the denominator, change to a mixed number. An example is:

$$\frac{23}{7} = 3\frac{2}{7}$$

Subtracting fractions

1. All the rules are the same as for addition except rule 4.
2. For rule 4, subtract instead of adding the numerators. An example is:

$$\frac{3}{7} - \frac{1}{13} = \frac{39}{91} - \frac{7}{91} = \frac{32}{91}$$

Multiplying fractions

1. To multiply fractions, multiply the numerators together and the denominators together. Write the result as a fraction. An example is:

$$\frac{5}{6} \times \frac{2}{5} = \frac{10}{30} = \frac{1}{3}$$

2. To multiply a whole number and a fraction, multiply the whole number by the numerator and place the result over the denominator. An example is:

$$5 \times \frac{2}{3} = \frac{10}{3} = 3\frac{1}{3}$$

Dividing fractions

1. Turn the divisor upside down and multiply. An example is:

$$\frac{4}{9} \div \frac{1}{3} = \frac{4}{9} \times \frac{3}{1} = \frac{12}{9} = 1\frac{3}{9} = 1\frac{1}{3}$$

2. Whole numbers can be written in the form of a fraction with 1 as the denominator. An example is:

$$3 = \frac{3}{1}$$

3. Therefore, to divide a fraction by a whole number, write the whole number as a fraction and invert. An example is:

$$\frac{4}{9} \div 3 = \frac{4}{9} \div \frac{3}{1} = \frac{4}{9} \times \frac{1}{3} = \frac{4}{27}$$

2. If two numbers have opposite signs, then the sum is the difference between them with the sign of the sum being the sign of the larger number. Thus 4 plus –7 is –3, and –4 plus 7 is 3.

3. If you have to add a series of numbers which have different signs, find the sum of the positive numbers and the sum of the negative numbers separately and then find the *algebraic* sum of the two. To add –5, 3, –1, 6, –2, –7, and 8, first find the sum of –5, –1, –2, and –7, which is –15. Then find the sum of 3, 6, and 8, which is 17. The sum of –15 and 17 is 2. If you use a hand calculator, you don't need to find the separate simple sums; you can just add the numbers together, but you need to press the right sign keys. Thus, in doing the above sum you would press the minus key, then 5, then the *plus* key, then 3, then the minus key, then 1, etc. When you have entered all the numbers, you press the equals (=) key.

4. For algebraic *subtraction*, you change the sign of the number to be subtracted and then add. Thus the difference between 8 and –3 is 11. When you subtract numbers opposite in sign, you are finding out how far apart the numbers are. For example, if the temperature this morning is 8 degrees in Cleveland and –3 in Minneapolis, the difference in temperature is 11 degrees.

Algebraic addition and subtraction are easy, but you have to be alert to know which operation to apply to a particular problem. This may particularly be difficult when the problem is put in words. (If it is –3 in Minneapolis and 8 in Cleveland, what is the difference in temperature?)

Some Basic Rules of Algebra. If you are going to take a course that makes some simple mathematical demands—physics for liberal arts students, for example—you need to brush up on a few basic rules of algebra, even if it is only to follow what the instructor is saying when he or she is working at the chalkboard. If you really are panicked by the matter, you should get hold of a book that reviews basic mathematics and assure yourself that you can do such things as add and subtract polynominals, that you can solve equations for numerical values, and that you know how to simplify factors and rearrange terms. There are a lot of such books available, many of them in student outline series.

There are a couple of aspects of rearranging terms that are so important that you will run into them even if you never take a course in the physical sciences. They are (1) how to move simple terms from one side of an equation to another, and (2) how to move part of a fraction or a product from one side of the equation to another. It was this operation we had to employ in order to set up the equation $x = 360/0.6$.

1. In order to move a single number such as 253 or 4 or a single term such as x or a or y from one side of the equation to the other, you add or subtract the number or term on each side of the equation, thus removing everything but the variable from the left side. Thus, to solve the equation

$$x - 5 = 30$$

you add 5 to each side of the equation:

$$x - 5 = 30$$
$$\underline{+5 \quad +5}$$
$$x + 0 = 35$$

Thus,

$$x = 35$$

2. In order to move the denominator of a fraction to the other side, multiply the term on the other side, and in order to move one term of a product to the other side, divide it into the term on the other side. Thus,

$$\frac{x}{5} = 4$$
$$x = 4 \times 5$$
$$= 20$$

and

$$4x = 20$$
$$x = 20 \div 4$$
$$= 5$$

These simple rules won't tell you what to do with complicated expressions, but if you understand them you should have no trouble learning how to deal with the rules that tell you how to decompose complicated expressions and treat the simple terms the way we did the ones above.

Many students are defeated by algebra, but remember someone once said that algebra is ninety percent notation and ten percent thinking. Pay attention to parentheses: 6(5+4) is 30 [six times five] plus 24 [six times four] or 54.

Powers, Roots, and Logarithms

As recently as thirty years ago, every serious student of the physical sciences or engineering had to have two things: (1) a slide rule and (2) a book of mathematical tables. He or she needed the book of mathematical tables for many purposes, for example, to look up powers, roots, and logarithms. The slide rule also served a lot of purposes but was used mainly for calculation. There is the old story of the engineering student who, when asked what the square root of 25 was, whipped out his slide rule and said approximately 5. Slide rules were not precision instruments, though the best of them could allow their users to calculate figures accurately to four places.

The slide rule is now an antique (the best of them are collectors items), and books of mathematical tables are much less often used than they once were. The reason is the development of the computer and, before that, the hand calculator. A good inexpensive calculator will enable you to calculate any power, any root, and any logarithm and do any arithmetic operation with an accuracy that would have been all but impossible for the ordinary student fifty years ago. But even if you don't have to learn how to use a slide rule or read a book of tables, you still must know what the concepts are that we've just talked about. Many of the quantitative rules in modern science are written in something called "scientific notation," and that is based upon powers and logarithms.

Powers. The power of a number results from multiplying the number by itself. Thus 3×3, or 9, is a power of 3. It happens to be the second power of 3 because there are *two* numbers, 3 and 3, that are multiplied together. Usually we call the second power of a number its square. So 3×3, or 9, is the square of 3. We can write it this way: 3^2. The number on the right, called the "exponent," tells the number of terms multiplied. Then, in addition to 3^2 we can have 3^3. That number, 3^3, tells us that there are three numbers multiplied together: $3 \times 3 \times 3$. The result of 3^3 is 27 (3×3 is 9, and 9×3 is 27). The third power of a number is called the "cube." Higher powers don't have any special

names. Thus 3^5 is just that, $3 \times 3 \times 3 \times 3 \times 3$, or 243. Powers very quickly become big numbers. The tenth power of 2, 2^{10}, is 1024, and just two powers higher, 2^{12}, is 4096. Scientific notation is useful with very big numbers. Instead of writing out 120,000,000,000, we can say that it is 1.2×10^{11}, or $1.2 \times 100,000,000,000$. Your astronomy professor might say, "The sun is on the order of magnitude of 9.3×10^7 miles from earth." You would know that the sun is ninety-three million miles away.

Roots. Roots are the opposite of powers. The square root of 9 is 3. So a root is the number you need to multiply by itself to get the number you started with ($3 \times 3 = 9$). The square root of a number is most often written in the style $\sqrt{9} = 3$. You can also have cube and higher roots. Thus, the cube root of 27, written as $\sqrt[3]{27}$, is 3. Calculating roots used to be one of the things you had to endure in the sixth grade, but most of us have forgotten how to do it. The fact of the matter is that all but the very cheapest hand-held calculators have a square root button, and the more expensive calculators have a button for computing any root, generally identified as $\sqrt[x]{y}$. But *do* understand the principles of roots and squares. If you don't, you will be in trouble in such things as elementary statistics.

Logarithms. What are logarithms? Logarithms are special kinds of powers. There are two kinds, decimal logarithms and natural logarithms. Natural logarithms are important mathematically, but students who are not going to be mathematics or science majors are not likely to encounter them. Almost any student, however, is likely to run across decimal logarithms. Decimal logarithms are powers of the number 10. Thus, the second power of 10 (10^2) is 100, and in logarithmic terms is just called 2 (remember that it is a logarithm). The third power of 10 in logarithmic notation is 3 (10^3), which is 1000. If you think about it a bit, you will see that the logarithm, or power of 10, is simply the number of zeros you write after the first digit. Thus, 100,000,000,000 is the logarithmic number 11. The way we say this is that log 100,000,000,000 is 11.

To write the number 314,000,000,000 in scientific notation, you separate it into two parts: First you write 3.14 (you put in the decimal to separate the first digit from the others), and second you multiply it by 10^{11}. Thus, 314,000,000,000 equals 3.14×10^{11} or log 314,000,000,000 is 3.14 × 100,000,000,000. But logarithms have uses other than to represent very large numbers. They can be used to represent and do calculations with more complicated large numbers, such as 5,011,872. That number can be represented as $10^{6.7}$. To put in terms of logarithms: log 5,011,872 equals 6.7.

Now when you see a number like $10^{3.2}$ you will know that it is simply another way of writing an ordinary number, in this case 1,584.89. How do we get from $10^{3.2}$ to 1,584.89 or from $10^{6.7}$ to 5,011,872? Until recently most of relied on published tables of logarithms to do that. But nowadays, calculators and computers do it for us. If you have a scientific hand-held calculator, the key for going from log notation to ordinary notation is simply marked "10^x" while the key for going from ordinary notation to logarithms is marked "log."

In any event, you should not panic when you see something like log 3,476 or an expression like $10^{2.476}$. You will know that these are other ways of writing the kind of numbers you are used to dealing with all along.

Other Mathematical Functions

We have only scratched the surface of the kinds of mathematical problems you will encounter if you take anything but the most elementary kind of mathematics or science course. There is, for example, a whole family of important mathematical functions called the "trigonometric functions." We haven't described these because they are more likely to be found in engineering and science courses than in the kind of courses you are taking if you have to read this section carefully. But they're not really difficult to understand. As with most things in mathematics, mastery is a matter of systematic study, building on concepts and operations that you have already learned.

Watching Notation

All mathematics, in principle, consists of simple, easy steps. But you have to know what you are doing. A lot of mathematical knowledge consists of learning how to break down complicated operations into easy steps. That is why learning how to set up problems properly is so important.

Equally important for getting those operations into the proper steps is to master the notation. A basic rule in dealing with mathematics is: *Know exactly what each symbol stands for.* If you are not sure, you are in trouble. Surprisingly, mathematical symbols are sometimes, like ordinary English, ambiguous. Any time you have the least doubt, check the textbook or ask. So far as ambiguity is concerned, you can be pretty sure what π means, but a symbol such as σ or λ has several different meanings, depending upon the scientific context. Also, different mathematical symbols may be used for the same thing by different authorities. Make sure you know how a symbol is being used in the context of the particular course you are taking. It goes without saying that when dealing with computers you *must* be absolutely clear about what a particular symbol means.

STUDYING THE SCIENCES

As you know, there are natural and social sciences. The natural sciences (e.g., physics, astronomy, chemistry, geology, biology) study nature, and the social sciences (e.g., sociology, economics, political science) study humanity. Psychology is both a natural and a social science. In its biological aspects it is a natural science, and in other aspects it is a social science. Physical anthropology is a natural science; cultural anthropology is a social science.

Science is basically a matter of solving problems in order to increase knowledge. Like all human knowledge, scientific information demands certain assumptions. These assumptions are likely to be dealt with in courses in the philosophy of science, but courses in the special sciences will generally take them for granted. Most science is inductive; it begins with the systematic collection of data and goes from there to the building of theories which summarize and interrelate those data. Other science is deductive; it begins with theories and then goes to the collection of data in order to find out whether the theories are right or not. Theories arrived at by both methods stand or fall by their correlation with further experimentation.

All stages of science depend upon solving problems. Collecting data requires scientists to be clever in devising methods for so doing. Thinking up theories, refining them, and finding ways to test them also require problem solving, and solving practical problems by applying science is also, by definition, problem solving.

Different sciences go about solving problems in different ways. Physics and certain branches of engineering and chemistry rely most heavily upon mathematics. Chemistry and engineering, however, are likely to rely also upon models or pictures to help interpret and design things. Almost all of the natural sciences tend to make more use of mathematics than do the social sciences, though once again there are important exceptions. If you are planning to major in economics, you can expect a reasonably heavy dose of mathematics.

Like mathematics, much of science—the natural sciences—is structured and builds concept upon concept; therefore, it involves sequential learning to a greater extent than do the social sciences or the humanities. This means you must attend class and keep up with your assignments or you will soon find yourself overwhelmed.

Scientific Language

All sciences make use of technical language. Sometimes it is a matter of giving a highly restricted and particular definition to a common word. For example, in introductory physics you learn to define the word "force" by an equation: Force = mass × acceleration. All the other meanings of force that you use in your daily life are irrelevant; you must learn to forget them when you are working on the mechanics section of beginning physics. At other times sciences invent special terms to describe theories, concepts, structures, and principles. For example, if you take a course in atomic physics, you will learn about things called "quarks" and "mesons."

Scientific language is meant to be more precise than ordinary language. That is why so many strange terms are invented—to avoid confusion with ordinary meanings. Unlike ordinary words, scientific words cannot be easily learned from context. You will be required to read and understand precise definitions of terms. Usually in scientific textbooks, technical terms are defined the first time they are used. If you somehow miss such a definition and find yourself lost, turn to the glossary. If the book doesn't have one, look in the index for the first reference to the term. The chances are good that a definition and perhaps an example of its use will accompany it. Occasionally

the writer of a scientific text will not define some particular term because he or she assumes that you will have learned it in a more elementary course. In that case, the thing to do is to find an elementary text and consult it.

Be aware, though, that knowing the definition of a scientific term is not enough—you must know how it relates to other terms and to the concepts you are learning. You may begin your study of a topic by memorizing the definitions of terms, but you will fully understand them by using them and building on them as you go further into the subject.

A special note about words in psychology and the social sciences in general is in order. Many of the terms you will encounter in these subjects will, like the word "force" in physics, be familiar to you. But beware. Whereas in physics you are likely to sense that ordinary words are used in special ways, in psychology or economics you may assume that you know the meaning of certain terms because you already know a lot about people and money. But you will find that the psychologist or economist will use a familiar word in a highly restricted way just as well as the physicist, and he or she will expect you to use the word that way too.

The Big Three: Chemistry, Biology, and Physics

If you're reading this chapter, you're likely to be taking, or thinking of taking, an introductory course in one of the three basic sciences. Although these sciences draw on one another for a complete understanding of the natural world, they differ in content and approach. We offer the following sections to point up some of these differences and give you an idea of what to expect in these college-level courses.*

Studying Chemistry. You may be studying chemistry because you intend to major in it or in a related field of science, or you may be taking it

---

*For students who are particularly anxious about taking science courses in college we recommend *Breaking the Science Barrier: How to Explore and Understand the Sciences* by Sheila Tobias and Carl T. Tomizuka (1992, College Board Publications, New York). Students apprehensive about chemistry will find valuable tips and insights into the *process* of learning chemical material in *The Success Manual for General Chemistry* by Elizabeth Kean and Catherine Middlecamp (1986, McGraw-Hill, New York).

COMPUTERS, MATHEMATICS, AND SCIENCE • 111

merely to satisfy the requirements of another area of study. Whatever your degree of interest in the subject, you must have heard that the introductory course in college chemistry is a killer—the course that separates the science-able from the science-hopeless. No question about it, there's a lot of complex material to learn in a short period of time. There's a lab, and there are homework assignments.

If you took chemistry in high school, you will have an easier time in college chemistry—in the beginning. But beware, your familiarity with the terminology and the topics covered may give you a false sense of mastery, and you may find yourself lagging behind. With this warning given, we will offer a few insights into studying chemistry that may help you if you are new to the subject or if you have some trepidation about taking it at all. Of course, you'll be wise to bring to the course the basic study habits and skills we've presented in earlier chapters.

Although chemistry deals with "chemicals," much of chemistry is abstract. With the help of diagrams and models, you will become accustomed to thinking visually about invisible things like atoms and molecules. You will learn how chemists compress a lot of information, in a very workable shorthand, into chemical formulas and reaction equations and how you can extract and make use of that information.

In chemistry you'll have to memorize certain facts, such as the symbols for the ninety-two natural elements. You will have to understand thoroughly a good many concepts such as molarity and reduction before you can successfully apply chemical rules and solve chemistry problems. When you study your lecture notes and read your text, it may help if you keep these categories—facts, concepts, rules—in mind. You might ask yourself, "What are the facts I need to memorize about this topic? What concepts are introduced, and how do they relate to one another? Are there any rules given?" Some rules (also referred to as "laws" and "principles") will be stressed by your lecturer and emphasized in your text; others may not be so obvious. Be sure you understand the concepts behind the rules of chemistry. For example, Boyle's law states that the volume of a gas is inversely proportional to its pressure when the temperature and number of moles of gas are con-

stant. Obviously, you cannot apply this law if you don't know what a mole is.

This brings us to solving chemistry problems, which can be the moment of truth as to whether or not you have mastered the material. Chemistry problems are usually stated in words, and similar type problems may be worded differently. When you approach a problem, read it carefully. Try to identify the rule or rules that apply.

It's one thing to solve a chemistry problem on a topic you're currently studying; it's another to solve a problem among many different types on a midterm or final exam. Our advice is to go to the exam with the basic types of problems and the steps and strategies for solving them firmly in your head. This means keeping track of the basic (generic) problems you encounter as you make your way through the course. A few days before the exam, review the list and work out as many types of problems as you can. If a problem on the exam seems unfamiliar, it may be a variation of one of the basic types.

Studying Biology. Biology is not considered to be as rigorous a course as chemistry, mainly because it's not so problem-oriented. However, because it is in part descriptive, the vocabulary of biology is larger; there are a lot of facts to memorize and a lot of concepts and processes to learn. Not that there's no chemistry involved in studying biology. There is. Your biology course will typically begin with atoms and molecules because these are the building blocks of biological molecules as well as of nonliving matter. You can learn the chemistry that pertains to biology as you go along—your textbook sets it all out—but it will be tough going without at least a high school chemistry course behind you.

Chemical reactions underlie all change within living things, and underlying all chemical reactions is energy. Cellular respiration and photosynthesis are the central energy pathways that sustain living organisms. These processes and all their ramifications are probably the hardest part of biology for students to master. The Krebs cycle, with its intricate "turns," is a notorious roadblock. The diagram can be memorized, but you will not be able to follow related discussions or answer exam questions correctly unless you truly understand the steps of the cycle. But don't be discouraged by this example. In biology, perhaps more than in the other natural sciences, you can't expect to fully understand everything when it's first presented. You'll be studying topics in a particular sequence, but they won't come together until you've studied a whole unit, or even finished the course. Then all those biochemical pathways and energy transformations will link up and the mechanisms of cellular reproduction and heredity will fall into place in a most satisfying way.

Your course in biology is likely to follow a general sequence based on levels of organization. Even if this isn't apparent, keep this concept in mind so you'll be studying within a broad framework. You'll start with atoms and biological molecules and then go on to cells, the basic units of life, and learn how they harness energy and how they reproduce. The genes control the development of organisms; organisms form populations, communities, and ecosystems. Evolution and ecology may be unifying themes as well as separate chapters.

Roughly the middle of the course will be about "natural history"—the zoology and botany you may be looking forward to. Here, though, there is much to learn and remember—the major groups, their origins and interrelationships, their anatomies and physiologies. The organizing scheme here is the system of classification created by the Swedish biologist Carolus Linnaeus in the mid-eighteenth century and still followed, with modifications. The hierarchy is kingdom, phylum, class, order, family, genus, and species. Today, most biologists recognize five kingdoms; along with Linnaeus's Plantae and Animalia are Monera (bacteria and cyanobacteria), Protista (mainly protozoans and some types of algae), and Fungi (molds and mushrooms and the like). Linnaeus's system names organisms by the binomial system: genus and species, as in *Canus lupus*, wolf. You'll have to memorize a certain number of these classification names. It will help fix them in your mind if you know some Latin and Greek roots, prefixes, and suffixes. For example, it's easy to remember that the order Chiroptera is bats if you know that *"cheir"* is "hand" and *"pteron"* is "wing" in Greek.

We mentioned earlier that biology is not as problem-oriented as chemistry. But there is one subject that does involve problems, and that is genetics. However, the genetics problems you are likely to encounter in an introductory course are not too complicated, and they're fun to work out.

Studying Physics. Physics approaches the natural world in terms of fundamental principles and laws. It is more "compact" than either chemistry or biology, as it deals much more with universals than with specifics. Its main divisions correspond to certain classes of natural phenomena and to particular structures in nature. These main areas of physics (both classical and modern), are mechanics, electricity and magnetism, thermodynamics, optics, electrodynamics, relativity, quantum mechanics, and particle and nuclear physics.

Physics has fewer terms to learn than chemistry, and certainly fewer than biology, but the terms and concepts it has must be thoroughly understood. Behind the clearly stated laws of physics are a wide range of observations about nature, some commonsense, such as Newton's first law of motion, some not, such as the theory of relativity. The tool of physics is measurement. There are six basic quantities, expressed in units, from which all other quantities can be derived. These are length (the meter), time (the second), mass (the kilogram), temperature (the kelvin), electric current (the ampere), and luminous intensity (the candela).

If the tool of physics is measurement, the language of physics is—let's face it—mathematics. In the typical physics course, equations and quantitative problems abound. We noted in the section on studying chemistry that the key to solving problems is applying the right principle or law. In physics, the universality of physical laws may make your task easier. One law may apply in many problems. The best strategy is to reduce each problem to its essentials and consider the steps you will need to follow to get the answer. And be sure to watch your units. In every mathematical operation, the units (e.g., lb, cm, m/s^2) must be carried along with the numbers and must undergo the same mathematical operations as the numbers.

The first course you take in physics depends on your career goals and on your science and mathematical aptitude and background. Before you sign up, read the course description carefully—you can't always go by the course title. "Introduction to Physics" may be very different from

"Introductory Physics." Some "General Physics" courses require a knowledge of calculus whereas others call for only high school algebra and trigonometry. "College Physics" is usually calculus-free; "University Physics" is typically built around calculus. "Ideas in Physics," "Physics for Poets," "Physics for Nonscience Majors," and the like approach the subject intuitively with a minimum of math. If your aim is a premed or pre-engineering course of study, be sure the physics course you take meets those requirements. It will almost certainly be the course that requires you to know differential and integral calculus.

Laboratory Work

Most introductory science courses have laboratories, and you may be required to take at least one during your four years, whatever your major. Labs in different courses emphasize different skills. Traditionally, physics labs require precise measurement, chemistry labs careful procedures, and traditional biology labs detailed observation. All, however, are designed to demonstrate the scientific method—to show you firsthand how to draw inferences from observation and experimentation.

Because the kinds of experiments and observations you will do in lab have been done by thousands, indeed millions, of students before, there is a tendency to regard them as mechanical chores to be gotten through as painlessly as possible. Avoid that view. Many of the experiments you will do are repetitions of fundamental discoveries in science. Try to put yourself in the position of the person who first made those observations.

Needless to say, you should be careful and accurate in making measurements and recording data. Check all your calculations. Keep a full record of everything you do. If you have a workbook, keep it neat. By and large scientists are neat, at least about their science, and a sloppy workbook is going to be looked down upon by a laboratory instructor. You will usually be given a set organization by which to report the results of your experiments. Hold to it strictly. Scientists set great store by orderly procedures, and if you follow the rules both in the conduct of laboratory experiments and the reporting of them, you will be getting into the habitual ways of doing things in that particular science.

Reading Science Texts

In Chapter 4 we said that different subjects require different strategies in reading. In this section we will say a few things about reading from scientific texts.

Problems. In scientific texts, examples and problems are worked out for you in the text itself. Don't just read these. Even if you think you understand, if you only read you may skip over some crucial step that you really don't follow. Work each problem out yourself just as it is presented in the text. That way you will really know if you can do each step. If you can get the same answer at each step as that given in the textbook, the chances are that you know how to do all the operations. Occasionally in texts in the physical sciences and engineering the obvious steps in some mathematical derivation are skipped. But when you try to do the derivation or solve the problem, don't skip. Make sure that you know all the intervening steps that the author did not bother to include.

Graphs and Diagrams. Scientific texts are full of graphs and diagrams. These aren't just decorative devices used to break up pages of solid print (though you may be used to some high school texts that have illustrations for exactly that purpose). They are usually essential to an understanding of the text. Be sure to read them and to make sure that you understand every aspect of them.

Graphs are among the most common illustrations found in scientific texts. Graphs are used in books in economics, psychology, physics, engineering, chemistry, biology—in fact, in almost all of the natural and social sciences. Most graphs illustrate a mathematical relation between two variables. These variables are represented by numbers on the vertical axis and the horizontal axis of the graph. The vertical axis is called the y-axis and the horizontal axis the x-axis. A line or curve on the graph shows you each value of y that corresponds to a particular value of x. The line works exactly like an equation. It will give you the same result as substituting for x or y in an equation. For example, the straight line in the illustration Reading a Graph on page 114 corresponds to the equation $y = 0 + 0.5x$. If you substitute 4 for x, then $y = 2$.

In scientific graphs the x-axis is customarily the independent variable and the y-axis the de-

Reading a Graph

Each line represents an equation on two variables x and y. For any given equation, you can find the value of y that corresponds to given value of x. The straight line represents the equation y = 0 + 0.5x, and the curved line represents the equation y = 2 + 0.5x².

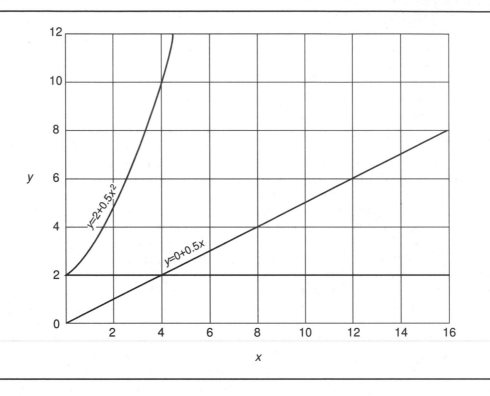

pendent variable. What that means is that the independent variable is the quality that the experimenter controls, while the dependent variable is the unknown quantity that depends upon changes in the independent variable.

One of the most elementary experiments in physics is to measure the time it takes a steel ball to pass successive distances when it rolls down an inclined plane (this experiment was first done by Galileo). The successive distances are the independent variable, and the time that it takes the ball to get from one distance to another is the dependent variable. This experiment is done in thousands of high school and college physics labs each year, and it tells you the effect of gravity upon the acceleration of motion. If you do the experiment, you will find that the distance traveled increases as the square of the distance already traveled. If

you were to make a graph of the result it would look like the curve for the equation $y = 2 + 0.5x^2$ in Reading a Graph.

Not all diagrams are graphs. Instead, some illustrate spatial relations or such abstract relations as the direction in space of a force applied to a body. If you have studied physics, you will recognize such diagrams as illustrating vectors and vector addition.

The term "vector" scares a lot of students, but it shouldn't. It is just a way of saying that forces differ in magnitude and direction. If you give a book a light shove toward the center of your desk, it will travel a short distance. You would represent that by a short line pointing to the middle of the desk. If you give the same book a hard shove, it may travel to the edge of the desk. You would represent that by a longer line reaching from

Reading a Table

Value of y for different values of x in different equations.

| x | y = a + bx | | y = x² | y = log x |
	a = 2; b = 1/2	a = 3; b = 1/3		
0.00	2.00	3.00	0.00	-∞
1.00	2.50	3.33	1.00	0.000
2.00	3.00	3.67	4.00	0.301
3.00	3.50	4.00	9.00	0.477
4.00	4.00	4.33	16.00	0.602
5.00	4.50	4.67	25.00	0.699
6.00	5.00	5.00	36.00	0.778
7.00	5.50	5.33	49.00	0.845
8.00	6.00	5.67	64.00	0.903
9.00	6.50	6.00	81.00	0.954
10.00	7.00	6.33	100.00	1.000
11.00	7.50	6.67	121.00	1.041
12.00	8.00	7.00	144.00	1.079
13.00	8.50	7.33	169.00	1.114
14.00	9.00	7.67	196.00	1.146
15.00	9.50	8.00	225.00	1.176
16.00	10.00	8.33	256.00	1.204

where you shoved the book to the edge of the desk. These lines would be vectors. Vector addition is a little harder, but it is based upon the same principle. Imagine you and your roommate giving a book a shove in different directions by flicking it simultaneously with your fingers. The resulting path of the book would be the addition of two vectors, the magnitude and direction of which would result from where you and your roommate aimed and how hard you both flicked.

Diagrams that illustrate how things work are just as common in the natural sciences. Examine these in every detail. Be sure to compare the labels with the information in the caption or legend for the illustration, or with the description in the text. Even photographs can be important in scientific texts, particularly in biology. Whatever you do, treat all the material in a scientific text as worthy of study. It is a good idea to sketch out diagrams yourself, just to make sure you haven't missed

something. This is particularly important in chemistry and biology, in which a series of reactions may be diagramed. Whether a diagram is one provided in the text or one you draw yourself, it should help you conceptualize and remember essential information such as the electronic configuration of sodium or the parts of a flower.

Tables. Students sometimes skip tables because they find them dull, detailed, and hard to read. Don't. The information that is in a table is important. At the very least make sure you understand *the principle by which the table is organized.* Sometimes tables say the same thing that a graph says. Instead of the *x*- and *y*-axes, you will find numbers listed in parallel columns corresponding to the *x*- and *y*-variables. Each *x*-value corresponds to the *y*-value opposite it. On this page you will find an exercise in reading simple numerical tables. Make sure that you understand how to read this table. If

Converting to the Metric System

Here are the metric equivalents of some of the more common British units.

1 inch	= 2.5400 centimeters	1 centimeter	= 0.3937 inch
1 foot	= 0.3048 meter	1 meter	= 3.2808 feet
1 yard	= 0.9144 meter	1 meter	= 1.0936 yards
1 mile	= 1.6093 kilometers	1 kilometer	= 0.6214 mile
1 quart	= 0.9464 liter	1 liter	= 1.0567 quarts
1 gallon	= 3.7854 liters	1 liter	= 0.2642 gallon
1 ounce	= 28.3495 grams	1 gram	= 0.0353 ounce
1 pound	= 0.4536 kilogram	1 kilogram	= 2.2046 pounds

you can't follow it, you will have trouble with almost any course in science.

Sometimes it helps to translate part or all of a table into a graph. Usually the equation relating the various parts of a table will not be given (we have listed the equations in the table on page 115), but you can visualize at a glance what the relationship between x and y looks like by plotting on graph paper a point for every pair of x- and y-values in the table. If you connect the points together you can get a geometrical picture of the relation. Often you will be required to do just that with the results from laboratory experiments. Your results will consist of x- and y-values, which you will first list in a table and then use to construct a graph. Sometimes you will be asked to draw a "smooth" curve through the points. Because there are random errors in collecting experimental data, the pairs of x- and y-values won't exactly correspond to the "true" mathematical relation that connects the points. There are various sophisticated ways of making smooth curves, but in elementary courses you will usually only be required to eyeball the relation.

The Metric System

If you take any course in the sciences, you will have to forget about feet, yards, quarts, and gallons and begin to think in terms of centimeters, liters, and grams. The United States is one of the few places left in the world that does not consistently use the metric system. Science, however, is an international enterprise, and American scientists, like all others, present their results in metric measures.

Even though the metric system may be unfamiliar to you, once you work with it, you will see its advantages. If you have a board that is two feet and seven inches and another one that is three feet and nine inches, and you want to know how long they would be together you would have to add the feet and inches separately and then convert the sixteen inches to one additional foot with four inches left over.

The trouble is that we do our arithmetic in a decimal system, and feet come in units of twelve inches (while yards come in units of three feet). Pounds come in units of sixteen ounces and gallons in units of four quarts. So there is no order to the system at all. The metric system is entirely in decimal units. One hundred centimeters make a meter, and there are ten millimeters to a centimeter. A kilometer is 1000 meters. The result is that you can convert from meters to kilometers, or from meters to millimeters, just by moving a decimal point.

Your problem is to learn to think in these units rather than in the familiar feet, yards, ounces, and pounds. Taking a course in science will help you to do this, and since the United States is more or less committed to making the metric system official in the future, you will have to learn to think metrically eventually anyway. Just having the experience of expressing results in the metric system will make it easier for you. Initially, you may want some help from the British system (as our system is generally called). It is like learning a foreign language; you go through an initial period of translating. But eventually you begin to think in metric terms. We have provided a conversion table for you on page 116, and this may help you in the translation process. Some hand-held calculators intended for scientific or engineering work contain keys for making British-to-metric conversions.

A CONCLUDING WORD

We have touched on only the most elementary aspects of science. In fact, except for tips on how to read texts and how to study for exams, there is probably nothing here that a lot of tenth graders who have had a little science and math do not know. Yet some of you who are good college material will be puzzled by what you read here. If you don't understand, don't let it go by. Don't put it down to being "dumb in math" or "having no head for science." You have just missed out on something.

Some of you may have been puzzled by so elementary a matter as graphs discussed a few pages back. That may be because no one ever showed you how to relate the numbers on the axes (you may not even know what an axis is) to the points and lines on the graph. Don't take it lying down. You don't *need to be* illiterate in science and math. If necessary, get someone to help you. Many colleges and universities run special remedial programs in math. If you are deficient and your institution has such programs, the sooner you take advantage of them the better.

Many students get anxious about math because it seems to go so fast and so much goes over their heads. Once again, being anxious about math is not necessary. It is something you can get over if you go about it in the right way. Once again, many colleges run math anxiety clinics, the purpose of which is not so much to cram a lot of mathematics into you as it is to get you to think about mathematics in a relaxed way. Math anxiety is something that is curable, and given the importance of mathematics, it is something you ought to work at to get over.

10
GETTING HELP

We have tried to show you how to become a better student by improving your classroom skills and learning how to study textbooks and write papers more effectively. There are other resources available to you, some of which may be recommended by your instructors and some of which you will have to seek out for yourself. Furthermore, there are some things you can do to improve the quality of your life in college, which is usually an important ingredient in getting the most out of your college years.

USING STUDY AIDS EFFECTIVELY

Workbooks and Study Guides

Workbooks and study guides, often combined, sometimes go along with textbooks assigned in college courses. They usually include special projects and exercises which illustrate and explain the textbook, along with review questions and self-test items that provide practice for examinations.

Some instructors will require the workbook; others may recommend it but not require it. Even if your instructor doesn't mention a workbook at all, you would do well to find out if one does accompany the textbook. Usually, the preface to the text will tell you whether or not there is a workbook or study guide. If you can find one, look at the workbook to see if it will be useful to you. Almost all workbooks are of some value, and some will give you a lot of help.

Outside Readings

Textbooks usually make up most of the reading for introductory courses. In advanced courses and in certain introductory courses, instructors assign outside readings or recommend them.

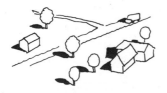

Many, maybe most, students don't bother with these outside readings, even when they are required. They are not likely to be the students who earn top grades, but students who are satisfied just to get by. That is too bad, because outside readings give depth to one's education. For one thing, they will help you better understand the textbook, and if there is no textbook, they are absolutely essential. For another, they give you a different perspective on the subject. Conscientious instructors, who know that everyone has some biases, often assign outside readings which take a different point of view. In the humanities, outside readings provide the real essentials. To read about Plato in a textbook on the history of philosophy is only an introduction to Plato himself. Finally, outside readings can make study more satisfying and arouse your curiosity. Often it is the outside readings that spark a deep interest in the subject matter. They may even lead you to a major.

Journals and periodicals of all kinds provide another perspective for your education. Aside from technical journals that probably will interest you only if you yourself are involved in research in a particular field, there are various journals and newspapers that provide everyone with background for a good education. Have you ever looked at *The Wall Street Journal*? Or *Business Week*? There are a whole host of periodicals which appeal to the educated mind. Among them are *Scientific American, American Scientist, The Economist, Harpers, The Atlantic Monthly*, and a pack of journals of opinion, which, whether you agree with them or not, provide educated and interesting reading. These include such diverse journals as *The New York Review of Books* and *The American Spectator*.

Find the general periodical room of your library and look through what it has to offer. Even a modest library will provide an astounding range of features of modern intellectual life. Once again, it is the good students who make use of such facilities. You could argue that they do so because they are interested in such things, but if you don't know about them, how can you become interested?

Films and TV Instruction

Films and videotapes are often used as teaching aids. When they are well done they combine the best features of an instructor's explanation with the visual presentation of things that cannot be brought into the classroom in any other way.

Such films and tapes are often entertaining, and therein lies a problem. Students sit back and relax when a film is being shown. Or worse, if the film is boring, they go to sleep. But if the film is doing its job, it has to be studied as carefully as a textbook or class notes. Pay attention to what the instructor says about the film. Take notes if you can or if it is appropriate; sometimes instructors will ask you not to take notes but just pay attention to what you are seeing. In any case, recite to yourself the important points the film makes. Look for the main ideas. Because a film moves fast, it is important that you jot down all the main points as soon as the film is over, or you will forget them.

At many colleges and universities, segments of courses and sometimes entire courses are videotaped and shown on closed-circuit TV. You may not like the idea, because TV is an impersonal teacher. But the kinds of things taught on TV would be impersonally taught in a big lecture anyway. And compared with the conventional lecture, TV has some advantages. Demonstrations are clearer, and TV tapes are usually very well prepared. The presentation usually is better organized than the typical lecture. If the tape is shown in a discussion section, the graduate assistant or the section instructor will be there, so you can ask questions. Do so.

There is little difference between what you do in a course taught by TV and in a conventional one. You do need to remember that TV courses, like films, generally move faster than conventional lectures. Be ready to take notes rapidly and carefully. Because TV lessons are generally well organized, however, it will probably be easier to take notes in outline form.

Programmed Texts and Self-Paced Courses

Programmed learning was developed before the widespread use of computers, but nowadays programmed instruction is heavily dependent upon computers and in particular upon interactive programs in which the computer can respond in appropriate ways to the kinds of answers the student gives. Even given the close relation between computer-based instruction and programmed learning, programmed textbooks are available for nearly all the basic courses in college. Workbooks in particular tend to be in the programmed mode.

What is the programmed mode? Programmed instruction is a way of getting you to work in small, carefully planned steps in which you test yourself regularly to make sure not just that you are making progress but that you understand everything that has gone before.

There are whole courses designed around programmed instruction in which you are self-paced. The great advantage of such courses is that you can do as much or as little as you want to in a given time. In self-paced courses you can do a whole semester's work in a couple of weeks.

The other advantages of programmed instruction are (1) that it provides you with immediate testing and the opportunity for correction, and (2) that it allows you to go at a pace suited to your own temperament and level of preparation. As you might suppose, programmed instruction in general is best suited to situations in which you have to learn how to do something. In that case, working through steps one by one enables you to make sure that you understand everything. In fact, most instruction disks designed to tell you how to operate a particular computer are designed this way. Some programs (including those to tell you how to operate your computer) are designed to be "error-free"; that is to say, the material is broken down into such small steps that you almost never get a question or some instruction wrong.

The disadvantage of programmed learning is that many students find such error-free or near error-free programs to be boring and frustrating. They want to go faster. If you have this reaction to programmed instruction, we suggest that you distribute your time at the program as much as possible. Spend twenty or thirty minutes on a fair-sized segment of the program, rest briefly, review the segment, take another rest, and then turn to something else. After you have studied another subject, come back to your program and tackle another segment. This gives you an opportunity to check on how much you remember, for if you begin where you left off and you start making a lot of mistakes, you know that you have to review the earlier segment.

If you are having trouble with some course that requires you to learn a lot of facts or how to do various things, you might well want to consider shopping around for an auxiliary programmed text to help you out. Then, too, you will find that many such courses are now being computer-based. Increasingly courses in applied statistics, for example, are based on interactive computer programs.

Test Files

On any campus you will find test files all over the place. Sororities, fraternities, dormitories, and student cooperatives all keep files containing old examinations and often old course outlines, notes, and even term papers. Some colleges and individual instructors arrange for files of old exams to be placed on reserve in the library so that they will be available to anybody who wants them.

How useful are these files? Not as much as students think. In fact, they can be a source of trouble if they are used as a substitute for good work habits. But for certain courses, you may want to take a look at them. Old tests can give you an idea of what a given professor's exams are like. Or you can see how someone else organized the course, and you can see what some other students thought important enough to write down. Old term papers with good grades can help you get ideas for papers and tell you how they should be written.

Beyond these uses, however, test files are of little value. Most professors change their courses, the reading assignments, and their lectures every year. Instructors who use objective questions usually draw these from a large pool of questions so that only a small percentage will be the same for any two exams. Then too, sometimes you *don't know* whether your instructor is the same one who wrote the exams on file. Using files of old exams to predict what will happen on an upcoming exam is risky. It can mislead you into not studying something you may need to know.

Don't even consider using old course notes and outlines as a substitute for class attendance. If you do, you will never know what has changed. And old notes vary in quality. You could be depending on inferior material.

But, the worst thing about old files is that they encourage poor study habits. Their availability may tempt some people to turn in someone else's work as their own. Plagiarism is a serious offense in college, and in some schools you could easily be dismissed if you are caught using someone else's work.

That brings us to the subject of commercially sold term papers. Aside from the dishonesty of passing off someone else's work as your own, there can be unfortunate consequences to buying term papers. It is actually illegal to do so in some states. Professors are not as unworldly as they sometimes seem; commercial papers are easy to detect. But most of all, you are cheating mainly yourself by using them. The things you came to college for—to learn to think, to analyze ideas critically, and to learn how to express your own ideas—are lost if someone else does your work for you.

GETTING HELP FROM SPECIAL SOURCES

There are times when everyone needs help from other people. In college, such help is routine—academic advising, for example. Some of it is there for students who have particular difficulties. Every college and university provides you with special help if you need it. The various services that exist for your benefit often mean the difference between academic success and failure, not to mention the difference between being miserable and being happy.

Academic Advising

Every school has its own system for helping students to choose courses, to decide on a major, to understand what they may and may not do under college rules. In most places, every student is assigned a faculty advisor. The advisor's duty is to help the student in all matters academic. How the relationship works out in practice depends upon both you and your advisor.

First of all, do for yourself all that you can do. Read the catalog and the various books and handouts provided for students. Consult the schedule. Do the arithmetic to determine how many credits you will need to complete each semester. When you have worked out a tentative schedule and thought about any questions you have, see your advisor. Remember that the advisor's job is to advise, not to make your decisions for you. Your advisor can give you information you can't get yourself, and he or she can give you opinions,

usually based on a lot of experience. But the choices are yours.

If you don't get along well with your advisor, or he or she doesn't take the job seriously, consult an academic dean. In most colleges and universities, the dean's office coordinates faculty advising, and in some institutions the dean's office itself bears the sole responsibility for advising. In that case there is usually a large and well-informed staff to do it.

Many students don't like to go to the dean about their academic problems. But remember, the whole purpose of a dean's office is to help students. At some small colleges you will probably get to know the dean personally. At large universities, there is usually a staff of associate and assistant deans whose primary job is to be completely accessible to students. Don't be bashful. If you don't like your particular dean, don't hesitate to ask for another one.

The dean's office is the best source for information about college rules and regulations. If you are not sure about such things as the number of credits required for graduation, the number of pass/fail courses you can take, distributional requirements, and other such matters, go to the dean's office. Don't rely on the student grapevine for answers to questions about policy. At the very least, if you consult an official source, that will be a matter of record, and if you receive the wrong advice you may be able to absolve yourself.

Suppose you are working hard in one of your courses, but you just can't seem to master the material. What do you do?

The first thing is to face your problem as soon as possible. Don't drift along hoping that things will take care of themselves. Don't wait for an F on the midterm to tell you what you probably knew all along. As soon as you sense difficulties ask yourself the following questions: "Am I adequately prepared for this course? Do other students have a background which I lack? Is there some one thing that gives me trouble? Do I understand the terminology? Do I have trouble doing calculations, problems, or lab work? Am I swamped by the reading?"

The next step is to decide whether you can do something about your problem or whether you must think about dropping the course. Here you need advice. Confer with the instructor, or if you are uncomfortable about doing that, talk to your dean. You may have gotten yourself into a course that is too advanced for you. This happens often in foreign languages or mathematics which you started in high school or in another institution. Or you may have signed up for an advanced course without realizing that you lacked the background.

If you seek help early enough you can either improve your work or you can drop the course. If you do it early enough you may be able to rearrange your program. It is not a good idea, however, to drop a course impulsively and without seeking the advice of your instructor, faculty advisor, or dean. This is particularly true if the course is a required one. Most colleges ask that a student get approval from both the instructor and the advisor in order to drop a course, just to ensure that the student is taking a wise action.

Suppose that you have waited too long to drop the course without some kind of penalty. It is still not too late to confer with the instructor to see what you can do to retrieve the situation. If you're really interested in improving, instructors are almost always willing to show you what you have done wrong on an exam or a paper and what you should have done. Of course, you may not be able to do enough to avoid failing the course. Even so, you may have learned something about how to avoid similar difficulties in the future. A grade of F does not mean that you are a failure as a student. In fact, regard it as a kind of warning signal.

Counseling Services

Personal problems often get in the way of academic work. If you have personal worries or difficulties that make it hard for you to work, you ought to be able to tell these problems to your advisor or academic dean and look for help and guidance. Often, just stating your problem to someone helps, because doing so points the way to a solution. Or your advisor may be able to offer you a word of wisdom. If, however, you have long-standing problems or problems that are too personal, the chances are that your faculty advisor or dean will have neither the time nor the background to deal with them. In that case, he or she would probably refer you to the counseling center or to a qualified professional counselor in the community.

Your counseling services are especially prepared to deal with you. Conflict with parents, poor self-esteem, feelings of insecurity, interpersonal problems, sexual problems, and an inability to concentrate are examples of the sort of things counselors deal with every day.

If one of these problems or one like it bothers you, you are fairly typical. Most people can live through these problems on their own, but if you feel that you can't, seek help.

Medical Services

The college years are not the healthiest years of a person's life. Poor eating habits, insufficient sleep, crowded and badly ventilated classrooms all contribute to a lowered resistance to infection. Minor respiratory diseases and stomach complaints are endemic on campus. Then there is mononucleosis. And, of course, there are sexually transmitted diseases from herpes on up. If you even *suspect* that you have one of these, make it your first priority to consult your medical services about it.

Even commuter colleges have some sort of student health service. These are usually prepared to deal with acute and not too serious illnesses. Any complaint that requires extensive diagnostic testing or hospitalization is going to be referred to a local physician or hospital. But don't let fear of such a referral lead you to postpone consultation with medical services.

Not only are sexually transmitted diseases a problem, but for women students, the fear of pregnancy is ever present. College students, or those planning to be, presumably know all there is to know about contraception. But that does not prevent many of them from getting into trouble. Prevention is the name of the game, even if it means abstinence. If you are pregnant, you have to deal with the problem with someone. If you find it difficult or impossible to approach your parents, once again the college's medical services may help. Abortion is about the worst method of birth control you can imagine, because it is expensive, emotionally draining, and potentially physically dangerous. But you need to consider your options within the framework of your and your family's beliefs. Whatever you do to seek counseling, remember that the ultimate decision is yours.

Tutorial and Remedial Services

If you are having trouble with a particular course, you can quite likely find someone to tutor you. Many colleges and universities maintain special tutorial referral services staffed by advanced undergraduates and/or graduate students. Tutoring is usually available in the harder basic subjects such as chemistry, biology, physics, mathematics, and foreign languages.

Some instructors have extra sessions for students who are having trouble with something in their courses. These sessions are usually held in the evening or late afternoon. Too often, the students who turn up are those who least need it. But remember, extra sessions are meant for students who *think* they are in trouble. If you find work in some course too difficult, be sure you go to every extra-help session that is offered, even if you have to give up something else to do it.

Students often study in joint sessions, particularly for exams. This is useful if it is done properly. You can learn from other students as well as give something of your own. Before you go into a review session with other students, you should have studied the material thoroughly; don't expect other students to teach you. When the group first meets, it should plan what to do and set up an agenda. Each student can take a turn at summarizing important points. Don't get bogged down arguing about trivial points. Anything new that a student says ought to be checked for accuracy. The best things about group studying are that it gives you a chance at oral recitation, and it allows students to correct one another's mistakes.

If you don't understand something in a course and you know that another student does understand that point, ask her or him to explain it to you. If, on the other hand, someone asks you for help on a point, take the time to go over it with him or her. Besides being a friendly thing to do, it will help you because it gives you a chance to recite what you know. There is no better way to learn something than to teach it to someone else.

Open enrollment is common at most community colleges, and there are a fair number of city and state universities that admit students who are capable of doing college work but who lack skill in reading, writing, and mathematics. Most of these schools provide a full range of remedial services, sometimes offered through noncredit courses in basic mathematics and English, and sometimes through remedial centers in which students can get personal tutoring.

Joe was a student who grew up as one of seven children in a poor family. His father, who had been an unskilled worker, died when Joe was ten. Joe liked school and did well, but when he reached the eighth grade, he was advised by the school counselor to enter a vocational program in high school. A college preparatory program wasn't even a possibility. Joe did make it through high school, and he got a job as a mechanic in a neighborhood garage after he graduated. He was good at his work, and one day one of his customers said, "Joe, you're smart; you ought to be an engineer or something."

This casual remark set him to thinking. He went to the public library, and, with the help of the librarian, found some books and pamphlets about various careers in engineering. He found out about things he had never dreamed of. The librarian suggested that Joe talk to someone at the local community college. The upshot was that two years after his high school graduation, Joe entered the college as a part-time student.

He was insecure, and the work was much harder and more theoretical than he had imagined it would be. Fortunately, he was in a good place; his college was equipped to meet his needs. He took three remedial courses during his first year: one in mathematics, one in reading, and one in composition. During his second year he made an A and B in chemistry and a B in calculus. He got enough financial aid to let him attend full time. At the end of his third year at the community college, he applied for admission to the school of engineering at the state university. He was accepted.

But his troubles only began. He was to be away from home for the first time, and he had to borrow money to make a go of it. He was in a far more cosmopolitan environment than he had ever been before. He had lived his entire life in a little community in which all the parents were either immigrants or first-generation Americans and in which nearly everybody his age went into blue-collar jobs when they got out of high school (if they didn't drop out). What is more, he was taking professional courses for the first time, and they nearly floored him.

He brought his problems to his advisor, who suggested that Joe take advantage of a new tutorial program that the school of engineering had set up. The result was that his first-semester grades were okay, and his second-semester grades were good.

Two years later, he received his bachelor's degree in electrical engineering.

A lot of students have histories like Joe's. Where remedial help is available, many people who otherwise could not make it manage to correct the deficiencies of their early education.

Career Counseling

If, like Joe, you are in a school of engineering, you have already made a tentative decision about what you want to do. Students in liberal arts, on the other hand, may have only a vague idea about what they want to do. They panic in their senior year: "What am I going to do, work at MacDonald's?"

Even students who enter college thinking that they know what they want to do, change their minds. Premedical students decide that medicine isn't really for them. A student who enters college with a vague plan to apply to law school may discover that he or she really likes sociology or psychology—and that opens up a whole range of occupations which that student may not have known about. Such uncertainty and change are natural and to be expected. In college you are learning new things about the world, and you should not be surprised to find that you have changed your mind or discovered something new.

Most colleges and universities maintain an office concerned with career planning and placement. Freshmen who have no idea how to focus their interests in order to choose a major are just as much the concern of such an office as seniors who know what they want to do but need to find a job to do it. The former need to assess abilities, interests, values, priorities, and goals; the latter need to know how to prepare resumes and how to be interviewed. Students who intend to go on to graduate or professional schools need to know what the admission requirements are and how to apply.

One of the most valuable services an office of career planning and placement can offer is to keep a file for you in which you can place letters of recommendation from professors or deans. Your professors will come and go. Some will retire, and some will move on to other places, or have a year in Afghanistan just when you need them. Go to your office of career planning and placement (or whatever it is called) and set up a file. Get the professors who know you best to write letters for that file. Five, ten, or even twenty years from now you may be very grateful.

If you are really panicked about life after college, you will want to go to your office of career and placement as soon as possible. The people there are in the business of helping you determine what your interests and abilities are. You may not know that of all students who enter college, only little more than half will finish with a bachelor's degree within five years. Although there are many careers open to people without college degrees, there are many more available to college graduates. If you really want to enter an occupation requiring a degree and you are doing only marginal work, you will need to do something, even if it is dropping out for the time being. The average age of college students has been rising for a decade. In any event, keep your options open, and one of the ways of doing that is to leave college for a while so that you can sort out your priorities.

If you decide on a college program that doesn't prepare you for what you eventually want to do, you can always get yourself qualified if your original college record is strong enough. Jill's and Karen's cases illustrate that.

Jill, a good student, entered her state university with the idea of becoming a doctor. She took the basic premed chemistry course in her freshman year, and though she did well enough in it, she didn't really like it. She discovered the intellectual excitement of studying philosophy, and she enjoyed her literature and history courses. She finally decided to leave the sciences and concentrate on the humanities with a major in history.

Jill assumed that after graduation she would probably go to law school because she had heard that law schools had no specific course requirements other than a background in the liberal arts, high grades, and good LSAT scores. When she reached her senior year, however, she knew that she really didn't want to go to law school. She graduated with high honors, took a civil service exam, and got a job in the planning office of the suburban county where she had grown up. The job grabbed her, and after two years, she applied for graduate work in architecture. She had a talent for it, and in the summers she works in a prestigious firm of city planners. When she gets through her schooling in architecture, she will have a job in the firm and, what is more important, an occupation she really likes.

Karen is a *magna cum laude* graduate of one of New England's best colleges with a major in English. Unsure of what she wanted to do, she worked for three years as a sales clerk and came to the conclusion that she really wanted something stable that would provide her with a good income. She enrolled in an accounting course at night at a local university. She completed the program in accounting, passed the CPA exam, and is currently a member of the largest accounting firm in her home town. She likes her job. It challenges her, and she knows that there are chances for professional advancement.

From medicine to architecture and city planning, from literature to accounting. A lot of people do find themselves. So don't be discouraged if you don't really know what you want to do in life (much less in your freshman year!). Many students make poor beginnings but end up on top. Ken was a mediocre high school student. He spent a year and a half at a local community college with his work going from bad to worse. Finally he flunked out. He was drafted and sent to Vietnam (this was a long time ago). During the three years Ken spent in the army, much of it in combat service, his attitude toward things changed and his goals became clearer. As soon as he was discharged he enrolled once again in the community college (community colleges are especially good for that kind of flexibility). He did honors work in the liberal arts transfer program and transferred to a local university as a mathematics major. The last we heard of him he was a second-year student in one of the country's best law schools. We presume he's now in legal practice.

The point is this: If you don't yet know what you want to do or if you think that your past performance blew your chances of ever doing what you want to do, there is no need to be discouraged. You can make a choice later on; just don't drift.

Transfer Student Services

Today's college students are much more likely than students of even a decade ago to take their degree from a different institution than the one they entered. They transfer for a variety of reasons. Sometimes it is a personal matter, and sometimes students just don't like where they are. If you are in a community or two-year college and you want to go on, you have no choice. Whatever the reason, you need to think even harder about where to go the second time than you thought about the first.

Students who know why they are transferring and who know what to expect at the new institution do well. A few students who transfer, however, are not prepared for the adjustment they have to make. Often transferring means facing severer academic standards in a more competitive atmosphere. Even if it doesn't, just being in a new place with new customs and rules can spell trouble. It is not at all unusual for transfer students to see their grade point averages fall in their first semester at the new institution. The student who transfers from a small college to a large university has to face bigger classes and an impersonal atmosphere. Transfer students have to make new friends and form new associations. This is not always easy to do if you are transferring into a large university, especially if you don't live in a dormitory or residence hall. Let's face it, if you are a transfer student, most of your classmates will have gotten accustomed to the place and some of them probably even know one another, even if it is Enormous State University.

Most colleges and universities recognize the problems transfer students face and provide support services. There is usually a special orientation program for new transfer that includes social gatherings along with academic orientation. Transfer students can get to know one another and become acquainted with student government officers.

Some schools arrange for student volunteers to meet individually with transfer students and to be available on a friend-to-friend basis to answer questions and provide introductions.

If you are or will be a new transfer student, take advantage of all the programs available to make your adjustment easier and faster. Don't, however, expect everything to be done for you. Take the initiative. Confer with your faculty advisor, who, chances are, has been specially selected to deal with transfer students.

If you have real problems, the worst thing you can do is to sit alone and feel sorry for yourself. Get help. And remember that although many transfer students do have trouble, it is usually temporary. Transfer students, by and large, do as well as students who started at the institution. One of us knew a student who transferred from a community college to a large state university in his junior year. By his senior year he was president of the student body.

Older Students in College

There was a time when nearly everybody in college was between seventeen and twenty-two years of age. Beginning with the college generation after World War II, when older veterans returned to their studies, the number of older people entering college for the first time and returning to complete a degree after many years has increased steadily. A recent survey placed the average age of college students at thirty plus.

If you are an older student you have one big advantage over your younger fellow students—maturity. Chances are you know who you are and where you're going. A lot of problems that younger people have to deal with you have already solved. This leaves you free to apply your energy to what college is all about—the life of the intellect. It makes it possible for you to enjoy learning in a way that younger people cannot always manage.

Some older people hesitate to return to school because they think that they have forgotten their academic skills, and they are afraid they won't be able to compete with sharp younger minds. That just isn't so. The evidence suggests that older students make better grades than their younger colleagues—even when they have to hold down jobs or have small children at home.

Flora Wilson had two years at a top women's college thirty years ago. She married at the end of her second year, and she settled into being a full-time homemaker, caring for four children. Through PTA activities she got interested in community affairs. By the time her last child was in high school, she was a respected civic leader with an important role in local and state politics. Despite her success, she felt self-conscious about her lack of a college degree. After a lot of thought and a good deal of uncertainty and with plenty of encouragement from her family and friends, she returned to college. Although she was well into her fifties, she was accepted by a very strong local university, and she was able to get nearly all of her earlier credits transferred. She worked a little harder at first than she needed to, but she enjoyed

it, and she got to know a lot of young people, some of whom came to visit at her house regularly. When she graduated after two years, she promptly got a job on the staff of an important local politician, and she is thoroughly engrossed in her work.

When John Kovacks attended college in the 1950s, he hadn't been terribly interested in academic work. His grades were mediocre. After two years he dropped out and went to work in a bank. A renewed religious commitment led him to question what he was doing. He thought he would like to be a social worker, an occupation that would let him work with people who needed help. He was married and had two teenage sons to support. Nevertheless, by relying on his wife's income as a teacher, by cutting out luxuries, and by taking a second mortgage on his house, Mr. Kovacks got through two more years of college and a two-year program in a school of social work for an MSW. He is now doing family counseling for a social agency, and he feels happier and more useful than he has ever felt before.

You don't have to want to change occupations to go back. Frank Seidman had two years at the local university—one of the strongest in the nation. After the war he entered the brokerage business and was both prosperous and happy. But he wanted a college degree. He went back to the evening division of the university and got his degree in the same year that his daughter went off to college. An acquaintance of his, a Harvard graduate, president of a bank, and a member of the board of trustees of Frank's university, went back at the same time to get a master's degree in the evening division.

Betty Little got married before she even finished high school. She and her husband had three children. Somehow, she managed to work part-time and take care of the children while her husband finished his education. When he got his bachelor's degree he said, "Betty, now it's your turn." She made up her high school deficiencies and enrolled in a nearby university as a freshman. She was twenty-eight with three children under ten. It wasn't easy for her; the demands on her time were horrendous. But she was well organized, and above all she liked being in college. As soon as she gets her degree, her husband will start work on a Ph.D. in education. She is already thinking about going back for her own graduate education.

These instances are typical of the experiences of older students. Problems? You bet. Insurmountable problems? Sometimes, but not often. More and more colleges and universities recognize the needs of older students. Some private colleges have both provided a useful service and rejuvenated themselves by specializing in the admission of older, part-time students. Women's colleges have been the leaders in this enterprise, because it is women who more often than men defer the completion of their education.

The scheduling needs of older students are often complex. They usually need more help in this respect than younger students, though they don't need advice and counseling as much. If you are an older student returning to college, be sure you know how to find someone who can help you solve your problems and bend the bureaucratic rules.

MAKING A GOOD PERSONAL ADJUSTMENT

The college years are a major transitional period in a person's life. As students make new academic and personal adjustments, they are aware that in a short time they will be on their own. The world outside of the academic walls can seem threatening. Getting that first job after graduation, finding a place to live, making all sorts of decisions that will affect their professional and personal lives—there is no way of running out of things to worry about.

Though you will probably love your college years and look back on them with nostalgia, you may also find the period to be full of stress. There is no simple formula for getting you through the adjustment problems you may have, but there are some good principles, most of them common sense, that may help you.

1. Be realistic. Well-adjusted people are realistic about most things. They know what they want, they set reasonable goals for themselves, and they know how to avoid trouble. Find out what you can reasonably expect to achieve and adjust your efforts and goals accordingly. Don't underestimate yourself. If you make mediocre grades, find out why. Are you bored? Do you lack the right background? Are you studying the wrong things?

Don't overestimate yourself either. For example, you might want to question your goal of becoming a doctor if you can't hack chemistry and your work habits are less than excellent. You'd also want to think about how much money a medical education is going to cost. The point is be realistic and know yourself and your circumstances. Take Forrest, for example:

When Forrest was accepted at a prestigious university, he intended to be premed, and he wanted to do all the extracurricular things. Soon after he entered, he joined the local symphony orchestra and he got into student politics. But he didn't like his studies; he didn't work hard enough academically to meet his ambitions. He dropped out of school, became an original jazz musician (his classical background helped out), and now, in his mid-twenties, he is in a successful career with his own band. Some day he may want to come back to school, but probably not in the premed curriculum.

Face your personal problems as objectively as you can. Sometimes your friends can be more objective about you than you can be yourself, but you may put them on the spot. They may not want to hurt your feelings. But it is better to talk to your friends about something that is bothering you than to keep it to yourself. An advisor or counselor can help. Beyond that, most campuses abound with groups that offer peer counseling about special problems, such as sex or drugs. A peer counselor is a responsible fellow student who can be more objective about your problems than you or your friends.

2. Accept anxiety. Anxiety is the natural result of fear-provoking situations. It can never be completely eliminated. Most of the things we fear, however, don't turn out to be as bad as we had imagined them to be, and anxiety dissipates. So accept anxiety and deal as best you can with the unpredictable, difficult, or threatening situation you are in.

Sometimes, however, anxiety becomes unreasonable. If that happens to you, you should be concerned. If you experience *free-floating anxiety*, that is to say, a feeling of dread that doesn't attach itself to any one particular thing but which seems to invade the whole of your life, then you need to do something about it. And a refuge in drugs, alcohol, inaction, or aimless watching of TV all day won't help.

3. *Don't be defensive.* All of us have conscious or unconscious ways of dealing with anxiety. Some of these are realistic and helpful. When you are anxious about an examination, you study for it. If you are prepared, you will feel less anxious. And if you do well, you won't be so anxious the next time. Suppose you do badly. You are now more anxious than ever, and you can't find any realistic way of doing something about it.

When we are anxious and we have no obvious way to do something about it, we try to fool ourselves in various ways. You might say, for example, that the exam you failed was unfair, that the instructor misled you about what to prepare for. This takes the blame away from you and externalizes it.

There are a number of ways of externalizing things as a defense against anxiety. Psychologists call these defense mechanisms, for what they do is defend our egos from anxiety, fear of failure, and feelings of personal inadequacy. Defense mechanisms are often harmless and convenient ways of making us feel better about the bad things that happen to us. But if they become a substitute for working to eliminate the source of our troubles and are used to sidestep persistent and severe problems, they can be a source of real trouble. Finally, our defenses have a way of breaking down under severe stress, with the result that a person is suddenly flooded with feelings of anxiety or depression. These feelings are not only uncomfortable, but they can totally incapacitate a person.

4. *Understand what you want and set goals.* Defenses are sometimes ways of fooling yourself about your own motives. Here, you need to face the questions: "What is it I really want? Am I willing to work to achieve what I want?" When your grades are poor, it is easy to blame everyone but yourself—your instructor, a bad cold, family problems, etc. But an honest answer to the question "What do I really want?" might lead you to see things differently. You might see that while, sure, you want good grades, you really *don't* want to work to achieve them. It's hard to be the sparkling center of the social life of your sorority or fraternity and at the same time make the grades to get you into the Harvard Law School. We can't have everything we want, and rather than let circumstances decide what you get, decide for yourself.

5. *Alter goals appropriately.* If you understand your motives well enough, one of the things you can do is alter your goals when this becomes necessary. Sometimes our goals come not from ourselves but from other people. Fred, for example, came to college with the idea of being a doctor, only to be frustrated by his lack of interest in premedical courses. In the middle of his sophomore year, his anxiety about the difficulties he experienced in chemistry reached the acute state. He sought help at the counseling center, where, after a few sessions, he acknowledged that medicine was a goal his family had set for him and that being a doctor was not what he really wanted for himself. He realized that his poor performance in premed courses was in part a rebellion against parental pressure. Though he had to face a row with his parents, he set his career goals toward things that were closer to his own interests and abilities.

6. *Learn to postpone satisfactions.* When two motives conflict, one way to resolve the conflict is to postpone the satisfaction of one of them. This is a way of taking control of your own life rather than letting circumstances and other people control it for you. Most college students know that, but sometimes they don't practice it on a daily basis. If you are going to participate in student government, or work on the student paper, you will have to postpone something to make the time. Or maybe it's the other way around. You may have to drop off the student paper because it takes too much time from something else. The point is, examine your options and choose one. If you don't, circumstances may choose something worse for you.

7. *Keep busy.* Keeping occupied with useful things is another mark of the well-adjusted person. This doesn't mean you should forever be running around frantically doing things; what it means is doing things so that you have some sense of satisfaction from accomplishment. It also may mean doing enough to keep yourself from ruminating on your troubles, or from resorting to alcohol or drugs. Work is not a cure for emotional problems, but it often keeps us from making those problems worse, and in the long run it might provide some deep satisfaction.

All this may sound a little old-fashioned in an age in which we are supposed to be free to do what we want to. But the idea that we are completely free to do whatever is in our power is a delusion. The minute we do one thing, we make it impossible to do something else. If you are going to master organic chemistry, you can't spend every evening getting mellow on alcohol or marijuana. And if you don't recognize your own real self—your goals, aspirations, prejudices, sexual feelings, emotions, abilities—you will end up being victimized by your ignorance.

If you are really at sea about yourself, insecure, or dependent upon drugs or alcohol, reading this or any other book won't help you very much. You need to explore your problems with the kind of give-and-take that occurs in a personal or group counseling situation. It doesn't matter so much what the setting is—health services, a psychological clinic, your physician's office, or the chaplain's office—as it does that you recognize you have a problem you can't solve on your own.

College isn't training for life; it is life. This book has been mostly about coping with the intellectual demands of college because these are the central purposes of college. You can't meet those demands unless you have both the skills to apply them and the personal adjustment to free you to do so.

Provisional Working Schedule

Time \ Day	Monday	Tuesday	Wednesday	Thursday	Friday	Saturday	Sunday
7:00							
8:00							
8:30							
9:00							
9:30							
10:00							
10:30							
11:00							
11:30							
12:00							
12:30							
1:00							
1:30							
2:00							
2:30							
3:00							
3:30							
4:00							
4:30							
5:00							
5:30							
6:00							
6:30							
7:00							
7:30							
8:00							
8:30							
9:00							
9:30							
10:00							
10:30							
11:00							

Provisional Working Schedule

Time \ Day	Monday	Tuesday	Wednesday	Thursday	Friday	Saturday	Sunday
7:00							
8:00							
8:30							
9:00							
9:30							
10:00							
10:30							
11:00							
11:30							
12:00							
12:30							
1:00							
1:30							
2:00							
2:30							
3:00							
3:30							
4:00							
4:30							
5:00							
5:30							
6:00							
6:30							
7:00							
7:30							
8:00							
8:30							
9:00							
9:30							
10:00							
10:30							
11:00							

Final Working Schedule

Time \ Day	Monday	Tuesday	Wednesday	Thursday	Friday	Saturday	Sunday
7:00							
8:00							
8:30							
9:00							
9:30							
10:00							
10:30							
11:00							
11:30							
12:00							
12:30							
1:00							
1:30							
2:00							
2:30							
3:00							
3:30							
4:00							
4:30							
5:00							
5:30							
6:00							
6:30							
7:00							
7:30							
8:00							
8:30							
9:00							
9:30							
10:00							
10:30							
11:00							

Final Working Schedule

Time \ Day	Monday	Tuesday	Wednesday	Thursday	Friday	Saturday	Sunday
7:00							
8:00							
8:30							
9:00							
9:30							
10:00							
10:30							
11:00							
11:30							
12:00							
12:30							
1:00							
1:30							
2:00							
2:30							
3:00							
3:30							
4:00							
4:30							
5:00							
5:30							
6:00							
6:30							
7:00							
7:30							
8:00							
8:30							
9:00							
9:30							
10:00							
10:30							
11:00							

INDEX